AUA Guidelines for Backfilling and Contact Grouting of Tunnels and Shafts

EDITED BY
Raymond W. Henn

PREPARED BY
Technical Committee on Backfilling and Contact Grouting of Tunnels
and Shafts of the American Underground Construction Association

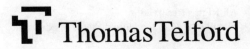

Abstract: This book focuses on backfilling and contact grouting performed to fill the voids between the excavated surface and the tunnel and shaft linings, as well as voids between the final structure and the initial support. Although only two types of underground facilities, "tunnels" and "shafts," are used in the title and are referred to throughout, the book is intended to be used in reference to all types of lined underground structures. For example, in addition to transportation, water, and wastewater tunnels, this book can be used for lined underground storage facilities, powerhouses, railroad stations, sports complexes, warehouse and document storage facilities, housing facilities, and other types of lined underground structures.

Library of Congress Cataloging-in-Publication Data

American Underground Construction Association. Technical Committee on Backfilling and Contact Grouting of Tunnels and Shafts.
    AUA guidelines for backfilling and contact grouting of tunnels and shafts / edited by Raymond W. Henn ; prepared by the Technical Committee on Backfilling and Contact Grouting of Tunnels and Shafts of the American Underground Construction Association.
        p. cm.
    Includes bibliographical references and index.
    ISBN 0-7844-0634-0
    1. Underground construction. 2. Grouting. 3. Fills (Earthwork) I. Henn, Raymond W. II. Title.

TA712 .A55 2002
624.1'9--dc21   2002038403

**AMERICAN UNDERGROUND
CONSTRUCTION ASSOCIATION**

The American Underground Construction Association (AUA) is an organization of professionals involved in every aspect of the underground design and construction industry. Many professional disciplines are represented in the membership including engineers, contractors, and equipment and materials suppliers.

The goals of the Association are:

- to serve as an advocate for its members and the underground construction industry.
- to promote the development and use of underground facilities
- to create greater understanding of the potential and benefit of siting facilities underground
- to encourage appropriate policies and planning for successful development, construction and use of underground facilities

The Association serves as a network within the industry and a point of contact between the industry and the public. The Association represents the United States in the International Tunnelling Association, a non-governmental advisor to the United Nations on matters related to the development and use of underground facilities.

ACKNOWLEDGEMENTS

The chairman and committee members would like to acknowledge and thank the American Underground Construction Association (AUA) and its' Board of Directors for their support and encouragement of the guidelines. The chairman would also like to thank all the members of the AUA Technical Committee on Backfilling and Contact Grouting of Tunnels and Shafts for their contribution of time and expertise in helping make these guidelines a reality, and especially those committee members who were lead chapter authors.

A special acknowledgement is made to Haley & Aldrich, Inc. for allowing the use of staff time and resources in assembling this guideline.

Finally, the chairman and committee members wish to acknowledge Patrick Stephens, Robert Pond, Glen Rorison, David Bixler, and Patricia Henn for their review of the draft manuscript.

AUA Technical Committee on
Backfilling and Contact Grouting of Tunnels and Shafts

Chairman
*Raymond W. Henn, Lyman Henn, Inc., Denver, CO

Secretary
Margaret A. Ganse, Lyman Henn, Inc., Denver, CO

Members
*Tim Avery, Master Builders, Phoenix, AZ
Jack E. Brockway, Herrenknecht Tunneling Systems USA, Inc., Enumclaw, WA
*Donald A. Bruce, Geosystems, L.P., Venetia, PA
*Patrick J. Doig, Hatch Mott MacDonald, Pleasanton, CA
*Amanda Elioff , Parsons Brinckerhoff, Los Angeles, CA
Michael Gay, GDC Constructors, Inc., Naples, FL
Marco Giorelli, Lovat, Inc., Etobicoke, Ontario, Canada
Gary Greenfield, Daigh Company, Inc., Cumming, GA
*David Jurich, Jurich Consulting, Inc., Denver, CO
Bert Kriekemans/Brian Iske, DeNeef Construction Chemicals, Inc., Waller, TX
Steven E. La Vallee, AJ Voton LLC, Melrose Park, IL
Stephen J. Navin, Parsons Engineering Science, Inc., La Jolla, CA
Sten-Åke Pettersson, Atlas Copco, Märsta, Sweden
Michael F. Roach, Traylor Brothers, Inc., Apex, NC
*Victor Romero, Jacobs Associates, San Francisco, CA
*James Warner, Consulting Engineer, Mariposa, CA
*Lee C. Warnock, Hatch Mott MacDonald, San Diego, CA
*Shane Yanagisawa, Frontier-Kemper Constructors, Inc., Seattle, WA

Guideline Reviewers
Patrick Stephens, Pacific International Grout Co., Bellingham, WA
Robert Pond, Frontier-Kemper Constructors Inc., Evansville, IN
Glen Rorison, Jay Dee Contractors, Inc., Livonia, MI
David Bixler, Student, Colorado School of Mines, Golden, CO
Patricia Henn, Consultant, Littleton, Colorado

* Lead Chapter Authors

Raymond W. Henn has more than 32 years of heavy and underground construction experience with a concentration in tunneling, transportation, water and wastewater, and hydroelectric projects. He holds degrees in geology, engineering, and construction management. During his career, Mr. Henn has held positions from field engineer through superintendent to construction manager on both direct-hire construction and construction management assignments. He has a strong background in general civil construction, mass and specialty concrete placement, grouting, deep foundations, and shaft and tunnel excavation and lining. Mr. Henn served as President of the American Underground Construction Association for the 2003–2005 term. He is the author of the ASCE-published *Practical Guide to Grouting of Underground Structures*. Mr. Henn is the recipient of the American Society of Civil Engineers 2002 Roebling Award.

Margaret A. Ganse has 11 years of geotechnical engineering and tunnel design experience throughout North America. She is experienced in geotechnical investigations for underground projects, ground characterization, tunnel lining design, cost estimating, and preparation of contract documents and reports. Her tunnel experience ranges from soft ground to hard rock, and includes transportation, water, and wastewater applications. Ms. Ganse serves on the Tunneling Committee of the Association of Engineering Geologists and is a member of the American Underground Construction Association.

Timothy S. Avery has more than 16 years of heavy construction and underground experience with a concentration in dam foundation grouting, tunnel grouting, and tunnel construction projects. Mr. Avery is currently president of GEO*Solutions*, a specialty consulting firm focusing on grouting and geotechnical construction methods.

Jack Brockway is a professional mechanical engineer with a bachelor of science degree in aeronautics and astronautics from the University of Washington. He has more than 30 years of experience in the tunnel boring machine (TBM) industry. He has held positions of design engineer, project manager, European sales manager, general manager/vice president, and senior vice president within the TBM supply industry. He has been involved in hundreds of hard rock, shielded, and soft ground TBM projects throughout the world.

Donald Bruce earned degrees in geology and civil engineering from Aberdeen University, Scotland, after which he worked for specialty geotechnical contractors worldwide for 20 years. In 1996, Dr. Bruce formed Geosystems, L.P. in Pittsburgh, Pennsylvania. He specializes in drilling, grouting, soil nailing, anchoring, micropiling, and deep mixing technologies. He was awarded the Martin Kapp Foundation Engineering award by ASCE in 1998. He is also a research professor at Polytechnic University of Brooklyn, New York.

Patrick J. Doig has more than 30 years of global experience in underground excavation and construction on projects for transportation, water and wastewater, power generation, and mining. He has represented both owners and contractors, and is experienced in an array of underground excavation methods, specialist subsurface ground treatment techniques, and support and lining systems. He has published more than 10 papers on his work.

Amanda Elioff is a senior professional associate with Parsons Brinckerhoff specializing in geotechnical and tunnel engineering. Presently she is working on extensions to the Los Angeles Metro Rail System.

Michael Gay is a registered professional engineer with more than 30 years of experience in all aspects of heavy and underground construction. He has worked on major transit, highway, and wastewater mega projects all over the United States, Canada, and the Caribbean in his 27-year career with Kiewit Construction Co. He is a member of the Moles and currently is the president of GDC Constructors Inc., an international construction and consulting firm located in Naples, Florida.

Marco Giorelli is a civil engineer with 15 years of experience in tunneling. He is presently the sales manager of Lovat, the world-renowned manufacturer of Tunnel Boring Machines.

Gary N. Greenfield has more than 32 years of involvement in the underground mining and tunneling industries in the Western Hemisphere. His extensive field experience also led to his site-specific introduction of improved ultrafine cements and tunnel backfill grouting control equipment and related admixtures. Mr. Greenfield served as a director of the American Underground Construction Association (1991 to 1995), was the Associations Conference Chair for NAT '98, and was named an Honorary Lifetime Member of AUA.

Brian Iske has more than 20 years of experience in underground waterproofing and all types of grouting. He is experienced in infiltration control in tunnels and shafts ranging from soft ground to hard rock. He has published papers on structural rehabilitation of concrete and groundwater control. Mr. Iske is a member of the American Society of Civil Engineers, International Concrete Repair Institute, Sealant and Waterproofing Institute, and the American Concrete Institute's Strategic Development Council.

David M. Jurich is a licensed professional engineer and professional geologist with 22 years of experience in the geotechnical investigation, design, construction, and repair of dams and tunnels for water resources and hydroelectric projects worldwide. He has a strong background in TBM and conventional tunneling in a wide range of geological formations and ground conditions. Mr. Jurich is a member of the American Underground Construction Association, the American Society of Civil Engineers, and the Association of Engineering Geologists.

Bert Kriekemans has more then 20 years of experience in grouting of underground structures and hydroelectric plants. He has a background in chemical engineering and has been president of De Neef Construction Chemicals Inc., a chemical grout manufacturer, since 1981. He is active in the following associations: International Concrete Repair Institute, American Concrete Institute, American Underground Construction Association, and, International Tunneling Association. He lives in Belgium.

Steven E. La Vallee has been involved with the production, process, and placement of foam concrete in a wide variety of geotechnical applications over the last 15 years. He has a strong mechanical background in the development of production equipment with general civil construction experience in the design of materials and placement techniques on large volume, heavy/highway and underground construction projects.

Stephen J. Navin has more than 40 years of experience in management and design of underground engineering projects. He is experienced in geological evaluations, estimating, lake taps, shaft sinking, and ventilation. His tunnel experience ranges from soft ground to hard rock, and includes tunnels using EPB (Earth Pressure Balance), TBM, roadheader, and drill and blast methods. Mr. Navin is a member of the American Underground Construction Association, the Society of Mining Engineering, and the Underground Technology Research Council.

Sten-Åke Pettersson has more than 30 years of experience from civil construction projects around the world. He authored Atlas Copco's text *Grouting and Drilling for Grouting*. His main background is in ground support, blasting works, and underground civil and mining grouting.

Michael F. Roach has more than 20 years of heavy civil and underground construction experience. He has a strong background in tunnel and shaft excavation and lining. Mr. Roach has extensive experience with precast concrete segmental tunnel liner systems.

Victor S. Romero has more than 10 years of underground design and construction experience. He has worked on a range of projects from pressure tunnels for water supply to mass transit subways, including serving as resident design engineer for the Tren Urbano – Rio Piedras design/build project. Mr. Romero holds engineering degrees from the Colorado School of Mines and University of California at Berkeley, and is currently Underground Technology Research Council committee chairman for the use of cellular concrete in tunnel applications.

James Warner is a consulting engineer operating from Mariposa, California. His international practice involves analysis and solution of geotechnical, structural, and material problems, with a strong emphasis on grouting. In 1977, he helped organize a week-long short course on grouting now sponsored by the University of Florida. The course has been held annually since that time and Mr. Warner continues as a principal instructor.

Lee C. Warnock started his construction career in 1966 as an ironworker. He has more than 27 years of professional experience in hard money contracting operations, contract development, and disputes resolution. His expertise includes heavy civil construction for water programs, pipelines, tunnels, utilities, aviation and industrial facilities, and oil and gas projects, both publicly contracted and privately negotiated. Mr. Warnock has extensive experience in developing and executing project delivery strategies and contracting plans, with enhanced skills in presentations, contract negotiations, and contracts troubleshooting.

Shane Yanagisawa has more than 20 years heavy civil construction experience. The last 14 years have been spent working as an engineer or project manager for contractors participating in the construction of underground structures including subways, sewers, and hydropower projects. He has written papers on the practical aspects of tunnel driving that have appeared *in World Tunnelling* magazine and the proceedings of the Rapid Excavation Tunnel Conferences.

CONTENTS

PREFACE

The need to place material behind tunnel and shaft linings in an effort to fill voids created during the excavation and subsequent lining process is a common requirement associated with most types of underground facility construction. There are two types of void filling operations-backfilling and contact grouting. They are performed as part of the construction process for both soft ground (soil) and rock tunnels and shafts.

This book focuses on backfilling and contact grouting performed to fill the voids between the excavated surface and the tunnel and shaft linings. Although only two types of underground facilities, "tunnels" and "shafts," are used in the title and are referred to throughout, the book is intended to be used in reference to all types of lined underground structures. For example, in addition to transportation, water, and wastewater tunnels, this book can be used for lined underground storage facilities, powerhouses, railroad stations, sports complexes, warehouse and document storage facilities, housing facilities, and other types of lined underground structures. This book does not attempt to address geotechnical grouting for primary groundwater control or ground stabilization of the geologic material surrounding underground excavations.

The underground engineering and construction industry's need for guidelines discussing backfilling and contact grouting first became clear shortly after the American Society of Civil Engineers published *Practical Guide to Grouting of Underground Structures* (Henn, 1996). The author, Raymond Henn, began receiving inquiries regarding specific issues relating to void filling behind tunnel linings. The issue of void filling behind tunnel linings was addressed in some detail in *Practical Guide to Grouting of Underground Structures*. However, as indicated by the inquiries, a more detailed discussion was in order.

Based on the nature and specifics of the inquiries, Henn suggested to Russell Clough and George Teetes that the three write a paper on backfilling and contact grouting of tunnels for presentation at the North American Tunneling Conference in 1998 (NAT '98). All three agreed on the need for such a paper and were willing to write one. The paper, *Clarifying Grouting Requirements Associated with Soil and Rock Tunnel Liners,* was presented and published in the proceedings of NAT '98. The paper was based primarily on the results of a questionnaire, developed by the authors, and sent to approximately 150 members of the underground engineering and construction industry. The paper was also based on a literature search, interviews with members of the underground construction industry, and the authors' experiences.

Of the 150 questionnaires sent out, 64 responses were received. In reviewing and tabulating the results it became apparent there was a wide range of opinions throughout the industry regarding backfilling and contact grouting. These issues were broadly grouped (e.g., definition of backfilling and contact grouting terms and methods; timing of the backfill and contact grout placement; backfill and contact grout materials; mix designs; injection pressures; purposes for backfilling and contact grouting; backfill and contact grout compressive strength requirements; quality control; and so on). Based on the results of the questionnaires, the three authors agreed additional work beyond the publishing of the paper was needed. The formation of a technical committee was suggested to address backfilling and contact grouting associated with underground structures.

Henn proposed such a technical committee to the American Underground Construction Association's (AUA) Executive Director, Susan Nelson. The proposal was accepted by AUA's Board of Directors, the committee was formed, and the first meeting of the full committee was held in Newport Beach, California, in conjunction with NAT '98.

The committee was named "AUA Technical Committee on Backfilling and Contact Grouting of Tunnels and Shafts." It was intentionally composed of professionals from a wide range of backgrounds and specialties within the underground construction industry. Currently there are 20 committee members representing engineering firms, contractors, equipment and materials suppliers, and consultants.

One of the original goals of the committee was to prepare and publish a guideline-type document that could be used by the underground construction industry to assist in minimizing misunderstandings related to backfilling and contact grouting terms and methods; improving the quality of both contract documents relating to backfilling and contact grouting and the in-place material; reducing costs and schedule time; and aid in avoiding or minimizing potential claims.

The guidelines are intended to be used by an audience ranging from the undergraduate university student to the mid-level professional, as well as the senior experienced underground construction practitioner. It is with this wide range of experience levels in mind that subjects such as geology, excavation methods, and liner systems are covered in rudimentary detail.

It is very important for the reader to keep in mind that this work is a "guideline" and not a "specification." It was written to accomplish the goals stated above. In some cases the materials and opinions put forward in the guidelines are a result of a consensus of the committee rather than a result of complete agreement by the committee. With these facts in mind the guidelines should be used in conjunction with good scientific engineering judgment.

CHAPTER 1
INTRODUCTION

1.1 Background

A common requirement found in most contract documents for underground construction projects is to fill the annulus or void between a tunnel or shaft lining and the surrounding ground. The terms "annulus" and "void" are used interchangeably in these guidelines. Voids are filled to:

- Stabilize the liner during construction
- Put the liner in full contact with the surrounding ground to allow load transfer
- Secure lining systems, such as pipes, penstocks, non-expandable precast concrete segmental liners, and liner plates, on final line and grade
- Help reduce permeability of the final liner system
- Reduce groundwater flow around (behind) the final liner
- Add corrosion protection to the final liner
- Help reduce surface settlement above tunnels and around shafts excavated in soft ground or weak rock
- Meet contract document requirements

There are two distinct void-filling methods used in underground construction, as well as in these guidelines: "backfilling" and "contact grouting." Backfilling and contact grouting are among the last major activities in the tunnel and shaft excavation and lining process. However, sometimes contact grouting is required early-on in the excavation and support process to fill voids behind the initial support system. Backfilling and contact grouting can represent a sizable cost and scheduling component of an underground project, depending on site-specific geologic and groundwater conditions surrounding the underground structure, the excavation method and the lining type used, requirements for ground/lining interaction, surface settlement issues, and operational requirements of the completed facilities.

Because of interaction between the shaft or tunnel lining system with the backfilling and contact grouting, these methods should be considered a form of structural material placement rather than a form of geotechnical grouting. It is generally believed by the American Underground Construction Association

1

(AUA) Technical Committee on Backfilling and Contact Grouting of Tunnels and Shafts that underground engineers and designers take great care to address geotechnical issues, such as geotechnical grouting for groundwater control and grouting for ground stabilization and strengthening. It also is believed that structural issues relating to tunnel and shaft lining systems receive great attention during design. However, backfilling and contact grouting of the interface between the excavated surface and the liner system receives much less attention during design and in fact is often thought to be simply incidental to the liner placement operation. This is a common misconception among engineers, designers, and many contractors as well. Hence, backfilling and contact grouting activities, and the time and cost required to perform them, are often underestimated in construction schedules, engineers' construction cost estimates, and contractors' bids. Further, there are discrepancies in the industry regarding the purpose of backfilling and contact grouting, the types and uses of different materials and placement methods, and terminology, resulting in numerous disagreements, delays, disputes, claims, and litigation on underground projects.

This guideline document provides a source reference document on backfilling and contact grouting. It contains standardized terminologies and definitions; objectives and reasons for performing backfilling and contact grouting; an overview of methods, mix designs, and equipment; and examples of effective record keeping, quality control, and contract documents. It is intended that the guidelines will be useful in reducing misunderstanding, eliminating unnecessary construction costs, maximizing production, improving the overall quality of the in-place backfill and contact grout, and minimizing or avoiding disputes and claims.

1.2   Organization of the Guidelines

The guidelines are presented in twelve chapters, as listed and described below:

- Chapter 1 establishes the background and purpose of the guidelines and defines "backfilling" and "contact grouting."
- Chapter 2 is an overview of geological conditions that can affect backfilling and contact grouting, such as geology, groundwater, and environmental conditions.
- Chapter 3 covers structural and operational requirements of completed underground facilities and how these can influence the backfilling and contact grouting program.
- Chapter 4 discusses liner types for tunnels and shafts and relates grouting to construction methods and liner designs.

2

- Chapters 5 and 6 focus on materials and mix properties, respectively, that are appropriate for use in various applications.
- Chapters 7 and 8 discuss backfilling and contact grouting, respectively, providing the reasons, mix designs, and methods used to perform backfilling and contact grouting of tunnels and shafts.
- Chapter 9 describes equipment used for backfilling and contact grouting.
- Chapter 10 addresses record keeping and its importance in each phase of a backfilling and contact grouting program.
- Chapter 11 describes quality control that will assure that mix designs, construction methods, equipment use, and completeness of work meet project requirements.
- Chapter 12 reviews contract documents with specific emphasis on the technical specifications as well as measurement and payment provisions.

1.3 Definitions

In addition to various different terms being used to describe backfilling and contact grouting, currently there is also fairly widespread use of the terms backfilling and contact grouting interchangeably. This can lead to misunderstandings, disputes, and claims. In an effort to mitigate problems, the following definitions are offered.

1.3.1 Backfilling

In various contract documents, backfilling is sometimes referred to as annulus grouting, back grouting, back pack grouting, fill grouting, void grouting, tailshield grouting, and tail void grouting. *"Backfilling" is simply defined as the filling of a void that was intentionally or unintentionally created between the excavated surface and liner as the result of the excavation and lining methods used. When implementing a backfilling program, the size, shape, and extent of the void is generally known prior to the start of backfilling operations.* Therefore, the volume of the void to be filled can be calculated with a reasonable degree of accuracy prior to the start of backfilling operations.

For example, when a void results from use of a tunnel boring machine (TBM) for tunnel excavation, and a non-expandable precast concrete segmental lining system is used, the excavated diameter and the outside diameter of the precast concrete segment ring are known. Therefore, the volume of backfill material required to fill the void can be estimated before backfilling starts. Another example is one in which a tunnel or shaft is excavated by the drill-and-blast (D&B) method and some type of pipe is used as the final lining system. The volume of backfill material required to fill the void between the excavated ground and the outside of the pipe can be fairly accurately calculated by performing a simple as-excavated survey prior to pipe installation.

Additionally, backfilling can be defined as the filling of a relatively large, approximately 50 to 600+ mm (2 to 24+ in.) deep annulus (void). The annulus occurs between the excavated surface or the initial (primary) tunnel or shaft support system and the outer surface of the final or secondary lining system. The void can vary in size and shape or be fairly constant and extend the entire length of the tunnel or depth of the shaft, such as in a drill and blast-excavated tunnel with a pipe liner system. The final or secondary lining system can consist of non-expandable precast concrete, cast iron, or fabricated steel segments; liner plate; steel penstocks or steel shaft liner; or manufactured pipe made of various materials. Figures 1-1 through 1-6 show several examples of backfilling applications.

The backfill materials used to fill the annulus can be a cementitious grout, conventional concrete, cellular concrete (foam grout), or flowable fill. The backfill material is normally injected at relatively low pressure (1 to 3 bars (15 to 45 psi)) above in situ hydrostatic pressure. It is injected into the annulus through the tailshield of earth pressure balance (EPB) or slurry shield (SS) tunnel boring machines, through injection holes (grout ports) drilled through or fabricated into the liner; or with a concrete slickline or grout pipe installed longitudinally at the tunnel crown in the void formed between the ground or initial lining and the secondary lining system. In shaft backfilling, a concrete or grout drop pipe is installed vertically within the annulus between the ground or initial support and the secondary lining system. In shallow tunnels, backfill material can often be placed directly into the tunnel crown from the surface through drilled drop holes. This method has the advantage of maintaining a head (pressure) of backfill material on the backfill placement until the material reaches initial set.

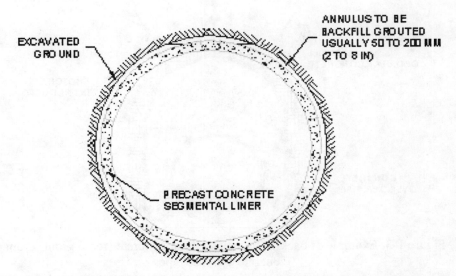

Figure 1-1. Example of backfill grouting behind a non-expandable precast concrete segmental tunnel liner.

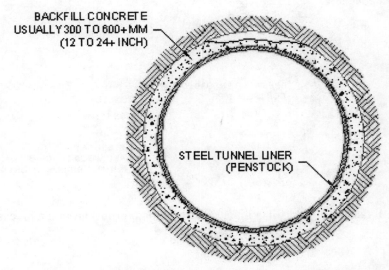

Figure 1-2. Example of backfill concrete behind a steel tunnel liner.

5

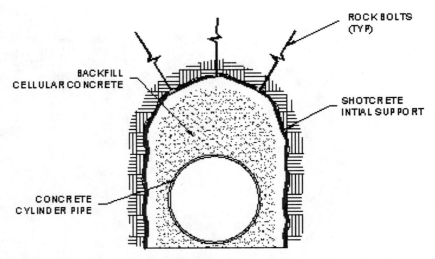

Figure 1-3. Example of backfilling with cellular concrete (foam grout) around concrete cylinder pipe.

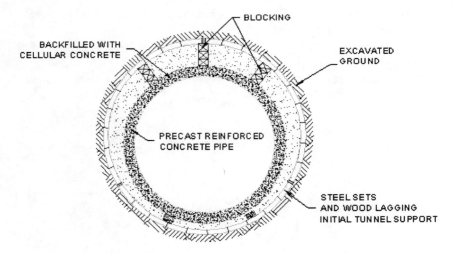

Figure 1-4. Example of backfill cellular concrete (foam grout) around a precast reinforced concrete pipe.

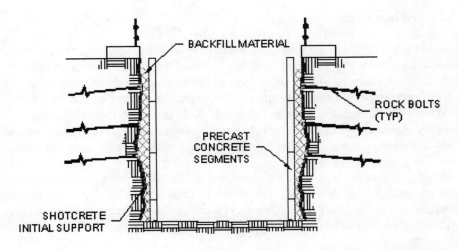

Figure 1-5. Example of backfill material placed behind a non-expandable precast concrete segmental shaft lining system.

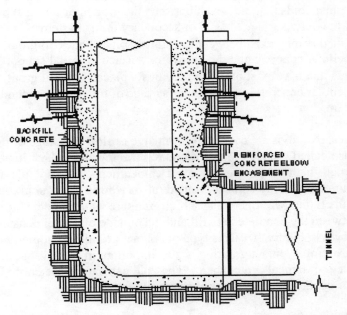

Figure 1-6. Example of backfill concrete around raised pipe in a shaft.

7

1.3.2   Contact Grouting

"Contact grouting" can be simply defined as the filling of voids that were unintentionally created as a result of the shaft and tunnel excavation and lining methods used. The size, shape, and extent of the void are generally unknown prior to starting contact grouting operations. Therefore, the volume of the void to be filled with contact grout cannot be calculated with any reasonable degree of accuracy. An example of this is a cast-in-place concrete tunnel liner that has small voids of varying sizes and shapes near the tunnel crown after the concrete has set.

Additionally, contact grouting can be defined as the filling of relatively small approximately 1.5 to 150+ mm (1/16 to 6+ in.) deep voids that may exist between the excavated surface and initial (primary) tunnel or shaft support system. This definition also applies to the following kinds of voids:

- Voids that exist between the ground or initial support system and panning material used for water control
- In the case of cast-in-place concrete and expandable segment lining systems, voids that may exist between the ground or initial support system and the outer surface of final or secondary lining systems
- Voids that may exist between previously placed backfill grout, concrete, or cellular concrete and the excavated surface or initial support systems
- Voids that may exist between previously placed backfill grout, concrete, or cellular concrete, and the outer surface of the final or secondary lining system

In most cases, the voids are caused by shrinkage or flow blockage of the backfill material (also called "shadowing") around reinforcing steel, shear lugs, electrical conduits, small-diameter piping, and other embedments. These voids, when they exist, are more commonly contact grouted (also referred to as "skin grouting") only when the tunnel will operate as a high-pressure water tunnel (for example, the void between the concrete backfill and the outside of a steel penstock tunnel liner, as shown in Figure 10). This type of contact grouting is sometimes referred to as skin grouting. Contact grouting is also important in soft-ground tunnels where surface settlement is a concern. The void can extend the entire length of the tunnel or depth of the shaft or only over an isolated area.

Figures 1-7 through 1-12 show several examples of contact grouting applications. Material used in contact grouting is usually a cementitious grout made with Portland or ultrafine (also called "microfine") cement. Contact grout is usually

8

injected at relatively low pressure, 1 to 3 bars (15 to 45 psi), above in situ hydrostatic pressure. Higher injection pressures are sometimes used, usually associated with pressure tunnels and shafts. When higher injection pressures are used, contact grout also can serve as a secondary means of geotechnical grouting of the surrounding geologic formation. Contact grout can be injected into voids behind tunnel linings through pre-installed grout inserts or field-drilled grout holes, utilizing pipe nipples or packers. In shafts constructed in soil, contact grout is often placed at shallow depths near the ground surface directly into the void between the excavation and initial (temporary) support using the chute of a transit mix concrete truck. At deeper shaft depths, contact grout is usually placed at pressure using small portable grout plants (see Chapter 9). Shaft contact grouting, when required at all, is usually only performed between the excavated ground and temporary support.

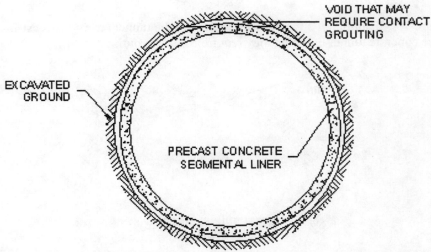

Figure 1-7. Example of a typical void located in the tunnel crown of a backfilled precast concrete segmental tunnel liner that may require contact grouting.

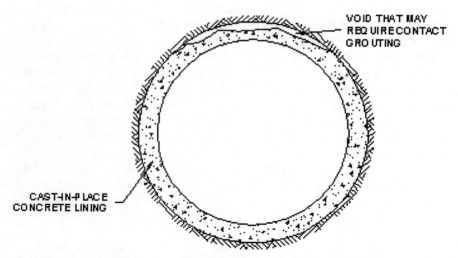

Figure 1-8. Example of a typical void located in the tunnel crown of a cast-in-place concrete tunnel liner that may require contact grouting.

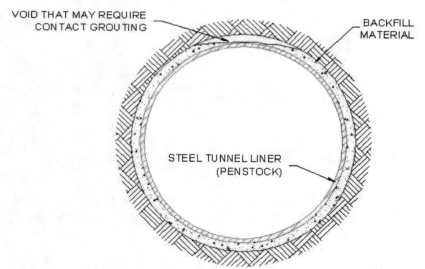

Figure 1-9. Example of void located at tunnel crown of a backfilled steel lined tunnel.

10

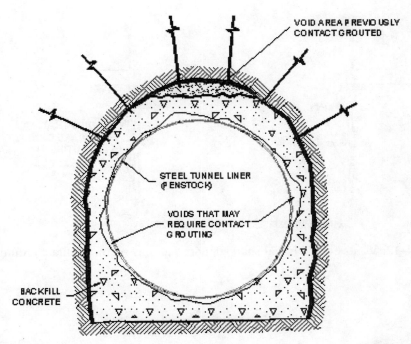

Figure 1-10. Example of voids between steel tunnel liner and backfill concrete that may require contact grouting.

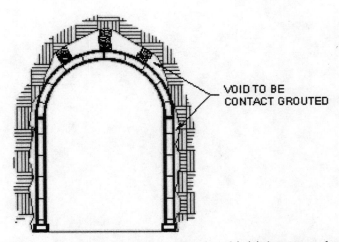

Figure 1-11. Example of voids between excavated ground and initial support that may require contact grouting.

11

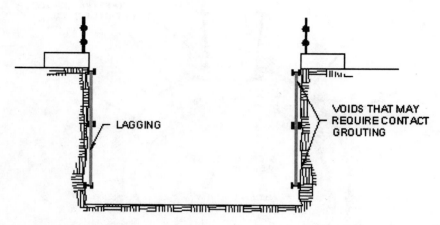

Figure 1-12. Voids behind initial shaft support that may require contact grouting.

CHAPTER 2
GEOLOGICAL CONDITIONS

While backfilling and contact grouting should be considered a form of structural material placement rather than a form of geotechnical grouting, geological conditions can play a major role in the placement and performance of backfill material and contact grout. The soil, rock, and groundwater surrounding shaft and tunnel excavations determine certain backfill and contact grout parameters, such as mix design, injection pressure, timing of the placements, the quantity of material placed, and material behavior during placement and in the long term.

Underground excavations are generally described in terms of soft ground (soil) or rock excavation techniques. Soil and rock properties and behavior are primary considerations in designing backfilling and contact grouting methods and placement timing. Two major functions of the backfill material or contact grout are to (1) fill voids to replace portions of "overexcavated" or "lost" ground, and (2) help minimize the amount of tunnel and shaft lining that is not in contact with the ground, ensuring that loads are distributed evenly on the lining. Depending on the lining system used (see Chapter 4), backfilling may help provide basic stability to the tunnel or shaft lining system and reduce surface settlement. Contact grouting, on the other hand, is not always required for tunnel stability. It is usually required for tunnels in soil or weak rock, where surface settlement is an issue, and for pressure tunnels in rock where the ground/liner load transfer interaction is important. Contact grouting also is usually not required in shafts except, in some cases, behind the initial support system. This is because backfill and cast-in-place concrete placed in shafts has the hydrostatic force of gravity working in their favor. The vertical head of the grout or concrete forces the backfill into any cracks, crevasses, and other irregularities in the surrounding ground, eliminating most if not all voids. However, form or liner vibration should be considered.

This chapter presents a general overview of geological conditions, i.e., ground (soil and rock) and groundwater, that are related to backfill and contact grouting. For reasons of brevity, underground excavations are referred to generically as "tunnels," but all comments apply equally to shafts, chambers, or any other underground structures. Issues requiring a significantly different approach in a shaft are noted.

13

2.1 Soil (Soft Ground)

From the perspective of excavating tunnels, soil is considered to be "soft ground." According to McCusker (1982), "soft ground is material which can be removed with reasonable facility using hand tools, even though such tools may not, in fact, be the ones employed." However, soft ground can include formations that would meet the geological definition of rock yet also meet McCusker's criterion. For the purposes of this discussion, the terms "soil" and "soft ground" are used interchangeably.

Soil is generally defined as the top layer of the earth's surface, consisting of rock and mineral particles mixed with organic matter. The origin of these constituents is described by White (1977), as follows:

"The soil and unconsolidated sediments which overlie bedrock have different origins. Most of these consist chiefly of particles derived from a previously existing rock. Some are detached from the parent rock by mechanical rock weathering or abrasion; the most common constituent derived this way is quartz. Others, like clay particles, are produced by the chemical decomposition of other minerals, such as feldspar. During volcanic eruptions, large quantities of minute particles are ejected from volcanic vents. In shallow lakes and sheltered coves the organic, calcareous, or siliceous remains of various organisms, such as algae, accumulate and build up what are known as "deposits of organic origin." These constituents can remain at the point of deposition or can be transported by water, glaciers or wind to other locations."

Some of the most common soil types are discussed below, including the impact of the soil on contact grouting and backfilling operations.

2.1.1 Backfilling and Contact Grouting in Soil Deposits

The characteristics and behaviors of the major soil types have a direct effect on the stand-up time of the soil during excavation and on how the backfilling and contact grouting operations are performed. Soil deposits are characterized by their original source, mode of transport to the point of deposition, depositional environment, grain size and distribution of the soil particles, chemical composition, and soil structure. Several common types of soil deposits are described in the following sections. The influence of each soil type on backfill and contact grouting also is discussed.

14

2.1.1.1 Alluvium

Alluvium consists of consolidated or unconsolidated sediments that have been transported from their point of origin by water via streams and rivers. Alluvial constituents include clay, silt, sand, gravel, cobbles, and boulders. The composition, distribution, and characteristics of the various particle sizes that compose a particular alluvium deposit depend on rock type and composition of the parent geologic material; energy of the stream or river; and distance from the parent material to the place of deposition, which influences the angularity of the particles. The nature of the resulting alluvial deposits, therefore, can be quite different from one locale to another, as can depth and lateral extent within a deposit.

Alluvial deposits can range from loose, granular, and highly permeable to hard and cohesive. Particle size distribution and density of an alluvial deposit can greatly influence backfilling and contact grouting placements. For example, a tunnel driven through loose, granular alluvium will generally experience much higher geotechnical grout takes (i.e., amount of grout injected per hole or linear foot of tunnel) compared to a tunnel driven through hard, cohesive alluvium, because the greater permeability of the granular alluvium results in loss of the backfill and contact grout material to the surrounding ground. This is a greater concern in contact grouting than in backfilling, since contact grouts are generally less viscous and more flowable than backfill material. Also, loose, granular alluvium will experience ground loss as material moves into the excavation, resulting in more voids.

2.1.1.2 Colluvium

Colluvium consists of unconsolidated deposits on a slope, at the base of a slope, or at the foot of a cliff, brought there by mass wasting. The characteristics of colluvial material vary according to the bedrock sources and the climate under which weathering and transport occur. Generally, colluvium is weakly stratified and consists of a heterogeneous mixture of soils and rock fragments ranging in size from clay particles to rocks 1 m (3.3 ft) or more in diameter. The particles are generally angular due to the short distance traveled before deposition. Colluvium deposits are usually thinnest near the crest and thickest near the toe of slope. At the base of slopes, colluvium may interfinger with alluvial deposits and may actually constitute the major portion of these alluvial deposits.

Like alluvium, the particle size distribution and density of the colluvium will influence backfilling and contact grout placements. Due to the heterogeneous nature of colluvium, it can be challenging to predict ground behavior during tunneling and the performance of contact grouting and backfilling.

2.1.1.3 Glacial

The physical characteristics of glacial deposits vary greatly in character due to the variety of ways in which glaciers transport and deposit material. Sediment deposited directly from basal ice differs from that deposited directly from ice along the glacial margin, and sediment winnowed by glacial meltwater differs from that derived directly from glacial ice. Sediments deposited from basal ice are called "till" and contain a wide spectrum of particle sizes, ranging from clay to large boulders, mixed randomly together without noticeable stratification. Because these deposits were overridden by ice, they are typically quite dense. Sediments deposited from glacial meltwater streams (outwash) or lakes exhibit better sorting and stratification, consisting of much finer grained particles with suspended well-rounded pebbles, cobbles, and occasional boulders. Glacial erratics—boulders carried by ice and deposited into lakes, streams, or other bodies of water—are often found in deposits where they are not expected to be found.

Because glacial deposits are generally dense, stand-up time during tunnel excavation is usually quite good. However, heterogeneity of the deposits could lead to markedly different ground behavior, such as when a cohesive clayey till deposit interfingers with a looser, sandy deposit. Glacial formations generally do not result in great loss of grout or backfill material into the formation, except in granular lenses/zones.

2.1.1.4 Lacustrine

Lacustrine deposits consist of sediments that have been deposited in lakes and owe their origin in some way to deltaic, fluvial, or glacial systems. Coarser grained gravel and sand carried into lakes are deposited in deltas at the lake margin, whereas the suspended load of silt and clay is transported farther out into the lake in suspension, where it settles out in quiet water. However, depending on climate and weathering, silts and clays may be the only deposits during the winter, when lakes become frozen over and inflowing meltwater streams have reduced discharges, carrying less coarse material. The majority of lacustrine deposits are fine-grained silts and thick, heterogeneous clays.

Typically, lacustrine deposits are homogeneous. Stand-up time during tunnel excavation will depend on the consistency of the clay deposit (soft vs. stiff). The fine-grained cohesiveness of lacustrine deposits means that contact grout and backfill material is generally not lost to the formation during tunneling.

2.1.1.5 Deltaic

Deltaic deposits are built by the accumulation of sediment deposited by streams discharging sediment loads into standing water. The distribution of water and sediment discharged into a body of water by a stream is determined largely by relative differences in density between the streamwater and the standing water, by the sediment load, and by the vigor of wave or current action in the lake or ocean. Deltas commonly exhibit numerous complex sedimentary depositional environments within the depositional system. Each of these is characterized by its own assemblage of sediments and sedimentary structures. A typical prograding delta ("prodelta") displays a coarsening-upward trend and a decrease in grain size in a seaward direction. These are generalities depending on the type of delta and the specific site of the stratigraphic section. In general, the delta plain, the most landward portion, is a mixture of sand, silts, and clay. The delta front, adjacent in the seaward direction, is dominantly sand, and the prodelta, the most distal portion of the delta, is silt and clay.

Overall density of the deltaic formation and constituents controls ground behavior and stand-up time during tunnel excavation. The delta front is generally granular and could experience flowing or running ground conditions during excavation. The prodelta, however, consists of cohesive materials, and can perform well during excavation if the deposits are sufficiently consistent. In general, cohesive deltaic deposits will experience less loss of backfill and grout into the surrounding ground than will granular deltaic deposits.

2.1.1.6 Marine

Marine deposits represent some of the thickest sedimentary sequences and are the most widespread of all sedimentary deposits. This type of depositional system lies seaward of continental margin and is characterized by truly deep-water sedimentation. Accumulations of marine deposits are composed primarily of exceptionally fine-grained clays, silts, and organic matter; however, because of a broad potential source area and rapid accumulation, these deposits tend to accumulate anything that is available. Sometimes nodules of manganese are formed, which are extremely hard and present a challenge to tunnel excavation operations.

17

Marine deposits are generally cohesive and, if of a stiff consistency, stand-up time of tunnel excavations can be quite good. Marine deposits located at shallower depths are often less dense or have a softer consistency due to mode of deposition and shorter consolidation time. Loss of contact grout or backfill material into the surrounding ground is generally not a great concern in marine deposits.

2.1.1.7 Loess

Loess consists of windblown (aeolian) silt and clay deposited as a relatively homogenous, unstratified blanket over the earth's surface. It is usually well sorted, consisting mostly of silt with smaller amounts of clay and fine sand. Typically, loess contains about 40 to 50 percent silt, up to 30 percent clay, and up to 10 percent fine sand. Clay-size loess can travel all the way around the world on high-altitude winds and is a major component of deep-sea sediments. An estimated 30 percent of the United States is mantled with loess, and as much as 10 percent of the earth's land area is covered by 1 to 100 meters (3 to 328 feet) of loess. The sources of most loess deposits are related to areas affected by glaciation, especially areas downwind from glacial outwash plains.

Loess deposits consist of cohesive particles of silt and clay. Stand-up time during tunnel excavation can be quite good because it supports vertical cuts. However, loess is sensitive to water and vibration, which dramatically impact its stand-up time and ground behavior. Loess does not generally lose backfill or grout to the formation, unless the formation is not well consolidated.

2.1.1.8 Pyroclastic

Pyroclastic deposits form directly from the fragmentation of magma and rock by explosive volcanic activity. Fragment size can vary from several meters to ash-sized particulates. They can be grouped into three generic types according to their mode of transport and deposition: falls, flows, and surges.

A fall deposit is formed after material has been explosively ejected from a vent, producing an eruption column. The geometry and size of a fall deposit reflects the eruption column height and the velocity and direction of atmospheric winds. As the plume expands, pyroclastic material falls back to earth at varying distances downwind from the source, depending on its size and density.

Flow deposits are pyroclastic debris controlled by gravity and topography to fill valleys and depressions. Internally, flow deposits are generally massive and poorly sorted, but sometimes they show grading of larger clasts.

A surge deposit transports pyroclasts along the surface as an expanded, turbulent, gas-solid dispersion. Deposits overlie topography but are also topographically controlled, tending to accumulate or are thickest in depressions.

Stand-up time during tunnel excavation is largely dependent on whether the particles are well cemented ("welded"). Loss of contact grout or backfill material will vary across the various types of pyroclastic deposits depending on the stratigraphy, permeability, and grain size distribution of the particular deposit.

2.1.1.9 Organic

Soils, especially silts and clays, are classified as organic or inorganic based on the amounts of organic material they contain. The organic content of soil is determined by vegetation and by animal and bacterial activity. Organic material in soils is usually derived from plant or root growth and consists of almost completely disintegrated organic matter, such as peat. Organic soils are usually characterized by their dark color and odor, and even small amounts of organic matter may significantly influence soil compressibility.

Organic soils are generally soft and can result in poor stand-up time and ground behavior during tunneling. Also, presence of organics can have a great influence on the behavior of the contact grout or backfill material. To be effective, mix designs for these materials must consider the organic nature of the deposit.

2.1.1.10 Residual Soils

Residual soils are rock that has been severely disintegrated by physical and chemical weathering. The rock is weathered to the condition of a soil with the original rock fabric intact and mineral grains mainly unaltered. With continued weathering, complete decomposition may occur in which most mineral grains are completely decomposed. Climate and rock lithology and mass characteristic are important in assessing the effects of weathering. The depth of weathering profiles and thickness of residual soils are highly variable, measuring 1 to 2 m (3 to 6 ft) in arid arctic conditions to more than 100 m (328 ft) for tropical weathering.

Tunnel excavation in residual soils results in impacts to stand-up time and behavior of backfill and grout material. Unlike thick, clayey, saprolitic soil deposits, residual soils derived from coarse sandstone, for example, could experience sloughing during excavation and lose backfill and grout to the formation.

2.1.2 Backfilling and Contact Grouting in Soft Ground

Backfilling and contact grouting soft-ground tunnels and shafts is controlled to a large degree by soil behavior during, and shortly after, excavation. The timing of backfilling placement is controlled by the stand-up time of the surrounding ground and the excavation method used. Contact grouting is sometimes required immediately after erection of initial support to help mitigate short-term surface settlement. Contact grouting is also performed after placement of the backfill material or the cast-in-place concrete liner to fill crown voids to help mitigate long-term surface settlement.

2.1.2.1 Soft Ground Classification

There are a number of soft ground classification systems and all are related to soil type (cohesive or granular) and the amount of water present. Terzaghi (1946) published *The Tunnelman's Ground Classification System* to describe the reaction of soils during tunneling operations. Terzaghi's system has been expanded by Heuer and Virgens (1987), as shown in Table 2-1.

2.1.2.2 Excavation Considerations in Soft Ground

Voids in soft ground are generally formed either intentionally ("overcut") or as a function of the excavation and support process (ground loss). The term "overcut" refers to additional excavation required beyond the diameter of the tunnel boring machine (TBM) body to ensure the machine can move through the soil without becoming mired. Overcut is used to reduce skin friction and to aid in TBM steering. TBM manufacturers generally suggest what is an appropriate overcut, given specifics of the machine, tunnel alignment, and geology. The tunnel contractor may alter this depending on site specifics and his own experience. When the machine is moving through a tight curve for instance, a larger overcut may be necessary. The overcut is achieved by oversized cutting tools mounted on the perimeter of the cutting head. Generally, these can be adjusted radially to increase or reduce the amount of overcut, especially for use during horizontal curves in the alignment.

Table 2-1 Tunnelman's Ground Classification System

CLASSIFICATION		BEHAVIOR	TYPICAL SOIL TYPES
Firm		Heading can be advanced without initial support, and final lining can be constructed before ground starts to move.	Loess above water table, hard clay, marl, cemented sand and gravel when not highly overstressed.
Raveling	Slow raveling Fast raveling	Chunks or flakes of material begin to drop out of the arch or walls sometime after the ground has been exposed, due to loosening or to overstress and "brittle" fracture (ground separates or breaks along distinct surfaces, as opposed to squeezing ground). In fast raveling ground, the process starts within a few minutes; otherwise, the ground is slow raveling.	Residual soils or sand with small amounts of binder may be fast raveling below the water table, slow raveling above. Stiff fissured clays may be slow or fast raveling depending upon degree of overstress.
Squeezing		Ground squeezes or extrudes plastically into tunnel, without visible fracturing or loss of continuity, and without perceptible increase in water content. Ductile, plastic yield and flow due to overstress.	Ground with low frictional strength. Rate of squeeze depends on degree of overstress. Occurs at shallow to medium depth in clay of very soft to medium consistency. Stiff to hard clay under high cover may move in combination of raveling at execution surface and squeezing at depth behind face.

Table 2-1 Tunnelman's Ground Classification System

CLASSIFICATION		BEHAVIOR	TYPICAL SOIL TYPES
Running	Non-cohesive running Running	Granular materials without cohesion are unstable at a slope greater than their angle of repose ($\pm$ 30°-35°). When exposed at steeper slopes, they run like granulated sugar or dune sand until the slope flattens to the angle of repose.	Clean, dry granular materials. Apparent cohesion in moist sand, or weak cementation in any granular soil, may allow the material to stand for a brief period of raveling before it breaks down and runs. Such behavior is cohesive running.
Flowing		A mixture of soil and water flows into the tunnel like a viscous fluid. The material can enter the tunnel from the invert as well as from the face, crown, and wall, and can flow for great distances, completely filling the tunnel in some cases.	Below the water table in silt, sand, or gravel without enough clay content to give significant cohesion and plasticity. May also occur in highly sensitive clay when such material is disturbed.
Swelling		Ground absorbs water, increases in volume, and expands slowly into the tunnel.	Highly preconsolidated clay with plasticity index in excess of about 30, generally containing significant percentages of montmorillonite.

"Ground loss" is the catch-all phrase for unintended overexcavation. The amount of ground loss is primarily the result of the material at the face and how it behaves or reacts to the excavation process. Non-cohesive soils, cobbley and bouldery ground, and groundwater inflows are conditions that can produce ground loss if the TBM is not designed and operated specifically to handle these geologic conditions. Limiting ground loss is largely a function of machine characteristics. Use of open-faced TBMs allows a higher potential for ground loss as the tunnel is exposed. The process can generally be better controlled with a closed-face TBM, and ground loss may be further reduced with an earth pressure balance (EPB) or slurry-shield (SS) TBM. Figure 2-1 shows a cross-section sketch of an EPB TBM; Figure 2-2 shows a cross section of an SS TBM. TBM operator performance also is a factor in containing overexcavation. Lack of expertise or attentiveness by the operator can override even the most sophisticated controls and machine design.

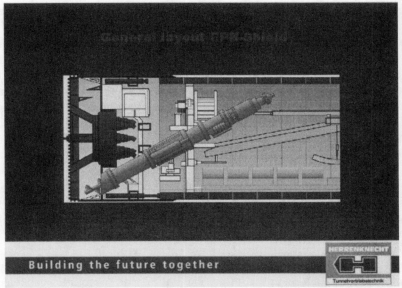

Figure 2-1. A cross section of an earth pressure balance (EPB) tunnel boring machine.

Figure 2-2. Cross section of a slurry shield (SS) tunnel boring machine.

Expandable supports may be used when tunneling in cohesive soil, and material that has a reasonable stand up time. These may be either concrete segments or steel ribs and lagging. In this instance, the support is expanded against the ground as it emerges from the tailsheild of the TBM and therefore the void is theoretically smaller and of unknown size. This small void may require contact grouting. Sometimes minor falls of ground can occur during expansion of the supports and these voids should be filled by contact grouting as soon as possible. More likely, unless specified by the Engineer, measures will be taken by the Contractor during final liner placement to address these voids. Because there may be some time between the original void formation and final liner installation, there is a distinct possibility the ground will move into the voids which can lead to surface settlement. It should be noted the use of expandable supports is almost unique to the United States.

The alternative to expandable supports is a bolted non-expandable segmental liner. These types of liner systems, used routinely in Europe and Japan, are gaining popularity in the United States. Bolted segmental liners are generally made of concrete. In Europe cast iron is sometimes used in poor ground conditions or when high water pressures are encountered. In the United States steel liner plate is another option. In wet conditions, these lining systems may employ water-tight gaskets in the joints. The bolted, and sometimes gasketed, liner is erected inside the tailsheild of the machine. When the liner emerges, the diameter is set and there is no facility for expansion. Therefore, there is an annulus between the liner exterior and the excavated surface. Modern practice is to backfill grout this void as the liner emerges, either through grout pipes installed in the TBM tailsheild or grout ports in the segments. In this manner the annulus is given immediate support and the potential for settlement is minimized. When tunneling in non-cohesive material with poor stand-up time, the ground support is erected within the tailshield of the TBM. As the machine moves forward, the ground support elements emerge from the rear of the TBM's tailshield. The annulus between the supports and excavated surface that remains is usually backfill grouted in the case of a non-expandable (bolted precast) liner system.

2.2   Rock

A dictionary definition of "rock" will generally employ words such as "hard," "solid," and "stone," while occasionally acknowledging that less-cohesive agglomerations of such material may also qualify. According to Bickel (1982), "rock tunnels are excavated in a firm, cohesive medium which may vary from relatively soft marl and sandstone to the very hard igneous rocks such as granite. Bedding and fissuring of rock layers, and the presence of water, control construction methods and difficulties." In general, it might be stated that, while soft ground can be excavated by hand with a shovel or pick, rock requires the application of some additional means. This might include the mechanical effort developed by machines, such as breakers, roadheaders, and TBMs, or by the dynamic force of explosives.

2.2.1   Backfilling and Contact Grouting in Rock

Backfilling and contact grouting in rock tunnels and shafts is only minimally controlled by rock behavior. There are exceptions, however; for example, backfilling and contact grouting may be used in blocky and fractured ground to stabilize the ground shortly after excavation. Normally, backfilling is used to fill voids and thus bring the liner in full contact with the surrounding ground for load transfer. Contact grouting helps to further ensure full contact between the liner and the ground.

2.2.2   Rock Classification

Rock is classified in a number of ways. Geologically, the primary classification is according to origin: sedimentary, igneous, or metamorphic. Rock types within these broad classes are distinguished further by their mineralogy, crystalline structure, grain size, or metamorphic facies. Classifying rock in this manner is useful to the tunnel engineer and gives some indication of the rock's properties, potential behavior upon excavation, and type of ground support required. Geology is also a good indicator of hardness and silica content, which affect, for instance, the ability to cut rock mechanically. However, to make more definite determinations about the type of excavation method, the nature and extent of support, and the design of the permanent liner, the condition and mechanical properties of the rock need to be known. Engineering classification systems have been developed for this purpose.

The rock classification system developed by Terzaghi (1946) is probably the most well known (see Table 2-2). This divides rock into seven classifications (with subclassifications) according to its potential behavior during and after excavation. Thus, rock may vary from "intact," through "blocky and seamy," to "swelling." In addition to helping the designer, these descriptive characterizations can alert tunnel excavation personnel to potential construction difficulties.

25

Table 2-2 Terzaghi's Rock Conditions

Rock Condition	Remarks
1. Hard and Stratified	Light lining, required only if spalling or popping occurs
2. Hard stratified or schistose	Light support
3. Massive, moderately jointed	Load may change erratically from point to point
4. Moderately blocky and seamy	No side pressure
5. Very blocky and seamy	Little or no side pressure
6. Completely crushed but chemically intact	Considerable side pressure. Softening effect of seepage towards bottom of tunnel requires either continuous support for lower ends of ribs or circular ribs
7. Squeezing rock, moderate depth	Heavy side pressure, invert struts required. Circular ribs are recommended
8. Squeezing rock, great depth	
9. Swelling Rock	Circular ribs required. In extreme cases use yielding support

(Notes on table: See reference for complete table with Rock load recommendations and figures).

Rock characteristics and properties also can be classified quantitatively. Several systems have been developed that use empirical data to classify rock and estimate ground support requirements. Deere (1964) developed the Rock Quality Designation or RQD Index, according to percentage core recovery from exploration holes. The RQD gives an indication of the degree of fracturing. Barton, Lien, and Lunde (1974) took the RQD and factored in joint characteristics, stress reduction, and other factors (such as groundwater conditions), to produce the Norwegian Geotechnical Institute index or Q system. Both RQD and Q are used extensively in presenting information on rock quality and to estimate ground support requirements. Hoek and Brown (1980) contains a comprehensive discussion of rock classification.

2.2.3   Excavation Considerations in Rock

What most classification systems acknowledge and what is highlighted in Bickel's (1982) observation, is that the rock conditions and the presence of water within the rock define how tunnel construction is conducted. Tunnels excavated in homogeneous, impermeable rock may be serviceable without a liner. Throughout the United States and around the world, there are many unlined rock tunnels in use for the transportation of vehicles and fluids. However, rock that is not entirely self-supporting, or that does or could yield transmit water, will require a liner.

26

The liner type installed in a rock tunnel will be a function of the physical characteristics of the host rock and the tunnel's intended purpose. Shotcrete, cast-in-place concrete, pipe, and penstock segments are all used extensively to line rock tunnels. For such liners to perform as designed, it is almost certain they will need to be in intimate contact with the excavated rock surface along their entire perimeter. Backfilling and contact grouting are the primary methods used to ensure full contact is achieved.

Whether in soil or rock, the interaction between liner and excavated tunnel surface is fundamental to liner design. The significance of this interface may be more pronounced in rock tunnels. Rock tunnels may be subject to very much higher ground loads and stresses, especially where there is groundwater. Complete void filling between liner and rock is essential to ensure loads are properly transferred and there are no stress concentrations that could cause liner distress or failure. Backfilling and contact grouting in softer rock such as shale may perform a similar function to backfilling and contact grouting in soil tunnels by helping limit settlement. However when performing such grouting, the grout must not be overpressurized, which would cause the surface to heave.

Voids behind the liner are most prevalent in drill-and-blast (D&B) tunnels. D&B tunnels are excavated as a series of relatively short segments, generally 1 to 5 m (4 to 16 ft) in length. The sawtooth profile created by the D&B excavation process and any overbreak (see Figure 2-3) makes complete filling with cast-in-place concrete or backfill difficult. The higher (overexcavated) areas tend to fill with air that cannot be easily displaced by the concrete or backfill material. Figures 2-4 through 2-6 illustrate additional overbreak profiles resulting from differing rock strata orientations. In addition to overexcavation and overbreak, loss of grout into open rock joints and seams can add to the quantity of backfill and contact grout placed. Figure 2-7 shows an example of open jointing, which could cause loss of backfill or contact grout.

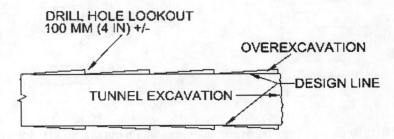

Figure 2-3. Sawtooth profile created by "looking out" of the drill holes in the drill and blast excavation method.

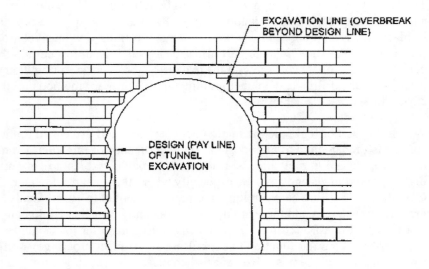

Figure 2-4. Rock bedding and jointing causing overbreak.

Figure 2-5. Rock bedding and overbreak creating a natural arch. B is the design (pay) line of the tunnel.

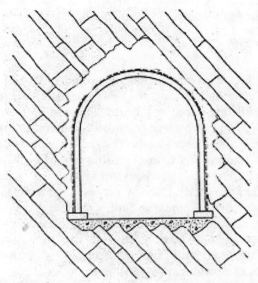

Figure 2-6. Rock bedding and overbreak in inclined strata.

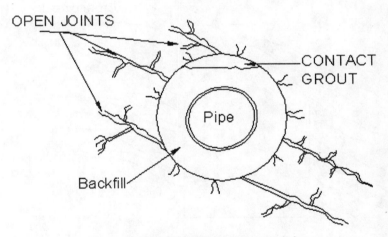

Figure 2-7. Loss of grout to open joints

Some tunnels are excavated by D&B rather than by TBMs for several reasons, such as the tunnel length is relatively short and does not justify the cost of the TBM, the size and shape of the tunnel does not lend itself to mechanical excavation, or the rock is too hard to cut by machine methods. Selection of the ground support system, along with the excavation method, can have a marked influence on backfilling and contact grouting methods used.

2.3 Groundwater

Because tunnels are often excavated below the groundwater table, water conditions can be a factor both in the design and installation of the liner and in how the liner is backfilled and contact grouted. Zones of high groundwater inflows resulting from highly fractured or faulted ground (see Figure 2-8) can be particularly challenging. The liner may be designed to keep water out and/or keep water in. In sewer and stormwater tunnels, infiltrating groundwater adds to treatment costs. In transportation tunnels, water inflows may cause operational problems for electrified rail transit and can increase maintenance of highway and rail tunnels, particularly in cold climates. Liners in these types of facilities will be designed to limit groundwater infiltration. However, in tunnels—such as pressurized headrace tunnels for hydroelectric stations, in water distribution systems that operate under pressure, and in pressurized sewer tunnels—the lining is designed to limit or even eliminate exfiltration.

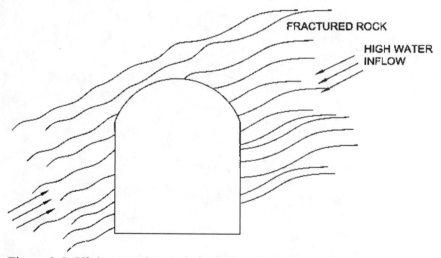

Figure 2-8. High groundwater inflow resulting from highly fractured rock.

2.4   Environmental Considerations

Backfill materials and contact grouts can impact or be impacted by the environments in which they are used. Reactions with chemicals or contaminants in groundwater can degrade the immediate or long-term performance of backfill and contact grout and liner materials. Gases that occur naturally in soil and rock can be potentially toxic or flammable. Also, backfill and contact grout used in underground developments constructed in urban and industrial areas can contain manufactured products and chemicals that could penetrate soil and underground systems. These environmental issues must be addressed to avoid potential safety and health risks in the construction and operational use of, and in the community surrounding, the excavated project.

2.4.1   Chemicals in Groundwater

In many developed urban and industrial areas, high levels of gasoline, dry cleaning solvents, and other types of chemical combinations may be present in groundwater, soil, and rock. Chemicals and contaminants in groundwater have the potential to attack lining concrete as well as cementitious backfill and contact grout materials. Materials such as sulfide-resistant cement can be used in concrete linings, backfill material and contact grout to ensure some protection from chemicals or minerals in the groundwater. A thorough geological and environmental site investigation should identify contaminants that are present. The project designer can then determine their potential to damage cementitious materials and the overall mix of the backfill materials and contact grout and specify appropriate admixtures.

2.4.2   Gases

Gas in the geologic formation creates the potential for adverse chemical reactions and is an additional consideration when backfilling and contact grouting the tunnel lining. In addition, the presence of toxic or flammable gases—such as methane in old trash dumps, or hydrogen sulfide in sufficient quantities to pose a health or safety hazard—must be addressed in the excavation methods used in tunnel liner design.

To combat gas infiltration into the finished tunnel or shaft, a gas-proof membrane can be installed between the excavated ground or the initial support system and the final cast-in-place concrete lining or backfill. Such membranes are typically made of high density polyethylene (HDPE) or polyvinyl chloride (PVC) and have welded joints to form a continuous barrier against gas transmission. The

31

membrane is affixed to the initial supports or the ground, and the cast-in-place concrete or backfill is placed directly against the membrane. The effectiveness of the membrane depends on the quality of the welding and the repair of any punctures inflicted during installation.

With cast-in-place concrete linings, contact grout holes are typically drilled through the finished lining to intersect the contact between the concrete and the ground or support system. This is not possible with a gas-proof membrane because of the likelihood that the drill bit will puncture the membrane, thereby providing a path for gas transmission. Therefore, if it is deemed necessary to use contact grout when a gas-proof membrane liner is used, pre-forming of contact grout holes could be done by positioning pipes within the liner so they will give access to the contact zone. The maximum testing pressures of the initial water test of these holes and of subsequent grout injection must take into account the strength of the membrane.

2.4.3   Grout Exfiltration

Preventing exfiltration of backfill materials and contact grout is a concern especially when the materials contain chemicals and admixtures that might be considered damaging. When preparing any backfilling and/or contact grouting program, the permeability of the surrounding formation and the presence of nearby water wells, structures, or facilities must be acknowledged and considered. In highly permeable sands or in rock with open fissures, there exists the potential for backfill material and especially contact grout to penetrate some considerable distance from the tunnel or shaft and emerge in unlikely locations, such as basements of buildings, electrical duct banks, and sewers. Injection pressures must be controlled and backfill and contact grout quantities monitored to ensure the material is entering and filling only the void as intended. The mix design and rheology of the backfill and contact grout should be appropriate to best suit the geologic and groundwater conditions.

CHAPTER 3
STRUCTURAL AND OPERATIONAL REQUIREMENTS OF THE COMPLETED FACILITY

To maintain the structural and operational integrity of the completed underground facility, criteria must be developed for design and construction of both the initial ground support and the final lining, and for any related backfilling and/or contact grouting programs. For example, to meet the operational requirement to prevent seepage into underground structures, both backfilling and contact grouting could be done to accommodate load transfer and control of seepage through the liner. The following are examples of additional operational requirements to be designed into a backfilling and contact grouting program:

- Load transfer from the underground structure to the surrounding ground
- Load transfer from the surrounding ground to the underground structure
- Surface settlement
- Safety of operations personnel and the public
- Working environment requirements for electrical, electronic, and mechanical equipment
- Line and grade tolerances of the lining system
- Groundwater inflow limits
- Liquid and gas inflow and outflow limits
- Life-cycle costs of a permanent dewatering system
- General cleaning and material costs associated with damp or wet conditions (maintenance)
- Affect of damp or wet conditions on the underground structure's permanent materials, concrete, reinforcing, or contents

Additional structural, operational, and construction requirements may be applied by the designer or owner on a project-by-project basis.

It is important to note that backfilling and contact grouting are not used as a primary means to control groundwater flows in to or out of the final liner. The primary approach is to stop or considerably reduce the groundwater flow in the surrounding ground before it gets to the liner. This can be accomplished by performing pre-excavation, postexcavation, and postlining installation geotechnical grouting, or installation of "waterproof" barriers (membrane liner).

Installing a high-quality, low-permeability liner will limit inflow and outflow through liners. Depending on liner type, this can be accomplished in the following ways:

- Specifying low-permeability concrete mixes for cast-in-place and precast linings
- Installing impermeable steel linings
- Designing tight pipe joints and construction joints
- Installing impermeable membrane linings
- Using bolted and gasketed connections for segmental liners
- Requiring high standards of workmanship
- Enforcing a good quality control program
- Having adequate and realistic construction budget and schedule

This chapter describes how backfill and contact grout contribute to the incorporation of structural and operational requirements in the design, construction, and use of underground facilities.

3.1   Load Transfer and Liner Stability

Load transfer and liner stability are among the primary functions of backfilling and contact grouting. Load transfer can be either from the underground structure to the surrounding ground, or from the surrounding ground to the underground structure. It is critical that designers consider all possible load conditions when designing and specifying backfilling and contact grouting programs. These conditions include, but are not limited to, temporary construction loads; loads imposed by backfilling and contact grouting; live and dead loads during normal operations (e.g., internal water pressure or vehicle loads in rail and highway tunnels); extreme load cases, such as water hammer and earthquake loads; and loads during maintenance when the structure might be in a dewatered condition. In soft-ground and weak-rock shaft sinking and tunneling, backfilling and contact grouting also serve an important function of helping to limit short- and long-term surface settlement.

Liner stability is important not only during underground facility operations but also during liner installation and construction. Annulus backfilling between the excavated ground and liner systems (e.g., non-expandable concrete segments or penstocks) is an example of liner stabilization. Backfilling helps keep the liner in position and prevents excessive stresses from developing in the liner during construction and after the facility has been put into service.

34

In addition to load transfer and liner stability, backfilling and contact grouting have the secondary benefit of limiting groundwater flows around and through the liner. Backfill material and contact grout can reduce flow of groundwater into the structure and reduce outflow of liquids and gases into surrounding ground. Backfilling with low-permeability material serves this function by filling the larger voids between the liner and the surrounding ground, limiting groundwater flow through the void. Specifically, when the backfilling is continuous and relatively uniform in thickness (such as when used with non-expandable concrete segments, penstocks, and other pipe lining systems), the backfilling and liner can be thought of as a composite liner, or the backfill can be considered a second liner. Contact grouting also fills voids, usually smaller and discontinuous ones that can act as conduits to carry water between the liner and the surrounding ground. Additionally, contact grout can fill shrinkage cracks, construction joints, cold joints, and other defects in cast-in-place concrete liners and in the backfill material. Also, since backfill material and contact grouts are usually injected at pressures between 1 to 3 bars (15 to 45 psi) above in situ hydrostatic pressure, they may permeate to some degree into the surrounding soil and rock. Contact grouting is sometimes injected at higher pressures (5 to 6 bars (75 to 90 psi)), based on specific project requirements, such as high operating pressures of a headrace tunnel. The structural integrity of the liner and the surrounding ground also must be considered. These higher contact grouting injection pressures are more common outside of the United States (Merritt, 2001).

Backfill materials and contact grouts that permeate the ground surrounding underground structures may help reduce the permeability of that ground and decrease inflows and outflows of gases and liquids in to and out of the facility. However, designers should not rely on backfilling and contact grouting to contribute to reducing the liner permeability. It is also important not to plan on having backfill material and contact grout act as a form of geotechnical grouting for groundwater control or strengthening of the ground surrounding the excavation. Curtain and consolidation grouting, two types of geotechnical grouting are the primary means for groundwater control and ground strengthening. Section 2.4 of the guidelines discusses this subject in more detail.

If backfilling and contact grouting are used to rehabilitate an existing underground structure, the impacts of such work should be assessed because rehabilitation can change the structural and operational requirements. Examples of changes include higher operating pressure for water supply or hydroelectric tunnels and shafts, more restrictive seepage criteria, new or additional construction in the area of the existing facility, increase or decrease in the regional groundwater level, increased vehicle loads. Additionally, the designer must evaluate potential adverse chemical reactions between existing underground structure materials and backfill and grout materials used in the rehabilitation.

An example of a rehabilitated existing water supply tunnel is the Larimer Poudre Tunnel in Colorado, originally constructed in the years 1910-11. The tunnel had a major collapse in the year 2000 at the approximate mid-point of the tunnel, the repair of which required a complete tunnel rehabilitation. Portions of the existing tunnel were unsupported, portions were supported with cast-in-place concrete, and other portions were supported with timber. After a complete inspection and analysis of the tunnel condition, it was decided by the designers to line the timbered portions of the tunnel with steel. The new steel liner was installed, and cellular concrete was used as the contact grout material between the new steel liner and the existing timber supports. Cellular concrete also was used to fill the voids between the timber support and ground. Figures 3-1a and 3-1b show the steel liner and the contact grout hoses installed through the spaces between the timber supports. The hoses delivered contact grout behind and around the timber and filled the void between the steel liner and the timber.

Figure 3-1a. Replacement steel liner, not yet expanded, inside of an existing timber lined tunnel. Note contact grout hoses installed into the void behind the timber. (Photo courtesy of Christoph Goss)

Figure 3-1b. Close-up look at contact grout hoses which were fitted through the prefabricated grout ports. Note: blocking not shown.
(Photo courtesy of Christoph Goss)

As with all well-engineered new and rehabilitation projects, the designer should solicit input from the owner and the owner's operation and maintenance personnel early in the design process. Regulations for an existing or new underground facility might exist that also may dictate additional requirements of the backfilling and contact grouting programs.

3.2   Facilities Constructed in Soil vs. Rock

There are significant differences in the structural and operational requirements of facilities constructed in soil and rock. Designers must consider excavation and support methods, physical properties of the material surrounding the structure, and long-term performance criteria of the completed structure. At a minimum, for structures located in soil, the structural properties of the backfill material and contact grout should be equal to or exceed the strength properties of the surrounding ground. When working with structures located in rock, the maximum compressive strength required for the in-place backfill material and contact grout is usually no greater than that of the concrete liner system used; often, it can be much less. An example is when a cellular concrete with a minimum 28-day compressive strength of 3.5 MPa (500 psi) is used to backfill a precast reinforced concrete pipe with a 28-day compressive strength of 21 MPa (3,000 psi). The higher compressive strength requirement for backfills and contact grouts is usually only required for pressure tunnels or where geologic conditions dictate. Physical strength parameters for the surrounding material—such as unit weight, porosity, Modulus of Elasticity, and/or Modulus of Deformation—also may influence the design of backfilling and contact grouting programs.

3.3   Load Transfer from the Underground Structure to the Surrounding Ground

Lined pressure water tunnels are designed to resist internal operating pressure either by a self-supporting liner, which is usually steel, or by interaction of the liner with the surrounding ground. In either case, designers must evaluate load transfer in both operational (pressurized) conditions and maintenance (dewatered) states. In many cases, the dewatered state is the controlling load condition for liner design.

The backfill material and contact grout helps develop an intimate contact with and provide a coupling between the liner and surrounding ground to improve load transfer and limit deformation of the liner prior to and during load transfer. Selection of injection pressures for backfilling and contact grouting of pressure tunnels is based on the operating and surge pressures of the liner and the stiffness of the surrounding ground.

In penstock and steel pipe pressure tunnels, two phases of contact grouting are often required. The first phase typically is performed between the concrete backfill and the surrounding ground, usually at the tunnel crown (see Figure 3-2). This "tunnel crown" void, typical in both backfilled and cast-in-place concrete tunnel linings, is a result of concrete shrinkage, gravity loads during backfilling and cast-in-place concrete placement operations, and poor workmanship of the placement crew.

The second phase of contact grouting is often necessary to fill voids formed between the backfill material and the penstock or steel pipe as a result of concrete or grout shrinkage during curing. Figure 3-3 shows typical locations of these types of voids. This second phase of grouting is sometimes called "skin grouting". Penstocks and steel pipes with stiffener rings, shear lugs, reinforcing steel, attachments of electrical conduits, attachment of small pipes, and other embedments/attachments can require extensive contact grouting to fill voids in the

38

backfill that form around the embedments/attachments. These voids form because the embedments and attachments inhibit the flow of the backfill material during placement. Voids around embedments and attachments can be filled during first phase and second phase contact grouting. However, because most embedment/attachment-type voids are located against the steel liner, only the second phase of contact grouting will completely fill this type of void.

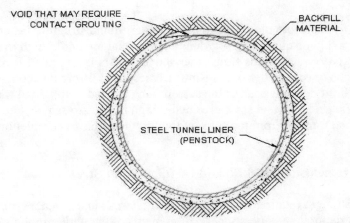

Figure 3-2. Typical location of contact grouting between concrete backfilling and the surrounding ground.

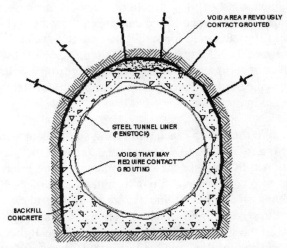

Figure 3-3. Typical location of voids between concrete backfill and penstock or steel pipe as a result of concrete shrinkage during curing.

39

For preliminary analysis of steel lined tunnels, Eskilsson (1999) recommends using a low modulus for the cracked backfill concrete layer on the order of 7,000 MPa (1 x 10^6 psi), or the same magnitude selected for the zone of disturbed rock, whichever is lower.

3.4   Load Transfer from the Surrounding Ground to the Underground Structure

Load transfer from surrounding ground to the underground structure generally occurs in soil and poor-quality rock/ground regions that are under high in situ stress from gravity, water, loads from other above- and below-ground facilities, and from regions or rock under high in situ stresses. Backfilling and contact grouting help limit deformations of the surrounding ground before load transfer to the liner occurs. Underground structures under high in situ stress may be subjected to load transfer from the surrounding ground prior to completion of the liner erection.

3.5   Requirements for Backfill and Contact Grout Strength

Compressive strength requirements for backfill materials and contact grouts are based on the structural and operational requirements of the underground structure, and on construction loading and surface settlement issues. Backfill material and contact grouts are designed to act in compression only. If tensile loads are anticipated, designers must employ structural elements, such as reinforcing steel, into the backfill design. The unconfined compressive strength (UCS) of backfill concrete and backfill grouts used for steel-lined pressure tunnels and shafts is usually in the range of 21 MPa to 35 MPa (3,000 psi to 5,000 psi). Cellular concrete backfill with compressive strengths ranging from 1 MPa to 5 MPa (150 psi to 700 psi) have been placed around concrete pipes and steel pipes in tunnels with various operation pressures.

The UCS of concrete for cast-in-place tunnel and shaft liners also is typically in the range of 21 MPa to 35 MPa (3,000 psi to 5,000 psi). Often, backfill grouts used in conjunction with precast concrete segmental tunnel liners generally require materials with compressive strengths in the range of 7 MPa to 35 MPa (1,000 psi to 5,000 psi). Segmental liners used for tunnels excavated in soil generally only require backfill grout with a compressive strength equal to or slightly greater than the strength of the surrounding soil. Higher compressive strength can be required for dynamic loading and geologic conditions.

Contact grouts are usually mixtures of Portland cement and water with a 1:1 or less water:cement ratio, and they generally have compressive strengths ranging from 14 MPa to 35 MPa (2,000 psi to 5,000 psi). A grout mix that contains only water and cement is referred to as a "neat grout mix." A grout mix containing sands or other fine aggregates is referred to as a "sanded grout mix" or "mortar grout." When the higher strength backfills and cast-in-place concretes are used for structural reasons, the contact grout strength should equal the backfill or cast-in-place concrete strength.

3.6   Groundwater Inflow and the Working Environment

Many underground structures contain sensitive equipment, including electrical, electronic, mechanical, and communications systems. Backfilling and contact grouting can help limit groundwater seepage and reduce undesirable moisture within the completed underground facility. Keeping in mind that this is not the primary function of backfilling and contact grouting, the designer should, therefore, consider additional means of seepage and moisture control, including the following:

- Mix design of the cast-in-place or precast concrete
- Bolted and gasketed segmental lining systems
- Pre- or post-liner installation geotechnical grouting to reduce permeability of the surrounding ground
- Membrane waterproofing
- Drainage systems
- Use of drainage gallery and drainage tunnels
- Maintaining the groundwater table below the tunnel invert
- Locating the facility above the groundwater table
- Use of steel pipe
- Good design of pipe and construction joints
- Good workmanship during manufacture and placement of the line
- A comprehensive quality control program

Seepage criteria should be determined early during facility design based on equipment sensitivity and the owner's operations and maintenance requirements. Detailed records of groundwater inflow made during excavation of the facility will provide valuable data that can identify troublesome zones that could require additional attention, such as geotechnical grouting to reduce permeability of the rock or soil. Many times, these groundwater inflow and grouting records can be invaluable to maintenance personnel for the life of the facility. Additionally, groundwater seepage relative to worker and public safety must be considered. Health hazards related to groundwater seepage can manifest as slippery floors, handrails, and ladder rungs; algae and mold growth; electrical shock danger; bad air; and ice formation. Contaminants and hazardous materials in groundwater that seeps into an underground structure may present a health hazard, as well as a fire and explosion hazard.

3.7   Gas and Liquid Inflow and Outflow

Inflows and outflows from underground structures are important issues. Liquids, such as raw and treated water and water for power generation, are a valuable resource that owners do not want to lose to the surrounding ground. Also, water flows into the surrounding ground can cause a rise in the water table, which, in turn, can cause problems for other facilities in the area. Likewise, a rise in the water table can cause slope and hillside stability problems in the surrounding areas. Also, when operating pressures are lower than the surrounding groundwater pressures, inflows from the surrounding ground may cause a lowering of the groundwater level. Any lowering could cause problems with water wells, surface water resources, and surface settlement. In the case of storm and sanitary sewers, inflow of groundwater means an increase in the volumes of sewerage for the treatment plant to process.

Concrete linings in tunnels and shafts are considered permeable or semi-permeable. These liners include precast segmental concrete, cast-in-place concrete, reinforced concrete pipe, and shotcrete. Backfilling and contact grouting is typically specified to help minimize water loss from pressurized water and sewer tunnels and shafts lined with concrete. Similarly, water seepage into tunnels may be mitigated with backfilling and contact grouting, but geotechnical grouting is inferred.

Leakage criteria are developed on a project-by-project basis. Lugeon water pressure tests should be conducted to determine the permeability characteristics of the surrounding ground. The lugeon test is a "pump-in" test where the volume of water taken in a section of test hole is measured during time intervals. It was derived by Lugeon in 1933, and the related unit of permeability has been named after him. One lugeon unit is equal to 1 liter of water taken per meter of test length, per minute, at 10 bars pressure (150 psi). The following gives a sense of proportion for the unit:

- 1 lugeon unit is the type of permeability where grouting is hardly necessary
- 10 lugeons warrants grouting for most seepage reduction jobs
- 100 lugeons is the type of permeability met in heavily jointed sites with relatively open joints or in sparsely cracked foundations where joints are very wide open (Houlsby, 1980)

When constructing hydroelectric and water transmission pressure tunnels and shafts in soil and rock which have permeabilities greater than approximately 10^{-6} cm/s or lugeon values greater than 10, geotechnical grouting should be used for leakage control.

The publication entitled *Guidelines for Tunnel Lining Design* provides recommended maximum infiltration rates for rapid transit and wastewater conveyance tunnels (O'Rourke, 1984). However many owners are now requiring stricter infiltration criteria than those given in that guideline.

Backfill and contact grout injection pressures must be sufficient to overcome any water pressure that may develop in the voids to be grouted. Water pressure can develop when the grout holes are packed or valved off prior to start of injection. Generally, 1 bar to 3 bars (15 psi to 45 psi) above measured groundwater pressure is considered sufficient for backfill grouting. Normally, contact grout injection pressures are about the same, however, outside of the United States, injection pressures of 5 to 6 bars (75 to 90 psi) are common, with some reported pressures as high as 13.5 bars (200 psi) (Merritt, 2001). The higher pressure suggests some geotechnical grouting may be performed during the contact grouting.

Other underground facilities, such as Compressed Air Energy Storage (CAES) caverns, require a high degree of impermeability. However, the surrounding ground for a CAES facility does not need to be highly impermeable if the cavern is located sufficiently deep enough beneath the groundwater surface. External hydrostatic pressure can provide the necessary confining pressure to prevent air leakage out of the cavern. This principle also applies to underground storage facilities for various other gases and petroleum products.

Backfilling and contact grouting of underground repositories for spent nuclear fuel present a unique challenge to designers. A great deal of research has been performed regarding temperature gradient around storage canisters that develops from the decay of the nuclear materials. Nolting, Duan, and Sun (1998) provides a more detailed discussion of the subject.

CHAPTER 4
LINER SYSTEMS

The selection of a tunnel and shaft lining depends on the geology and groundwater, excavation method, type of lining system (one-pass or two-pass), and completed facility's service requirements (transit, water supply, hydroelectric, wastewater, etc.). In many tunnel and shaft construction projects, two support systems are installed: (1) an initial ground support system erected during excavation to maintain stability and to protect worker safety; and (2) a final lining system to support long-term loads, to meet serviceability requirements, and to provide for the operational functioning of the facility for its intended purpose. This system—an initial support and a final lining—is often called a "two-pass" lining in the underground industry. However, it is not uncommon to have a "one-pass" lining in which a single lining or support system is installed during excavation that satisfies all the safety, load, serviceability, and operational requirements of a two-pass lining.

This chapter identifies various types of ground support and liner systems and their typical applications. Appropriate backfilling and contact grouting requirements also are described.

The type of ground support and/or lining installed in a tunnel or shaft depends on the purpose and use of the completed facility, the geology, and groundwater conditions of the project site. These factors in turn determine what excavation methods are feasible. As a generalization, geologic conditions can be sorted into two categories in tunneling, soft ground (soil) or rock. Furthermore, the behavior of materials within the excavation is described by such systems as the Tunnelman's Classification (Heuer and Virgens, 1987) for soft ground and the Terzaghi Method (Proctor and White, 1988) for rock tunnels. Chapter 2 gives a more detailed description of soil and rock. A key factor in the type of tunnel or shaft support installed during excavation is the stability of the ground, which is often referred to as "stand-up time." Tunnels and shafts excavated in soft ground usually require immediate support following the excavation to support soils that may have short to non-existent stand-up time. Rock tunnels and shafts may or may not require immediate support, depending on the stand-up time, which can range from hours to many years, in which case little or no support is required.

4.1   Types of Tunnel and Shaft Linings

This section describes and illustrates nine tunnel and shaft lining systems.

4.1.1 Steel Ribs and Lagging

Steel ribs and lagging are used in both soft ground and rock tunnels and shafts, usually as part of a two-pass system. The steel ribs and lagging serve as immediate, temporary support during tunnel or shaft excavation (Figure 4-1). The steel ribs usually consist of rolled structural sections bolted together in pieces to form "sets" or "rings" wedged against the ground. The ribs may or may not be expanded and are usually evenly spaced. The steel ribs serve to support ground pressures from soil or highly fractured rock, or they can support individual rock blocks in blocky ground. Wood blocking and/or steel shims are often used to wedge ribs into full contact with the surrounding ground. Wood lagging is required between individual steel ribs if smaller, unstable blocks or raveling ground is present; however, this can be omitted if the ground is stable between ribs, as shown in Figure 4-2. Lagging can alternately consist of steel mats, steel channels, concrete lagging, or steel plates. Shotcrete also is used to fill the spaces between steel sets, particularly in shafts. Steel ribs placed horizontally in shafts are referred to as "ring beams." In shafts, the lagging is placed vertically.

Figure 4-1. Steel ribs and continuous wood lagging support in a TBM excavated rock tunnel.

Figure 4-2. Steel ribs with minimal wood lagging in a drill and blast excavated rock tunnel.

Contact grouting is sometimes required behind the steel ribs and lagging to fill voids caused by overexcavation and/or loss of ground. Contact grouting can be required even when the ribs are expanded.

4.1.2   Liner Plate

Liner plate is typically used in soft-ground conditions where immediate ground support is required and is commonly used in shafts excavated in soft ground. Usually constructed of steel or cast-iron, liner plates consist of metal panels that are bolted together to form a continuous lining (see Figures 4-3 and 4-4). The liner plates can be fitted with gaskets to form a watertight lining. Steel liner plate is generally considered temporary and part of a two-pass lining system, whereas cast-iron liner plate can be used as a one-pass lining because of its corrosion-resistant properties. Steel ribs are sometimes used integrally or as inside supports. Galvanized liner plates are sometimes used as a final liner under railroads and highways. Steel liner segments also are used as a primary liner. Gasketed segments are often used under the groundwater table. Liner plate was once commonly used as a one-pass lining in soft ground transit tunnels, but it is now being less used in favor of precast concrete segmental lining. Because liner plate is not expanded against the ground, contact grouting is usually required to transfer ground loads more uniformly to the lining and to help reduce surface settlement.

Figure 4-3. Cast-iron liner plate supporting a tunnel.

Figure 4-4. Cast-iron liner plate support in a shaft.

4.1.3 Shotcrete

Shotcrete can be used as a form of lagging between steel ribs or other erected supports. Shotcrete is often applied to the excavated ground as initial support without the use of steel ribs. Shotcrete also can be built up to sufficient thickness to serve as a structural lining. Reinforcing of shotcrete is sometimes required if significant bending of the lining is anticipated. Shotcrete reinforcing usually consists of steel fibers, welded wire fabric, or small-diameter rebar, although synthetic fibers are seeing increased use by the underground construction community. Due to the method of application, shotcrete linings are usually used in tunnels and shafts excavated by hand, open-faced digger shield, roadheader, or drill and blast (D&B) methods. Shotcrete is generally not easily compatible with tunnel boring machine (TBM) excavated tunnels due to interference with trailing gear of the machine. Due to its construction versatility, shotcrete is ideal for sequential excavation in soft ground (Figure 4-5). It also is an excellent method for immediate support. Shotcrete has traditionally been considered a temporary lining as part of a two-pass system but is increasingly being seen as the final lining of a one-pass system. During 2001-2003, Colorado Department of Transportation constructed the Highway 160 Wolf Creek Pass tunnel using 75 mm (3 in) of shotcrete as initial support, plus 225 mm (9 in) of reinforced shotcrete as the final liner.

Shotcrete is used extensively in the New Austrian Tunneling Method (NATM), which also is referred to as the sequential excavation method (SEM). In sequentially excavated tunnels, a steel lattice girder or rib is often used as a template to define the tunnel section (Figure 4-6).

Figure 4-5. Shotcrete support in a soft-ground tunnel, excavated using the sequential excavation method, as part of a two-pass tunnel lining system.

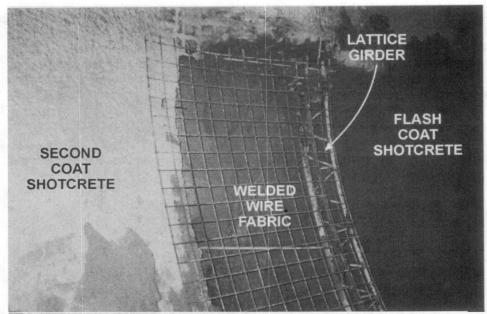

Figure 4-6. Details of a shotcrete lining with steel lattice girders as part of a one-pass system.

Grouting behind shotcrete linings per se is usually not necessary because the shotcrete, by virtue of the placement methods, is in intimate contact with the ground. However, contact grouting between an initial shotcrete lining and a cast-in-place concrete final lining is very common in two-pass lining systems. Likewise, backfilling between an initial shotcrete lining and a final lining, such as a pipe, also is quite common.

4.1.4   Expandable Precast Concrete Segments

Expanded segments are typically used in soft ground but are sometimes installed in hard-rock tunnels. This type of lining is usually the initial support of a two-pass system. It consists of precast concrete segments that are expanded as a ring behind an open-faced shield or TBM to provide immediate support (Figure 4-7). Expansion of the segmental ring results in a gap in the ring that must be supported with metal screw jacks, steel wedges, shotcrete, or a mortar grout. Adjacent rings are usually not connected to each other.

As with steel ribs and lagging, contact grouting is sometimes required behind the expandable precast concrete segmental lining to fill voids caused by overexcavation and ground loss.

Figure 4-7. Expanded concrete segments in a rock tunnel.

4.1.5 Non-expandable Precast Concrete Segments

This type of tunnel lining is increasingly the method of choice in soft-ground tunnels excavated with TBMs. When using a non-expandable system, individual precast concrete segments, usually with gasketed joints, are bolted to each other to form a ring (Figure 4-8). Subsequent rings are bolted to each other to form a watertight lining. This type of precast concrete segmental lining can be used as initial support for a two-pass system, or it can function as a one-pass system (Figure 4-9). A bolted, gasketed, non-expanded lining is almost always required for pressurized face excavation methods, such as a slurry shield (SS) or earth pressure balance (EPB) TBM. In these cases, the lining is assembled in the tailshield of the TBM and bolted together. The bolted lining is extruded from the tailshield, providing immediate support. The annulus between the excavated ground and the precast concrete segmental lining is then backfill grouted. The backfill grout can be injected through a piping system installed within the shield of the TBM or through grout ports in the segments. Backfill grouting behind the non-expanded segmental lining is required to maintain line and grade of the lining, to transfer ground loads more uniformly to the lining, and to help reduce surface settlement in soft-ground and weak-rock tunnels.

Precast concrete segments, both expandable and non-expandable, are used in shaft construction; however, this is not yet common practice in the United States.

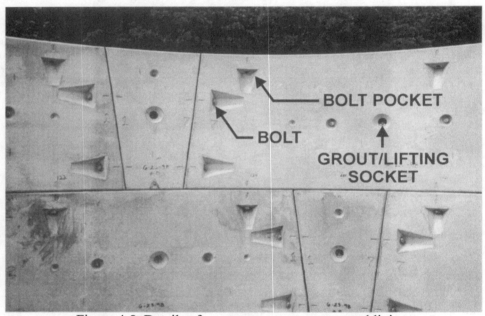

Figure 4-8. Details of a precast concrete segmental lining.

Figure 4-9. One-pass precast concrete segmental lining in a soft ground tunnel.

4.1.6 Cast-in-Place Concrete

Usually serving as the final lining of a two-pass system, cast-in-place concrete is a common method to line transit tunnels and water supply tunnels and shafts. It can be used in both soft-ground and rock conditions. The concrete placement operation usually occurs after excavation of the tunnel is complete (Figure 4-10). In transit tunnels, it is sometimes required to install a membrane waterproofing between the initial lining and the final cast-in-place lining to help limit groundwater or gas inflows. Most cast-in-place concrete linings are constructed using collapsible steel forms (Figure 4-11).

Contact grouting is almost always required between the excavated ground and/or initial support and the final lining to fill voids in the tunnel crown that are invariably left by the cast-in-place concrete placement process.

Figure 4-10. Cast-in-place concrete tunnel lining (note forms in foreground).

Figure 4-11. Collapsible tunnel forms.

4.1.7 Welded Steel Pipe

A steel carrier pipe is usually used for water supply tunnels and penstocks. When the carrier pipe is installed in a tunnel that is already supported by an initial support system, the carrier pipe forms a two-pass lining system. The carrier pipe also can be installed in a rock tunnel where the rock is of good enough quality to require little or no initial support.

The steel pipe/penstock is fabricated and delivered to the job site in sections, usually in lengths ranging from 2.5 to 18 m (8 to 60 ft). Figure 4-12 shows the shop fabrication of a large-diameter steel pipe. Figure 4-13 shows a section of a penstock that is 3.35 m (11 ft) in diameter at the job site, awaiting installation into the tunnel. Note the stiffener rings and small diameter pipes that will be embedded in the backfill. These are the types of embedments that can block the free flow of backfill, causing voids. When larger diameter pipe/penstock is required, e.g., 4 m (13 ft) and larger, it is usually fabricated at the job site. Steel pipe sections can be connected with butt welds or bell-and-spigot joints, with or without seal welding. The interior surface of steel pipe is normally coated with a mortar or epoxy for corrosion protection.

Backfilling between excavated ground and/or initial ground support and the steel carrier pipe is required to transfer loads and provide corrosion protection to the exterior surface of the steel pipe. When steel pipes are subjected to high groundwater pressures, the backfill enhances the buckling capacity of the steel pipe. A program of contact grouting is often required to fill any void left by the backfilling operation, similar to cast-in-place concrete lining. Some steel pipes and penstocks require a second phase of contact grouting between the steel pipe or penstock and the backfill.

4.1.8 Precast Concrete Pipe

Similar to steel pipe, precast concrete pipe is often used as a carrier pipe in a two-pass system and often in water supply and wastewater tunnel applications (Figures 4-14 and 4-15). Among the different types of precast concrete pipes are prestressed concrete cylinder pipe (PCCP), reinforced concrete cylinder pipe (RCCP), and reinforced concrete pipe (RCP). Large- and small-diameter glass reinforced pipe (GRP) also is used in underground applications.

Backfill and contact grouting operations for precast concrete pipes are similar to backfill and contact grouting for steel pipes.

Figure 4-12. Fabrication of welded steel pipe for a tunnel lining.

Figure 4-13. A 3.35 m (11 ft) diameter steel penstock at the job site awaiting installation into the tunnel.

Figure 4-14. 2400 mm (96 in.) inside diameter reinforced concrete pipe (RCP).

Figure 4-15. Pre-stressed concrete cylinder pipe during installation in a
wastewater tunnel.

4.1.9 Other Types of Pipe

In addition to concrete, fiberglass, and steel pipe, other types of pipe materials are used in tunnels, particularly in small-diameter water and wastewater tunnels. Many small-diameter water lines and sanitary and storm sewers are installed using trenchless technology methods, such as directional drilling and pipe jacking (microtunneling). Other types of pipe material include high-density polyethylene (HDPE), vitrified clay, and polymer concrete pipe, also known as polycrete pipe (Figure 4-16).

Pipes installed by trenchless methods may or may not require backfilling or contact grouting, depending on the size of the tunnel and the amount of surface settlement expected. An example is in the case where a pipe casing is first installed using the directional drilling method, and subsequently a smaller diameter carrier pipe or several utility pipes are installed within the casing pipe. The annulus between the carrier pipe(s) and the casing often requires backfill grouting. Contact grouting in trenchless technology tunnels is used to fill the annulus between the excavated ground and the pipe installed as part of the excavation process.

Figure 4-16. Polymer concrete pipe being installed by pipe jacking method.

4.2   Grouting in Relation to Lining Design

The design of the tunnel and shaft linings is typically based on a number of ground–liner interaction procedures first proposed by Peck in 1969 and expanded in later works (Ranken, 1978; Hansmire et al., 1989; and Kuesel et al., 1996). These methods recognize the flexibility of the tunnel/shaft lining to allow for stresses around the outside of the lining to equilibrate, thus reducing the moments imposed on the lining. The basis for the design procedure is that the lining has to be flexible enough in relation to the surrounding medium in order to deform. To some extent, tunnels and shafts are "self-correcting" against ground load. In other words, tunnels and shafts tend to deform in such a manner that their full strength is mobilized prior to failure.

Once expected moments and thrusts have been estimated by one of the various ground–liner interaction methods, the next step is to determine whether the lining is capable of supporting these loads. The expected combinations of thrust and moment are plotted on the moment–thrust diagram for concrete and shotcrete linings, or compared to yielding and/or buckling relationships for steel linings.

In addition to its primary function as a void filler of the annulus around a carrier pipe, backfill material and contact grout serve to transfer the radial ground loads to the carrier pipe lining. The design of the backfill and contact grout must account for this load transfer, as well as provide complete and uniform contact between excavated ground and/or initial ground support and the carrier pipe. It is critical to support carrier pipes to prevent flotation during backfilling operations. In addition, stulling (i.e., bracing) of the carrier pipe is often required to prevent its unacceptable deformation due to buoyant forces. In this regard, low-density grouts are advantageous because they impart lower buoyancy.

Like backfill, contact grout must provide intimate contact between the lining and the ground or initial support. The design of the lining being contact grouted must account for high-contact grout injection pressures that are often necessary to completely fill voids and overcome any groundwater pressures. Contact grout injection pressures are considered a temporary load, and therefore may justify lower load factors (or lower safety factors) for design. Contact grout is injected through discrete holes or ports, causing a concentrated pressure around the lining near the hole or port. Fortunately, this pressure decreases rapidly as distance increases from the injection point due to friction losses, grout migration into voids, and possibly some slight permeation of grout into the surrounding ground.

CHAPTER 5
GROUT MATERIAL

Grouts based on some type of cement are the most widely used category of grouts throughout the world. They are used in more applications than the other families of grouts, including colloidal and pure chemical solutions. Cement-based particulate grouts (Bruce et al., 1997), depending on their composition, may be stable (i.e., having minimal bleeding) or unstable when left at rest. Stable thixotropic grouts have both cohesion and plastic viscosity increasing with time at a rate that may be considerably accelerated under pressure. They exhibit a Binghamian performance (Figure 5-1a), compared to the evolutive or non-evolutive Newtonian characteristics of colloidal solutions and pure solutions, respectively (Figure 5-1b). Chapter 6 contains a detailed discussion of fluid behavior.

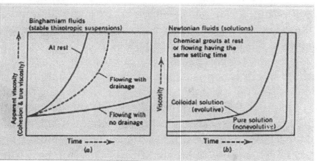

Figure 5-1. Rheological behavior of typical grouts
(Mongilardi and Tornaghi, 1986).

The water-to-solids ratio of cement-based particulate grouts is the prime determinant of their properties and basic characteristics, which, in addition to cohesion, viscosity, and stability, include durability and strength (Littlejohn, 1982). Five broad subcategories of particulate grouts can be identified:

1. **Neat Cement Grouts.** These are typically associated with high strength and durability.

2. **Clay/Bentonite-Cement Grouts.** Cement is stabilized with a clay mineral to provide specific fluid and set characteristics. Mix designs for waterproofing and low-strength backfilling applications will have much clay and relatively little cement, while the reverse is true for structural grouts. Jefferis (1982) described how the quality of mixing of such grouts

in particular can have a strong influence on the subsequent grout properties, especially bleed, penetrability, strength, and brittleness.

3. **Grouts with Fillers.** Adding non-cementitious substances substantially modifies the resultant properties and reduces the unit volume cost of the mix. The most common fillers are sands and pulverized flyash (p.f.a.), both Type C and Type F; but other materials have been used depending on local preferences and availability. These are usually fine and inert industrial byproducts that include mine tailings, kiln dust, pumice, silica fume, and other materials.

4. **Grouts for Special Applications.** Depending on specific project requirements for the grout in its fluid and/or set condition, there are requirements for grouts with controlled rates of hydration and rheology; foam, enhanced strength, and/or improved resistance to washout. Such grouts will be multicomponent blends of many materials, including typically admixtures and additives (Gause and Bruce, 1997).

5. **Grouts with Enhanced Penetrability.** To thoroughly and economically fill small voids while avoiding concerns typical of other categories of grouts, e.g., permanence, toxicity, strength, and cost. Additives are used to improve rheological properties and/or increase pressure-filtration resistance, while the use of ultrafine cements (Schwarz and Krizek, 1992) is increasing fast. Contact grouting the void(s) between a pipe or penstock and the backfill is a good example of small voids where ultrafine cements are often specified.

This chapter describes materials used in backfill and cement grout mixtures: cement, water, aggregates, mineral and chemical admixtures, and foam concentrates. The characteristics and behavior of these materials in backfill and contact grout, as well as applications for their use, also are discussed.

5.1   Cements

Generally, two categories of cements are used to make backfill materials and contact grouts: Portland cements and ultrafine cements. Different types of Portland cement are manufactured to meet various physical and chemical requirements for specific purposes. ASTM C150, *Standard Specification for Portland Cement,* provides for eight types of Portland cement. However, for most backfilling and contact grouting applications, only Types I, II, and III are used.

The Portland Cement Association publication *Design and Control of Concrete Mixtures* (Kosmatka and Panarese, 1988) gives the following definition for Types I, II, and III Portland cements:

1. **Type I.** Type I Portland cement is a general-purpose cement suitable for all uses where the special properties of other types are not required. It is used in concrete that is not subject to aggressive exposures, such as sulfate attack from soil or water, or to an objectionable temperature rise due to heat generated by hydration. Its uses in concrete include pavements, floors, reinforced concrete buildings, bridges, railway structures, tanks and reservoirs, pipe, masonry units, and other precast concrete products.

2. **Type II.** Type II Portland cement is used where precaution against moderate sulfate attack is important, as in drainage structures where sulfate concentrations in groundwater are higher than normal but not unusually severe. Type II cement will usually generate less heat at a slower rate than Type I. The requirement of moderate heat of hydration can be specified at the option of the purchaser. If heat-of-hydration maximums are specified, this cement can be used in structures of considerable mass, such as large piers and heavy abutments and retaining walls. Its use will reduce temperature rise, which is especially important when concrete is placed in warm weather. Frequently, the addition of flyash to concrete or grout can provide resistance to sulfate attack in place of Type II cement.

3. **Type III.** Type III Portland cement provides high strengths at an early period, usually a week or less. It is chemically and physically similar to Type I cement, except that its particles have been more finely ground. It is used when forms need to be removed as soon as possible or when the structure must be put into service quickly. In cold weather, its use permits a reduction in the controlled curing period. Although richer mixes of Type I cement can be used to gain high early strength, Type III may provide it more satisfactorily and more economically.

It is important to remember that, despite the existence of ASTM C150, cements of the same type will vary from one geographic location to another, from one cement plant to another, and even from one batch to another from the same cement plant. Therefore, prior to the start of field backfilling and contact grouting operations, trial batches of the backfill and contact grout should always be tested using the actual cement and other ingredients that will be used in production batching.

Ultrafine cements, also called "microfine" and "superfine" cements, are sometimes used in specialized contact grouting operations. These terms are considered synonymous, since at present there is no industry standard definition. Ultrafine cement can be manufactured from a Portland cement, a slag or a combination of these. Currently there is no established nomenclature or reference standard in terms of grain-size distribution for ultrafine cements. The American Concrete Institute (ACI) Committee 552 (Geotechnical Cement Grouting) has unofficially adopted a reference standard for ultrafine cement. In a draft report on state-of-the-art geotechnical cement grouting, this committee defines ultrafine cement particles as 100 percent finer than 15 μm (Henn, 1996).

5.2   Water

Almost any water that is potable and has no pronounced taste or odor can be used as mixing water for making backfill materials and contact grouts. However, some waters that are not potable may still be suitable for making backfill materials and contact grouts.

Water of questionable suitability can be used for making backfill materials or contact grouts if mortar cubes (ASTM C109, *Test Method for Compressive Strength of Hydraulic Cement Mortars (Using 2 in. or 50 mm Cube Specimens)*) made with it have 7-day strengths equal to at least 90 percent of companion specimens made with potable or distilled water. In addition, ASTM C191, *Test Method for Testing of Setting of Hydraulic Cement by Vicat Needle*, tests should be made to ensure impurities in the mixing water do not adversely shorten or extend the setting time of the cement. Acceptable criteria for water that can be used in concrete are given in ASTM C94, *Standard Specification for Ready Mix Concrete*. Tables 5-1 and 5-2 show examples of these criteria.

Table 5-1. Acceptance Criteria for Questionable Water Supplies (ASTM C94)

	Limits	Test Method
Compressive strength, minimum percentage of control at 7 days	90	C109[*]
Time of set, deviation from control, hr:min	from 1:00 earlier to 1:30 later	C191[*]

[*]Comparisons should be based on fixed proportions and the same volume of test water compared to control mix using city water or distilled water.

Table 5-2. Chemical Limits for Wash Water used as Mixing Water (ASTM C94)

Chemical	Maximum concentration[*], ppm	Test Method[**]
Chloride, as Cl		ASTM D512
Prestressed concrete or concrete in bridge decks	500[***]	
Other reinforced concrete in moist environments or containing aluminum embedments or dissimilar metals or with stay-in-place galvanized metal forms	1,000[***]	
Sulfate, as SO_4	3,000	ASTM D516
Alkalies, as (Na_2O + 0.658 K_2O)	600	
Total Solids	50,000	AASHTO T26

[*]Wash water reused as mixing water in concrete can exceed the listed concentrations of chloride and sulfate if it can be shown that the concentration calculated in the total mixing water, including mixing water on the aggregates and other sources, does not exceed the stated limits.
[**]Other test methods that have been demonstrated to yield comparable results can be used.
[***]For conditions allowing use of $CaCl_2$ accelerator as an admixture, the chloride limitation may be waived by the purchaser.

Excessive impurities in mixing water not only may affect setting time and backfill/contact grout compressive strength but also may cause efflorescence, staining, corrosion of reinforcement, volume instability, and reduced durability. Therefore, certain optimal limits may be set on chlorides, sulfates, alkalies, and solids in the mixing water, or appropriate tests can be performed to determine the effect the impurity has on various properties. Some impurities may have little effect on compressive strength and setting time, yet they can adversely affect durability and other properties.

Water containing less than 2,000 ppm of total dissolved solids can generally be used satisfactorily for making backfill materials and contact grouts. Water containing more than 2,000 ppm of dissolved solids should be tested for its effect on strength and set time.

The grout program designer should carefully select water acceptance criteria carefully. For example, if water acceptance criteria are set higher than is technically necessary for specific project requirements, unjustified additional costs may be added to the project. A situation in which this could happen is when a designer copies the water acceptance requirements from an existing reinforced concrete specification into a non-reinforced backfill or contact grout specification. While most commercial and onsite concrete batch plants can meet or exceed such water quality requirements, the same water-quality may not be readily available onsite for the project's backfilling and contact grouting programs. However, to meet the unnecessarily high water-quality standards required in the backfilling and contact grouting specification, water may have to be transported in, a supply line installed, or a well drilled. Any of these measures could result in additional, possibly unwarranted, project costs.

In the above example, the upper limits of the chloride concentration in the mixing water for the reinforced concrete may have been established due to the possible adverse effects of chloride ions on the corrosion of reinforcing steel in the concrete. A higher allowable limit of chloride concentration for the non-reinforced backfill or contact grout may be acceptable, however, if it is not going to be in contact with steel reinforcing, steel lining, steel embedments, or reinforced concrete linings (Henn, 1996).

AJ Voton LLC (2001), a foam concrete supplier/contractor, suggests limiting harmful ingredients in the mixing water of the slurry used to make foam concrete to the amounts given in Table 5-3.

5.3   Aggregates

Sand is the most common aggregate used in making backfill and contact grout. Coarse aggregates are used in making conventional concrete backfills, usually associated with penstock and other types of high-pressure pipe backfilling.

Sand is used as a filler to provide mix volume, usually when larger voids requiring filling are known to exist. Also, sand offers an advantage as it is considerably less costly than cement.

Table 5-3. AJ Voton LLC Suggested Limits of Harmful Ingredients in Mixing Water

Substances	Maximum Amounts in % by Mass
Non-soluble matter	0.5
Soluble matter	1.0
Alkali (bi) carbonates	0.1
Sulphates (determined as SO_3^{2-})	0.1
Sugars	0.01
Phosphates (determined as P_2O_5	0.01
Nitrates (determined as NO_3^-)	0.05
Zinc compounds	0.01

Chlorides should be limited to 500 mg/l. Acidity pH at least 4. Check water for presence of humic acid by mixing equal amounts with 3% NaOH; proper water should show no brown color.

Adding sand to a contact grout mix is usually warranted when the contact grout water–cement ratio (of the cement and water only), has been reduced to a point of thickening the mix to its minimum pumpable viscosity while the void being injected still shows no sign of a reduced injection rate. Also, starting contact grouting of the hole with a sanded grout mix may be warranted to fill larger voids, in the 50-mm (2-in) plus depth range, when they are known to exist prior to the start of injection. It is still a good idea to first inject a batch of non-sanded grout to fill adjacent smaller defects and "prime" the way for the less penetrable sanded mix. Exclusive use of a sanded grout may prevent neat grout from penetrating the finer cracks and voids that may allow water to flow along the annulus and ultimately have undesirable effects on the facility.

In addition to economical considerations, sand also is used to reduce shrinkage experienced by in-place hardened backfill and contact grout. Both concrete and grout undergo a reduction in volume as they change from the fluid state to the solid state. The amount of volume change is dependent on the water–cement ratio; that is, the higher the water–cement ratio, the greater the shrinkage.

Sand meeting the requirements of ASTM C33, *Specification for Concrete Aggregates,* can be used for backfills and contact grouts. The ASTM C33 gradation limits with respect to sieve size are given in Table 5-4.

The larger particles in C-33 sand, especially those larger than No. 16 sieve, will tend to rapidly settle out of the relatively thin mixes used in contact grout. They also will tend to plug small voids that surround the larger ones into which the injection is being made. Sand used for suspension grouts is typically on the fine side, often minus-No.-30 sieve. It is important to remember that sand is abrasive and its addition, especially to a contact grout mix, causes additional wear on pumps and grout distribution systems and can form sand plugs in the pumping/distribution system.

Table 5-4. ASTM C33 Gradation Limits

Sieve Size	Percent passing by weight
9.5 mm (3/8 in.)	100
No. 4 (4.75 mm)	95-100
No. 8 (2.36 mm)	80-100
No. 16 (1.18 mm)	50-85
No. 30 (600 μm)	25-60
No. 50 (300 μm)	10-30
No. 100 (150 μm)	2-10

5.4   Admixtures

The ACI defines an admixture as "a material other than cement, water, aggregate or fibers required for the manufacture of high performance concrete." Admixtures fall into two categories: mineral admixtures and chemical admixtures. Mineral admixtures generally act as fillers to replace cement, help reduce shrinking, increase pumpability, or give other specific properties to a mix. Chemical admixture technology generally always works on the cement portion of concrete, so the same attributes would apply to grout regardless of whether sand or aggregate is present. Mineral and chemical admixtures are described in the following sections.

5.4.1   Mineral Admixtures

Mineral admixtures are other materials added to the mix to provide volume, replace some cement, improve pumpability, provide compressability to the hardened material, and increase or decrease mix density. Some examples are bentonite, flyash, and vermiculite, as described below. Foam can be considered a special filler; it is made from organic or synthetic materials.

5.4.1.1 Bentonite

Bentonite is a colloidal clay from the montmorillonite group that is hydrophilic, or water swelling. Some bentonite can absorb as much as five or more times its own weight in water (Brady and Clauser, 1986). Bentonite is added to cement

67

grout to stabilize the mix by reducing settlement of cement particles and, when used, sand. It increases both grout viscosity and cohesion. Addition of bentonite will also improve the mix's pumpability and flowability. Bentonite is proportioned to the grout mix as a percentage of cement by weight. The amount of bentonite used usually ranges from 1 to 4 percent by weight of cement. The use of bentonite, however, will reduce backfill and contact grout strengths.

5.4.1.2 Flyash

Flyash, the most widely used mineral admixture in concrete, is a pozzolan. It is a finely divided residue (powder resembling cement) that results from the combustion of pulverized coal in electric power generating plants. Most flyash particles are solid spheres; some are hollow cenospheres. Particle sizes in flyash can vary from less than 1 μm to more than 100 μm, with typical particle size under 20 μm. Flyash is primarily silicate glass containing silica, alumina, iron, and calcium (Kosmatka and Panarese, 1988). Flyash can be used to replace a portion of the cement in backfill and contact grout mixes. The use of flyash will also reduce the heat of hydration of the in-place concrete and grout.

There are two types of flyash: ASTM Classes C and F. Class C ash is pozzolanic and cementitious and will set on its own when mixed with water. Class F flyash is pozzolanic but not cementitious; therefore, it will not set on its own in water, but requires a source of calcium to set, as when mixed with cement. The combination of cement and Class F flyash will always set more slowly than a mix with no flyash, yet it will typically achieve the same or even greater ultimate strengths but much sooner. This is advantageous if moderate late-age strengths are required but low early-age strengths are acceptable. Adding flyash to a mix will reduce the heat generated during hydration. This is particularly important in shaft and tunnel backfilling and contact grouting since the surface area to liberate heat is limited to the inside of the shaft or tunnel.

5.4.1.3 Vermiculite

Vermiculite, a foliated mineral, is an alteration of biotite and other micas. It is found in Colorado, Wyoming, Montana, and the Transvaal. When used, vermiculite is added to backfill mixes to create a low-density and/or compressible fill material. Compressability of backfill material is sometimes required in seismic areas and areas subject to high in situ rock stresses (rock squeeze).

5.4.2 Chemical Admixtures

Chemical admixtures generally cannot turn a bad backfill or contact grout mix design into a good one. Rather, they should be used to enhance the performance of a good mix design. Chemical admixtures can be used to increase the flowability of a mix, increase strength (by reducing mix water quantity), minimize bleeding and segregation, increase working time, prevent washout when placed in water, accelerate setting time, and reduce shrinkage.

ASTM C494 states that for an admixture to conform it must provide a certain measurable increase in performance over a control mix. The ASTM lists seven types of chemical admixtures. Designations for their performance are listed and described below.

1. **Type A (water reducing).** Against a control concrete mix, a Type A admixture must provide a 5- to 12-percent water reduction, provide a minimum 10-percent strength gain, and have no influence over the normal set time, neither increasing nor decreasing it.

2. **Type B (retarding).** Against a control concrete mix, a Type B admixture must provide an increase of 1 to 3.5 hr on the initial set and 3.5 hr on the final set.

3. **Type C (accelerating).** Against a control concrete mix, a Type C admixture must provide a minimum of 1- to 3.5-hr earlier initial set and 1-hr earlier final set.

4. **Type D (water reducing and retarding).** Against a control concrete mix, a Type D admixture must provide an increase of 1 to 3.5 hr on the initial set and 3.5 hr on the final set. It also must provide a minimum 10-percent strength gain.

5. **Type E (water reducing and accelerating).** Against a control concrete mix, a Type E admixture must provide a minimum of 1- to 3.5-hr earlier initial and 1-hr earlier final set. To satisfy the water-reducing aspect of this admixture, it also must provide a 10-percent strength gain in addition to the acceleration.

6. **Type F (water reducing, high range).** Against a control concrete mix, a Type F admixture must provide a minimum of 10- to 40-percent water reduction. It also must show a 40-percent increase in 1-day strength.

7. **Type G (water reducing, high range, and retarding).** Against a control concrete mix, a Type G admixture must provide a minimum of 10- to 40-percent water reduction, a minimum of 1- to 3.5-hours delay on initial set, a minimum 3.5-hour delay on the final set, and a 25-percent increase in 1-day strengths.

5.4.2.1.   Water Reducers and Superplasticizers

All superplasticizers are water reducers, but not all water reducers are superplasticizers. As stated in the ASTM C494, the degree of water reduction in a superplasticizer is much greater than in a normal water-reducing agent. Water reducers are one of the most important and versatile admixtures. The shrinkage potential of grout or concrete, as well as compressive strength and durability, is a function of its water–cement ratio. The minimum water–cement ratio required (by weight) for complete hydration of cement is approximately 0.22:0.25 (Kosmatka and Panarese, 1988). Any water in excess of this minimum amount reduces the strength of the hardened mix. However, more water than the minimum required for complete hydration is almost always needed to make a more pumpable or penetrable grout. The additional water for flowability and workability reduces the grout/concrete's compressive strength. Water reducers allow the amount of water in a mix to be reduced without affecting the workability of the mix.

5.4.2.2.   Retarders and Hydration Control Agents

Retarders extend the workability time of a mix, which is frequently required in tunnel work. Long transport and placing times often require extended set times. Most retarders provide only a given amount of retardation, generally no more than 3 to 4 hr. They act by delaying the hydration of only one of the four chemical compounds in the cement. Adding more retarder than recommended to achieve a longer retardation time is not advisable, since it could retard the mix far longer than desired or may even cause a flash set.

Hydration control agents work by delaying the set of all four of the cement chemical compounds. Contrary to the way retarders work, a hydration control agent can be used to extend the set time of cement in a controlled fashion by upwards of 72 hr.

5.4.2.3. Accelerators

Several types of accelerators are available for decreasing the set time of a cement-based grout or concrete. These accelerators can be calcium-chloride based or sodium-thiocyanate based, and shotcrete accelerators such as sodium silicate and aluminum sulfate. It should be noted that some of these shotcrete accelerators have deleterious effects (mainly corrosion of reinforcement) in long-term applications.

5.4.2.4. Other Admixtures

There are other types of admixtures not listed in or covered by the ASTM standards. This does not mean the admixtures are unacceptable for use; rather, there is no standard for assessing their performance. Three other such admixtures are listed and described below. Of these, anti-washout and anti-shrink admixtures have the most application in void filling.

1. **Anti-washout Admixtures/Viscosity Modifiers.** Anti-washout admixtures are perhaps one of the greatest admixture tools for void filling underground. It is common to have either standing or flowing water in the annulus during backfilling or contact grouting. Standing water can often be displaced during backfill and contact grout placements by the advancing mix itself pushing the water ahead of the advancing material. Flowing water, however, can be problematic, causing dilution and washout of the backfill and contact grout. The use of an anti-washout admixture greatly reduces dilution and washout of the material being placed.

   Bentonite, while it will increase the cohesion and viscosity of a grout, does not provide significant anti-washout properties. Bentonite also will reduce the compressive strength of the placed backfill and contact grout. Anti-washout admixtures will help prevent washout and not seriously affect the strength of the placed material. Anti-washout admixtures will increase cohesion and viscosity of backfill and contact grout. Their use will thus significantly reduce settlement of the solid in a grout, reducing or very nearly eliminating bleed. While these will "thicken" the grout, where required, the penetrability of backfill or contact grout can be increased by using superplasticizers.

   Unlike most admixtures, which treat the cement portion of the mix, anti-washout agents treat the fluid part of the mix. Therefore, the lower the amount of water used in the mix, the lower the dose of anti-washout admixture required. Anti-washout admixtures do not perform their intended function as well with mixes that have high water–cement ratios.

2. **Anti-Shrink Admixtures.** Eliminating or reducing shrinkage of the hardened backfill and contact grout mix can be accomplished by using expansive agents or by using admixtures that reduce shrinkage to an acceptable amount. Expansive agents slightly expand the mix to a greater amount than the mix shrinks. Alternatively, anti-shrinkage admixtures may be used. These admixtures do not completely eliminate shrinkage, but they can reduce it significantly. If desired, shrinkage of a backfill or contact grout mix should be measured by ASTM C1090.

   As with anti-washout admixtures, the anti-shrink and shrinkage compensating admixtures must be used in a balanced mix design, with a moderate to a relatively low water–cement ratio. There also are expansion agents that can be used in very fluid mixes with an accelerator, e.g., Sika/Intercrete

3. **Corrosion-Resisting Admixtures.** Corrosion resistance of backfill and contact grout mixes is generally not an issue. However, in some circumstances, it may be important that in-place backfill and contact grout prevent chloride or sulfate ingress into the tunnel or tunnel liner reinforcement system. This may be particularly true in deep tunnels or those mined near geothermally heated water, which often contains high concentrations of sulfites and sulfates. A backfill or contact grout mix can be made to be more durable against the penetration of these elements by one of the following means. First, a denser mix will always help in resisting water flow and hence chemical ingress. A dense mix is made using less water and more fines, such as cement, flyash, and silica fume. As a natural consequence of the denser mix, higher strengths are usually achieved. However, the mix may be less flowable, requiring the addition of plasticizers.

Admixtures also can be used to increase durability of the backfill material, contact grout, and steel reinforcement. They can provide corrosion protection by blocking pore spaces in the grout/concrete matrix, or by forming a coating on the steel, which prevents chloride attack.

5.5   Foam Concentrates

Foam concentrates are best treated separately from standard admixtures. Foam is more like a near "zero" weight aggregate or filler. Foam is added to a cement slurry to produce a cellular concrete or foam grout. Cellular concrete in underground applications can provide the following advantages over normal-weight backfills:

- Generally, lower unit cost than higher density backfill materials.
- Greater pumpability. The air in the slurry makes the cellular concrete very easy to pump; thus the material can be pumped very long distances.
- Greater flowability. Promotes complete encapsulation of initial support elements, the final lining, and embedments located in the annulus.
- Variable density (can be made lighter than water). By varying the amount of slurry to amount of foam, variable density cellular concretes can be easily made.
- Compressibility. A backfill material made with foam will compress as load is applied due to collapse of the bubbles, thus allowing the cellular concrete to yield under strain. The collapse of the internal structure of the cellular concrete is non-recoverable. This can be an advantage if a backfill material needs energy absorptive characteristics, such as at an active fault closing.
- Speed of placement. The addition of air not only makes the cellular concrete easier to pump, but also it increases the amount of material being pumped. The foam comprises a significant volume of a cellular concrete. Tremendous quantities of foam can be made easily and rapidly, which roughly doubles or triples the production rate of a normal-weight backfill operation.

A cellular concrete consists of foam solution, air, and a cement grout slurry. The cement slurry also can contain flyash. The foam solution consists of foam concentrate and water. Passing the solution and air through a conditioner (foam generator) aerates the solution, thus making foam. The foam is then proportionally added to a cement/flyash grout slurry and mixed, producing a cellular concrete.

Foam works simply by adding air to the mix. The amount of foam used in a mix varies from cellular concrete densities of 320 kg/m^3 (20 pcf) up to the density of a completely unfoamed slurry. The low densities, while sometimes desirable, are more difficult to maintain. In fact, most tunnel cellular concretes are rarely less dense than 720 kg/m^3 (45 pcf) density. The greatest concern when using a cellular concrete is that the material's density does not appreciably change from the point of mixing to point of final placement. Just as important, the foam must not dissipate prior to the setting of the cellular concrete. Figure 5-2 is a graph showing density versus strength of foam mixtures; these are approximate strengths. Designs should not be based on this graph; rather, it should be used as a measure of the strengths that are obtainable at various densities. All mix designs should be trial tested in a laboratory and field tested prior to placement.

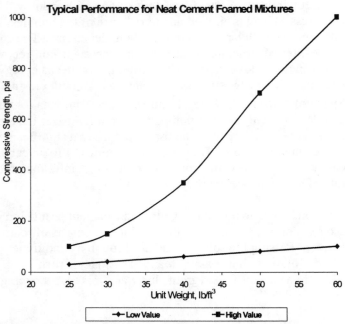

Figure 5-2. Graph showing density versus strength for neat cement foamed mixes.

CHAPTER 6
GROUT PROPERTIES

Some of the desired long-term properties of backfill materials and contact grouts run counter to short-term placement and workability properties of the mixes. For example, desired properties such as high compressive strength, durability, and low permeability are all results of a dense backfill material and contact grout. However, pumpability and workability require mobile mixes. Prior to the advent of water reducers and superplasticizers, a pumpable and workable mix meant that higher water:cement ratios were needed. However, a high water:cement ratio means lower compressive strength, less durability, and higher permeability of the final in-place product.

The amount of water needed to fully hydrate cement, by weight of cement, is approximately 23 percent. A mix with only this much water would have the consistency of stiff cookie dough and would not be workable. Most commonly, concrete mix designs use a water:cement ratio in the range of 0.35:0.70, which is often almost twice the water required for full hydration. The term "water:cement ratio" is more properly called the "water:cementitious ratio" since flyash and other pozzolans are sometimes used to replace a portion of the cement in the mix. Grout water:cement ratios are much higher and are expressed in water:cement ratio by volume or by weight. For example, contact grouts with water:cement ratios of 1:1 by volume are common.

This chapter describes properties of backfill and contact grout that are required for their optimum performance in an underground construction project. Methods for achieving the appropriate mixture to attain these properties also are provided.

6.1 Rheology

Rheology is the study of the deformation and flow of materials. As related to grouting, the American Concrete Institute (ACI), in their publication, ACI 116 *Cement and Concrete Terminology, 1990,* defines rheology as "the science dealing with flow of materials, including studies of deformation of hardened concrete, the handling and placing of freshly mixed concrete, and the behavior of slurries, pastes, and the like." Satisfactory rheological properties of a concrete or a grout in both the as-mixed and hardened states are fundamental to successful completion of any backfilling and contact grouting project. The mix must provide appropriate properties to enable proper injection and travel within the particular formations to be improved, in the case of geotechnical grouting; or within the void to be filled in backfilling and contact grouting applications. Obviously, the durability and long-term performance of the hardened material is fundamental to achieving the intended performance.

The flow properties of grout and concrete materials vary widely. Many grouts are subject to thixotropy, which is the performance at rest of a material as an immobile paste or gel or as a fluid when energy is exerted into it. A common example of thixotropic behavior is the pouring of catsup from a bottle: the catsup has a high resistance to flow out of the bottle at first attempt but flows readily after being shaken rapidly. Many grouts are thixotropic in that they require a positive pressure of some magnitude to initiate movement within the delivery system, but flow freely at lower sustained pressure, once movement is initiated. This factor is important in considering allowable injection pressure for a given application, and an adequate initial pressure level to start flow must be provided.

The flow behavior of fluids is a complex science. The following paragraphs describe in simple terms the basics of both fluid and plastic flow, which will provide a basis of understanding backfill and contact grout flow. A detailed technical explanation can be found in Tattersall and Banfill (1983) and Mehta and Monteiro (1993).

Fluids are described as either Newtonian or Binghamian. In Newtonian flow, the shear stress, which is the force required to move the fluid, is essentially constant, regardless of the rate of movement, or "shear strain." Water is an example of a Newtonian fluid. Bingham fluids, on the other hand, possess some thixotropy, which requires a measurable force ("shear stress") to start movement. The magnitude of that force is usually referred to as the "Bingham Yield Value," and sometimes, in reference to grout, as the "cohesion." With such grouts, the shear stress typically increases as the rate of shear (shear strain) increases. Typical stress–strain curves for both Newtonian and Binghamian flow are shown in Figure 6-1. The slope of the Bingham curve indicates viscosity. While some chemical solution grouts perform as Newtonian fluids, most fluid suspension and other grouts exhibit Bingham behavior.

76

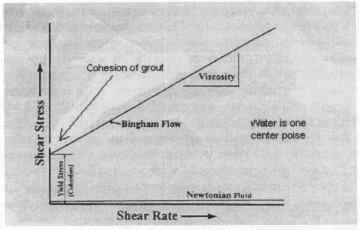

Figure 6-1. Newtonian and Bingham flow indicating Bingham yield stress (cohesion).

Behavior of non-Newtonian grouts is not always as simple as indicated by the straight-line relationship of the applied shear stress and the shear rate or strain, as shown in Figure 6-1. While the relationship of shear stress to shear rate can remain constant as shown, it also can vary, either up or down depending on the tendency of the material to thicken or thin with an increase in the shear rate. Figure 6-2 demonstrates an instance of shear thickening, where resistance to flow (pressure) increases with an increase in shear or flow rate. Some grouts will behave quite differently: their resistance to flow will decrease as the shear or flow rate increases (shear thinning) as shown in Figure 6-3.

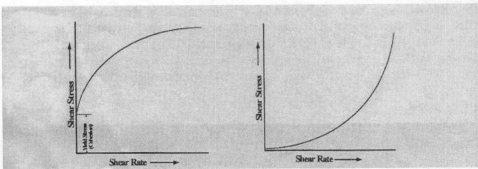

Figure 6-2. Shear thickening   Figure 6-3. Shear thinning

Although it is incorrect to do so, all too frequently only one or a few of the rheological properties of a particular grout mixture are used to describe the performance of that grout. One of the most frequent errors is using the viscosity alone to define the injectability; however, knowing the viscosity is of little value unless other important properties such as surface tension and the resulting wetability are known. Grout rheology is very complex and must consider many important properties of the mix and the surface(s) with which the mix will come into contact. Simple terms should be used to describe the properties of grouts, for example, "mobility" for relatively thick grouts, and "penetrability" for more fluid grouts that are intended to fully permeate soil, rock, or small voids and cracks (s below). Each of these terms include many rheological influences and effects which must be evaluated in total to rationally evaluate the properties of that grout for a particular application.

6.2   Mobility

Mobility denotes the ability of a grout or concrete material to travel through the delivery system and into the space to be filled within the void being backfilled o contact grouted. Of equal importance is the ability to limit travel of the material to prevent flow beyond the zone of desired deposition. This is of more concern with grouts than with conventional concrete backfills. Thus, for proper performance, the grout should be of sufficient mobility to travel within and completely fill the desired void, but it must be sufficiently limited so it will not flow beyond the desired injection zone and into the surrounding ground.

A common misconception is that a thick grout is always of low mobility wherea a thin grout is always highly mobile. Depending on the individual mix constituents, thin grouts can be of relatively low mobility, whereas even very thick, low slump grouts can be highly mobile and behave, for example, in a soil like a fluid. An example of the former would be fluid suspension grouts that contain blocking agents such as sawdust or mill feed (Technical Memorandum 646, 1957). Before it was possible to pump low-mobility, plastic-consistency grouts, low-viscosity fluid grout mixtures designed to restrict grout travel were quite common.

6.3   Penetrability

Penetrability defines the ability of a grout to permeate a porous mass, such as sand, or fill fractures in rock, cracks in concrete linings, or small voids. As previously discussed, viscosity alone is sometimes equated to the penetrability o a given grout. In actual practice, however, penetrability of a solution grout (which is a grout free of suspended solids), into soils, fractures, cracks, and small voids is dependent on a combination of viscosity and wetability. Within the viscosity ranges commonly found in pure-solution grouts and fluid suspension, wetability, which is measured and defined by the contact angle of a drop of the fluid with the receiving surface, is a far more important and significant property than viscosity. Wetability, in the case of backfilling and contact grouting, is a function of the surface tension between the surrounding ground and the liner surface, and the grout at the interface.

The attraction of the molecules in a liquid creates tension at the surface of that liquid. Because a sphere has the least surface area for a given volume, liquids tend to exist in spherical drops. When a drop of liquid is placed on a flat surface, an angle, tangent to the liquid and the flat surface can be measured. This is defined as the contact angle. A liquid wets a solid when the contact angle is less than 90 degrees. Should there be no measurable angle between a liquid and flat surface, the liquid would spread infinitely.

The surface tension depends on the chemical composition of the grout being used and the chemistry and physical conditions of the soil or rock and the liner surface. The affinity of the grout, which results from its wetability behavior in contact with the surrounding ground and the liner it is placed against, is thus of critical importance. This affinity, which includes the grout's surface tension properties, is fundamental to the penetrability of a grout. A simple example of the concept is the relative immobility of a drop of water placed on a newly waxed surface, compared with the rapid dispersion of a drop of the same water placed on a similar but heavily oxidized surface. The penetrability of a grout is thus not solely dependent on its viscosity. Low-viscosity grouts can have poor penetrability, whereas highly viscous grouts can be very penetrable in a given application.

In the case of grouts containing solids, such as suspensions and slurries, the particle (grain) size of the solids, cement, and pozzolans, also effect the grout's ability to penetrate. Theoretical research and discussion abound relative to the ratio of maximum particle size of cement/pozzolan that can penetrate a given crack and/or joint width in the grouting of rock. Although the subject is somewhat contentious, in rock grouting there is general agreement that the minimum dimension of the defect being grouted must be at least three to five times that of the maximum particle size in the grout. The maximum particle size unquestionably affects the penetrability of very small voids or fine cracks; however, it is only one consideration, and perhaps not the most important.

As an example: if a grout contained only a small percentage of the maximum siz particles, and those particles were well distributed so they were not adjacent to or in near proximity of one another, the maximum size of an individual particle would not be of great significance as long as its dimension was less than that of the void or crack being filled. Conversely, if the grout contained a larger proportion of the large size particles and/or they were in near proximity of one another, the risk of blockage would be much greater and the maximum size of the particle more significant. Regardless of the particle size, of particular importance in all cases is the amount of shear energy applied during the grout mixing. It has an important influence in the dispersion of the individual particles of cement and thus the penetrability of the resulting grout.

The shape of the cement particles and condition of its surface also is of great importance. Rough angular particles are far more likely to form blockages within very small void space or fine cracks than are smooth, round-shaped particles. Experience has repeatedly shown cementitious grouts containing large amounts o pozzolanic materials, such as flyash or silica fume, are more penetrable than are those containing only cement. This is no doubt the result of the near spherical shape of most pozzolans. Round-shaped particles tend to roll past and over each other, rather than bind together as would rough angular shapes.

6.4   Cohesion

A simple field test can be performed to determine the "cohesion" of a grout. Lombardi (1985) reported on the test but actually evaluated the Bingham Yield Value for the grout. The test involves dipping a 10-cm (4-in) square, slightly roughened metal plate approximately 3 mm (1/8 in) thick into a bucket of grout. Measuring the weight of the grout that remains on the plate after the plate is removed from the bucket reveals the grout's cohesion or yield value.

6.5   Bleed

When at rest, the individual particles of a fluid suspension grout will tend to settl out of solution. This is referred to as "bleed." To prevent grout from bleeding prior to injection, it is usually continuously agitated after mixing. Whereas excessive bleed cannot occur under proper agitation, it can occur when the grout is essentially at rest, during or after injection. This is of particular significance where large quantities of grout have been injected into a single void location, or where the injection rate is very slow. As bleed occurs, solids will settle to the bottom of the void being filled, and the top portion will be filled initially with water and then eventually with air, leaving void space. The bleed potential of a grout can be greatly reduced by very thorough, high shear mixing as well as through thoughtful mix design, use of lowest workable water:cement ratio, and judicious use of admixtures.

6.6   Pumpability

One of the major benefits of admixture technology is that it has enabled the concrete and grouting industries to make materials that have specific engineering properties while at the same time provide excellent workability.   Without admixtures, these two features are generally at odds with each other (for example, the development of high-strength concrete and grout mixes that also are highly workable and pumpable).

The pumpability of a mix can be viewed in two different cases. The first case is as a slurry, in which it is important to reduce line resistance, such as where long pumping distances are required.   The second case is as a mix containing sand and/or coarse aggregates (concrete), and separation of the liquid portion of the mix causes a plug blockage, reducing or eliminating the pumpability of the mix. Pumpability of slurries and concrete is further discussed in the following paragraphs.

6.6.1   Grout Slurries

A slurry is a mix made from water and any of the following components in various concentration: Portland cement, ultrafine cement, bentonite, flyash, blast furnace slag, pumice, silica fume, or limestone dust.   To provide a stable grout mix (for example, one that does not bleed or has relatively low bleed), the water:cementitious materials ratio should be kept low.   Decreasing the water:cementitious ratio will result in a relatively thick mix that may still be pumpable. However, pumping over longer distances will require increasingly larger, more powerful pumps and piping with heavier wall thicknesses, which is usually not practical.   The simplest and best method to reduce pumping pressures of grout slurries is to use a superplasticizer (high-range water reducer) in the mix. This will dramatically lower the viscosity and cohesion of a grout mix, allowing grouts to be pumped longer distances.   A graph showing relative viscosity, as a function of Marsh funnel time, was plotted for grouts with various water:cementitious ratios with and without the addition of a superplasticizer. The results are shown in Figure 6-4.

81

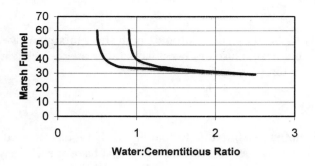

Figure 6-4. Marsh funnel viscosity as a function of water cementitious ratio.

6.6.2 Concrete

Conventional concrete is quite often used as a backfill material for penstocks and other types of pressure pipes within tunnels and shafts. The pumpability of a concrete mix is generally governed by the ability of the mix to withstand segregation and its ability to be self-lubricating where in contact with the delivery pipe. Segregation can be prevented by increasing the fines in the mix that provide sufficient cohesion. The mix must, therefore, be both plastic and cohesive and must contain enough water and fines to lubricate the delivery piping (slickline). Slump is not an accurate assessment of the pumpability of a concrete mix. In actuality, high-slump mixes may be less pumpable. The key to making a concrete pumpable is to keep the cement paste and aggregate together. Often, a concrete can be made more pumpable with addition of more cement and fines, such as flyash, blast furnace slag, and even silica fume (although expensive) to the mix. Certain admixtures also can improve the pumpability of a concrete mix, as can entrainment of air into the mix.

6.7 Setting Time

Setting time is usually more important in backfilling operations than in contact grouting operations. Setting time does become important, however, when contact grouting is injected into voids that contain flowing water. In many cases, control of the time required for a grout to set or harden can be crucial to proper placement and long-term performance. In both backfilling and contact grouting, rapid setting times are usually desirable when injecting into flowing water so the grout mass will set before it is washed away; the use of anti-washout admixtures should be considered. Even where water is not flowing, a rapid set will minimize dilution of the grout. Rapid setting times are also important to add stability to the lining system when backfilling behind segmental liners used in association with tunnel boring machine (TBM)-excavated tunnels. Conversely, where injection is to be made through a very long delivery system or into large void spaces, it might be necessary to extend the set time to prevent hardening of the grout within the delivery system or in the initially filled portions of the void. Admixtures are commercially available that can either accelerate or delay the setting time of all concretes and cementitious grouts. Type III Portland cement also can be used to replace Type I or Type II Portland cement where a more rapid set and strength gain are required.

6.8   Compressive Strength

The compressive strength of a grout or concrete mix is largely a function of the water:cement ratio. A rough approximation of strength is provided by the Abrams Law, which states that

$$\sigma = A/B^{(w:c)(1.5)}$$

where, $A = 14,000$ psi
              $B = 4$ (depends on cement)
              $w{:}c = $ Water:Cement Ratio (by weight)

Grout compressive strengths of 70 to 85 MPa (10,000 to 12,000 psi) are achievable using only cement, water, and admixtures. Concretes with compressive strengths in excess of 106 MPa (15,000 psi) can be made, but they also require admixture technology. On the other hand, adding bentonite or foam to the mix will reduce compressive grout strength. Rarely, however, are backfill materials and contact grouts required to have compressive strengths this high. Typical compressive concrete backfills are usually in the compressive strength range of 21 to 35 MPa (3,000 to 5,000 psi). Other backfill materials can have a wide range of compressive strengths, for example, 0.7 to 21 MPa (100 to 3,000 psi). Since most contact grouts are a mixture of Portland cement and water with a water:cement ratio of approximately 1:1, their compressive strengths usually range from 14 to 25 MPa (2,000 to 3,500 psi). Increasing the compressive strength requirement will almost always increase the cost of the backfill and contact grout. Therefore, the designer should only require the minimum compressive strength based on the actual structure- and project-specific requirements.

6.9   Shrinkage

Grouts and concrete expand slightly with the gain in moisture and contract with loss in moisture. Shrinkage is a phenomenon that occurs in both concrete and grout. The shrinkage of reinforced concrete is less an issue than with plain (non-

83

reinforced) concrete and grouts. The amount of shrinkage is proportional to the amount of water used in the mix. Figure 6-5 shows the shrinkage amount per inch, in millionths of an inch, that concretes with various water contents may exhibit. Drying shrinkage can be evaluated in accordance with ASTM C157.

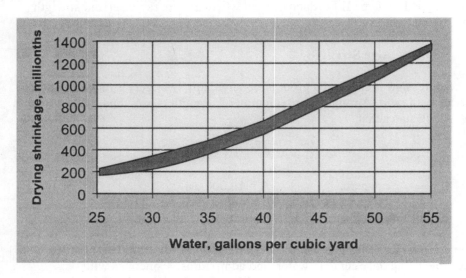

Figure 6-5 Shrinkage as a function of water.

Figure 6-6 shows a photo of a field demonstration of shrinkage based on the water content in a grout mix. Three cups of the same size were completely filled to the brim with grout, with a 1:1 mix, a 2:1 mix, and a 3:1 mix, respectively, and allowed to set overnight. The voids at the top of the cups indicate greater shrinkage in mixes that contained more water.

Curing conditions also influence the amount of shrinkage. The curing conditions for tunnel and shaft backfills and contact grouts may be considered ideal to moderate, depending on the surrounding geology, groundwater condition, and the liner type used. Ideal curing conditions are at or close to 100 percent humidity, such as in a shaft or tunnel that is below the water table. A shaft or tunnel above the water table may expose the backfill and contact grout to water-wicking forces that would accelerate and increase drying of the backfill and contact grout and, thus, increase shrinkage.

Figure 6-6. Office demonstration of shrinkage based on the water content in a grout mix.

Using fine and coarse aggregates in concrete and sanded grout mixes helps reduce shrinkage. Another method of reducing drying shrinkage is to use shrinkage-reducing admixtures, sometimes called "expansion agents." These admixtures, when used in a properly designed mix, may reduce drying shrinkage by as much as 40 percent.

The drying shrinkage of neat cement grout can be expected to be greater than that for a sanded grout or concrete due to the greater volume of shrinkage-prone material, namely the cement paste. Again, the best means of reducing shrinkage is to minimize the water: cement ratio. Contact grouts should have water–cement ratios of approximately 1:1, by volume, or less to help minimize shrinkage.

6.10   Durability

As with compressive strength, durability of backfills and contact grouts is largely a function of the density of the in-place material. A dense mix will greatly reduce the penetration of the in-place material by water or deleterious substances. The first step in making a durable backfill and contact grout mix is to limit the amount of mix water used. A low water:cement ratio mix will produce a hardened material that has a lower permeability, hence reducing the ingress of water or deleterious substances.

There are three durability issues to address in the design of backfills and contact grouts:

85

- Freeze–thaw conditions (usually more of a concern in the upper portions of shafts and at tunnel portals)
- Chloride attack if ferrous metal is present
- Sulfate or other chemical attack on the cement

Freeze–thaw of backfills and contact grouts should be considered in all geographic locations where freeze–thaw is an issue for above-ground concrete structures. An example of where freeze-thaw may be a concern would be the first 100 m (328 ft) in from the portal of a transportation tunnel, or any tunnel open to air flow. Another example might be the upper elevations of an access shaft. Each freeze–thaw case should be examined on a project-to-project basis. In many cases, freeze–thaw is not an issue, such as in water, sewer, and subway tunnels (except near portals); but there are exceptions. As stated in Chapter 5, a low water:cement ratio will help reduce freeze–thaw problems. Low water:cement ratios with the addition of entrained air tremendously increases the freeze–thaw resistance of concretes and grouts. The required air content is a function of cement paste quantity and maximum aggregate size.

Chloride attack may not be an issue for the actual backfill and contact grout; however, it may be an issue for the lining behind the backfill and contact grout. This is true when the liner is made of steel or precast reinforced concrete or reinforced cast-in-place concrete. If there is no steel reinforcing or metal embedments in the prefabricated lining or within the backfill, chloride attack usually does not raise durability issues. If there are steel reinforcing or metal embedments to protect, chloride attack can be an issue. As with all other durability issues, the first means of combating it is to reduce the water:cement ratio of the grout or concrete mix being used. Chloride-neutralizing admixtures also can be used in the mix. These admixtures neutralize and tie up chloride ions as they enter the concrete or grout and migrate toward the steel reinforcing or steel embedments or act as sacrificial anodes.

Sulfates contained in the soil, rock, or groundwater can attack backfill and contact grout materials, causing an internal expansion in the material to occur and fracture it. Perhaps the easiest method of protection against moderate sulfate attack on concrete and grout is to use a Type II cement. Also, a mixture of regular cement, Type I and Class C flyash (comprising approximately 20 percent of the cement–flyash portion of the mix) can be used, again along with a low water:cement ratio.

One other chemical attack that can occur with backfills and contact grouts is alkali-silica reaction. This is only an issue for concrete and sanded grout backfill and sanded contact grout.   Grout slurries containing cement, bentonite, and flyash (with no sand) are not susceptible to an alkali-silica reaction. There are now admixtures that stop alkali-silicate reactions in concrete. Using low-alkali cements are one method of reducing the alkali-silica reaction.   Another method is adding flyash to the mix or replacing approximately 30 percent of the reactive sand and aggregate with crushed limestone or non-reactive sand and aggregate. Again, using the lowest possible water:cement ratio is highly recommended.

6.11   Compressibility

Compressible grout and concrete mixes may be required to allow ground deformation yet prevent excess loading of the lining. Compressible grouts and concretes are used as backfill material around liners that pass through seismic areas, faults, or shear zones and zones of high in situ rock stresses.   To make a compressible backfill, there must be voids within the mix to allow the movement and compression to occur. Grouts and concrete alone have very little compressibility and would transfer the load directly to the lining. By incorporating voids into the grout or concrete, the in-place material can be made a somewhat compressible backfill. The voids can be created by using either a foamed slurry grout mix or a compressible aggregate such as vermiculite.   The compressibility of either mix is a function of the amount of foam or vermiculite it contains. The addition of foam or vermiculite will reduce the compressive strength of the in-place material.

CHAPTER 7
BACKFILLING

Backfilling is the process of filling voids that occur during tunnel and shaft excavations and lining processes. Voids that exist between the excavated ground or initial support and the final liner, and the annulus outside pre-formed liners—such as non-expandable precast concrete segmental systems, liner plate systems, penstocks, and various other types of pipe lining systems—all must be backfilled. Depending on the final liner type used, backfill mix designs and material placement methods will vary. The backfill material also will vary based on geology of the surrounding ground and the structural and operational requirements of the completed project. The terms "backfill material," "backfill grout," "backfill concrete," and "backfill cellular concrete" are used interchangeably, but they all are composed of neat cement grout, sanded cement grout, conventional concrete, flowable fill, or cellular concrete (foam grout).

This chapter consolidates and expands on information provided elsewhere in the guidelines, but the focus is on backfill: Reasons for backfilling, backfilling in soil and rock, lining systems, methods, and mix designs. In particular, backfill placement timings and methods that are appropriate for specific liner types are described.

7.1   Reasons for Backfilling

Some typical reasons to place backfill material in an excavated and lined tunnel or shaft project include the following:

- Stabilizes the liner during construction
- Puts the liner in full contact with the surrounding ground to allow load transfer
- Secures lining systems, such as pipes, penstocks, non-expandable precast concrete segmental liners, and liner plates on final line and grade
- Helps reduce permeability of the final liner system
- Reduces groundwater flow around (behind) the final liner
- Gives some added corrosion protection to the final liner
- Helps reduce surface settlement above tunnels and around shafts excavated in soft ground or weak rock
- Reduces rock deformation around the tunnel

7.2   Backfilling Tunnels and Shafts Excavated in Soil and Rock

Timing of the placement of backfill material in tunnels and shafts excavations is different for soil than it is for rock. In general, in soft-ground tunnels that are excavated with tunnel boring machines (TBM) and that employ non-expandable precast concrete segmental lining systems, the backfill must be placed simultaneously with excavation. The criticality of the actual backfill placement timing is based on the stand-up time of the soil. For example, in soils with little or no stand-up time, the backfill should be placed through the TBM tailshield. This is usually the case in soft-ground tunnels excavated below the groundwater table or above the water table in cohesionless soils. Other times, the backfill can be placed a short distance behind the TBM tailshield using pre-installed grout ports cast into the non-expandable precast concrete segmental lining systems. This is usually the case in soft-ground tunnels excavated above the groundwater table and in cohesive soil with good stand-up time.

When non-expandable precast concrete segments are not used, soft-ground tunnels commonly are supported initially using steel supports and wood lagging, both above and below the groundwater table. When excavating below the groundwater table, dewatering or ground treatment is employed to control water. When this method of excavation is used in conjunction with the installation of a pipe liner system, the pipe is installed and backfilled after excavation is complete. Expandable precast concrete segments and liner plates also are common methods of initial support in soft-ground tunneling. However, it is still good practice to place contact grout in the annulus between the ground and the initial support.

Backfilling TBM tunnels excavated in good rock (long stand-up time) using a non-expandable precast concrete segmental lining system can generally be delayed. This is because the backfill is primarily used to stabilize and maintain line and grade of the liner during construction loading rather than to control ground movement. In tunnels excavated in rock, depending on the type of lining system used, the start of backfilling is often delayed until all tunnel excavation is completed. An example of delayed backfill placement would be a rock tunnel completely excavated with only initial support, such as rock bolts, installed. Upon demobilization of the tunnel excavation equipment, a steel penstock liner is installed and subsequently backfilled with concrete.

Earth pressure balance (EPB) and slurry shield (SS) tunnel boring machines are designed primarily to excavate through soft ground below the water table, where a positive pressure at the face is required to maintain stability of the tunnel face. Soft-ground tunnels also can be excavated by closed-faced non-pressurized TBM, roadheader, open-faced shield, compressed air, the New Austrian Tunneling Method (NATM), hand mining, and other methods. TBMs also are designed to excavate tunnels in rock. These rock TBMs are generally not designed as closed-face pressure machines, but they can be used as such depending on geology and groundwater conditions. Rock tunnels also can be excavated by the drill and blast (D&B) method, with a roadheader and other mechanical equipment.

Shafts in soil can be excavated by augering or with smaller size conventional excavation equipment, such as hydraulic excavators, wheeled and track loaders, and clam bucket. Shafts in rock can be excavated by blind-bore or raise-bore drilling, D&B method, roadheader, and other mechanical methods. The same general rules that apply to the timing of backfill placement in tunnels also apply to shafts. However, most shafts excavated in soil are temporarily supported as they are excavated with ring steel and wood lagging, liner plate, or soldier piles and wood lagging. Shafts excavated in soil also can be frozen. The void between the shaft excavation and the temporary support system often requires contact grouting.

In soft-ground shaft excavation, there is really no equivalent to EPB or SS TBM soft-ground tunnel excavation. Therefore, backfilling through the tailshield, or backfilling through the segments immediately behind the tailshield, and shaft backfilling cannot be compared. For the purposes of this chapter, all types of rotating cutterhead tunnel-excavating machines are referred to as TBMs, even though there are many types and designs of tunnel boring machines.
Most backfilling in shafts is done using drop pipes, with backfill material supplied through pipes from the top of the shaft. An example of this is a riser pipe (final lining) being installed in a shaft. The annulus between the excavated shaft and the riser pipe is backfilled with concrete using a conventional concrete boom pump truck to place the backfill.

7.3   Backfilling Requirements for Liner Systems

The type of liner system used in an excavation project depends on the intended use of the completed facility, geology, groundwater conditions, and designer/contractor preference. This section describes backfilling requirements for four categories of lining systems: shaft linings, precast concrete segmental tunnel liner systems, pipe, and penstock and other high-pressure pipe.

7.3.1   Shaft Linings

The most common shaft lining systems that require backfill are made with pipe elements. Typical pipe shaft liner materials are steel, precast concrete, fiberglass, and corrugated metal. Cast-in-place concrete linings also are common but do not require backfilling, unless two-side forming is used. Precast concrete segmental lining systems also are used but are not common in the United States. However, backfilling a segmental system for a shaft is quite similar to backfilling a shaft with a pipe lining system. In deep or larger diameter shafts, the pipe liner is erected in sections starting from the shaft bottom. If the shaft is not very deep, for example, 6 to 18 m (20 to 60 ft), the pipe liner might be lowered into the shaft in one or two pieces. The diameter and wall thickness, and thus the weight of the liner pipe, also will be a factor in the length of liner pipe sections used. Depending on the annulus size, structural requirements of the liner, or the presence of annulus embedment, backfill material can be neat cement grout, a sanded cement grout, cellular concrete, or conventional concrete. The use of cellular concrete is common for shafts in soil. Neat cement grout, sand cement grout, and conventional concrete are more common for pressure shafts in rock.

7.3.2   Precast Concrete Segmental Tunnel Liner Systems

Precast concrete segmental tunnel liners are assembled in the TBM tailshield and pushed out the rear of the machine as it advances. The precast liner is brought into the tunnel in segments. Each set of segments is assembled to produce one hollow cylinder, commonly called a "ring." Modern rings typically have a width of between 1.0 and 1.5 m (3 and 5 ft), while the width of the advance stroke of the TBM ranges from 1.7 to 2.2 m (5.5 to 7.2 ft). Precast concrete segmental liners can be expandable or non-expandable.

Expandable segments are not backfilled since, in theory, there is no known large void to be filled. This is because the segments are expanded tight against the excavated ground as they leave the tailshield of the TBM. This system, however, often requires contact grouting between the segment and the ground to fill any of the smaller voids of varying sizes.

Non-expandable precast segmental systems, used most often with EPB and SS TBMs, which are both pressurized face type TBMs, are usually gasketed and bolted. Recently, dowels have begun to be used rather than bolts. Non-expandable precast segments also can be used in non-pressurized face TBM rock tunnels. The gaskets are placed between individual segments within a ring and between segment rings. Precast concrete segments used with rock TBMs working in ground with high water inflow also use gasketed, bolted systems. Each assembled ring abuts and is mechanically connected to the previously assembled ring, creating the tunnel lining. Gasketed, bolted segment systems are sometimes used as both initial support and final liner. Some projects require bolted and gasketed segments as initial support, with a pipe installed as the final lining after completion of tunnel excavation. In these cases, there are two phases of backfilling: one between the non-expandable segments and the excavated ground, and one between the segments and the pipe. Bolted, gasketed and dowelled, precast concrete segmental systems are often used as a one-pass lining system, supplying both initial support and the final liner.

The cutting wheel or cutterhead at the TBM face must overcut the radius of the machine slightly to provide steering clearance and to reduce friction between the skin (steel cylinder) of the TBM shield and the ground. The total annulus could be 125 mm (5 in) or more (see Figure 7-1). The annulus generated by this overcut provides a pathway for pressurized fluids at the face to move toward the back of the machine. The TBM tailshield also has a finite thickness, which includes the steel cylinder and the seal system. The seal system prevents pressurized fluids from leaking past the outside face of the segmental liner into the tunnel. Since bolted, gasketed segments are not expandable, there is an annulus at the rear of the TBM. Depending on TBM design, the annulus between the outside face of the segmental liner and the ground is normally in the range of 50 to 200 mm (2 to 8 in). Figure 7-1 is a sketch of the makeup of the total annulus. Note the total annulus is the radial difference between TBM overcut and the segment extrados. It consists of overcut, shield thickness, and size of the rear wire brush seals. The primary purpose of the precast segmental liner, during construction, is to maintain the ground in a stable condition, provide reactive forces to allow the TBM to be thrust forward, and to serve as a barrier to pressurized fluids entering the tunnel. In many cases, the segmental liner also serves as the final tunnel lining. Therefore, the quality of the liner and backfill is very important, and both must work together as an integral part of the overall lining system.

From the short-term perspective of construction operations, backfill stabilizes the assembled ring, prevents the ring from deforming into an oval, and stabilizes the assembled rings to withstand TBM jacking forces. The backfill also prevents the surrounding ground from entering the annular space, which, if allowed in soft-ground tunnels or tunnels in weak rock with shallow cover, could cause surface settlement. Backfill must be placed carefully to uniformly envelop the liner; otherwise, the liner may be subjected to uplift forces from the backfill or water accumulating in the annulus underneath the liner or from lateral forces from backfill placed too deeply on one side.

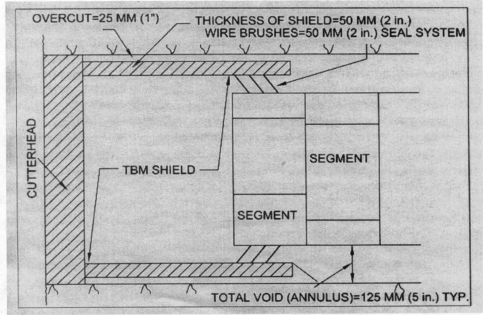

Figure 7-1. Sketch showing makeup of the total annulus (NTS).

A TBM consists of a boring machine and a long train of support equipment called the "trailing gear" or "gantry." The trailing gear is pulled closely behind the TBM and rides on a temporary rail, which, in turn, bears directly on the invert or segmental liner. These loads can be substantial and include the weight of the trailing gear with its various associated mechanical and electrical equipment, locomotives, muck cars or conveyors, segment cars, and grout cars. The precast concrete liner can be thought of as a tube supported at the advancing end by the TBM tailshield and at the back end by the set (hardened) backfill. In between is an approximately 9- to 18-m (30- to 60-ft) interval where the liner is supported in fresh, uncured backfill. Also, during soft-ground and some rock tunnel excavation, the TBM pushes directly off the in-place segments to develop its forward thrust. These axial loads, which are considerable, require a stable and structurally sound reaction structure (the segment ring) to develop the load without displacement. A fully backfilled annulus provides uniform support to the precast segmental liner so that it can safely carry the weight of the trailing gear and all the other construction loads listed above.

Pressurized face TBMs operate with a pressurized zone in front of the cutterhead to maintain ground face stability. EPB machines use muck generated from the in situ material to create a plastic soil plug of pressurized material consistency

93

within the muck chamber and the intake screw conveyor to maintain face pressure. If the in situ material does not contain enough clay to maintain the soil plug, bentonite and foams are added. SS machines introduce a bentonite-based slurry at the face to pressurize the face and transport cuttings out of the tunnel via a pipeline. Both EPB and SS machines must contain fluids at the face in order to maintain pressure. The precast liner being pushed out from the tailshield of the TBM is sealed from fluid intrusion by a series of closely spaced rubber- or wire-brush seals that encircle the inside of the tailshield. Figure 7-2 shows a detail of wire-brush seals. For safety purposes, up to five rows of brushes can be installed. When using wire-brush seals, the space between the brushes is filled with biodegradable grease. The grease is injected into the chambers between the individual rows of brushes and kept at a certain pressure, i.e., 1 bar (15 psi) above backfill injection pressure. The backfill around the precast liner is kept up to the tailshield to provide an additional barrier to pressurized fluid intrusion and to help prevent surface settlement.

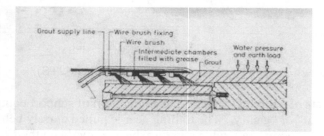

Figure 7-2. Detail of a tailshield wire brush seal located at the rear of the EPB or SS.

Quite often the TBM intercepts and passes through ground with water-bearing zones under pressure. If the annulus around the segments is not filled with pressurized backfill material after the TBM has advanced, the tunnel lining annulus becomes a horizontal drain and conducts groundwater and possibly contaminants up to the face of the TBM.

When backfilling behind segments in very wet conditions, it is necessary to ensure all water in the annulus is expelled and replaced by backfill to completely fill the void. Bolted, gasketed segments are essential in this instance. To ensure complete annulus filling when grouting through grout ports in the segments, grout injection should be commenced in the lowest grout ports in the segmental ring and move upward. The upper (crown) grout ports should be left open to relieve water pressure and trapped air. The injection point should be moved up when grout starts to come out (return) at the next higher level grout port.

Backfill also has important long-term benefits for precast tunnel linings. It provides uniform contact between the liner and the ground, which ensures the liner can develop load transfer as designed. If the annulus between the precast liner and the ground is not backfilled, the ground may collapse around the tunnel, which, in soft-ground and weak rock tunnels with shallow cover, could result in subsidence at the surface. Depending on the soil type, the ground could squeeze or collapse around the liner immediately after the liner is ejected from the tailshield, or the annulus could stay open for extended periods, collecting groundwater and various contaminants. The annulus backfill serves as a secondary defense against water infiltration through the segments by sealing the segment joints from the outside.

Figure 7-3 shows a picture of a cross-section of a wire-brush tail seal. Figures 7-4, 7-5, 7-6 show wire brushes installed in the tailshield of TBMs. Wire-brush seals and backfill grout pipe are pictured.

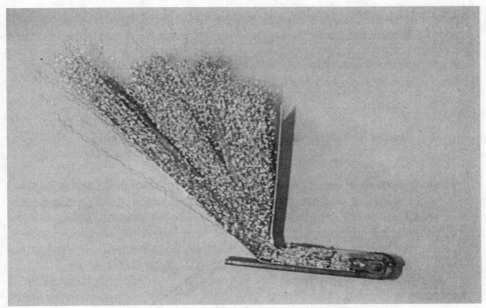

Figure 7-3. Cross-section of wire brush tail seal.

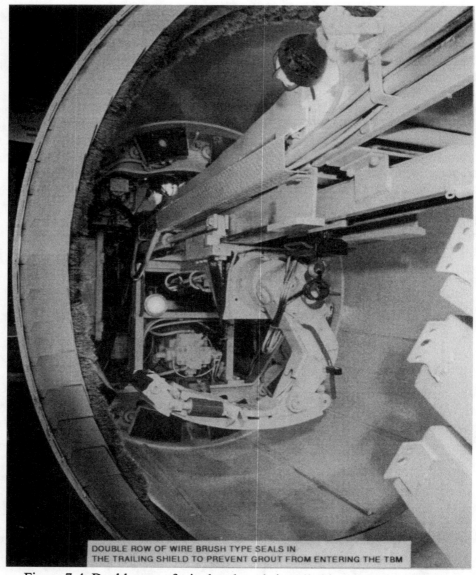

DOUBLE ROW OF WIRE BRUSH TYPE SEALS IN
THE TRAILING SHIELD TO PREVENT GROUT FROM ENTERING THE TBM

Figure 7-4. Double row of wire brush seals installed in tailshield of TBM.

Figure 7-5. Wire brush seals installed in tailshield of TBM.

TRAILING SHIELD C/W
TAIL SEAL WIRE BRUSHES AND GROUT LINES

Figure 7-6. Looking through the tailshield towards the cutterhead of the TBM. Wire brush seals and backfill grout pipe are pictured.

7.3.3   Pipe Installed Inside an Excavated Tunnel

In areas where open cut construction is impractical, a common method for installing low-pressure water and wastewater pipelines underground is to excavate a tunnel and then install a pipe inside. Low-pressure is considered 550 kPa (80 psi) or less internal operating pressure (Bishop, 2001). The space between the carrier pipe and the tunnel excavation is then filled with a suitable backfill material. The tunnel can be excavated by a variety of methods. The pipe can be made of various materials depending on its intended use, ground conditions, loading, and operating pressures. In addition to loads imposed during operation and maintenance, the pipe also must be able to hold its shape during backfilling operations.

Backfilling around a pipe in a tunnel serves several purposes. The void around the pipe must be filled with an inert material capable of supporting the ground and allowing load transfer. Many pipe tunnels excavated in soil use an initial support system, such as steel ribs and wood lagging, that is only intended to provide temporary support. Temporary support methods are not designed to prevent long-term infiltration of fines and water and may completely fail over time if not supported by backfill. Collapse of a tunnel that is not completely backfilled can cause damage or complete failure of the piping system. In soil tunnels and tunnels in weak rock, completely filling the void prevents the infiltration of soil and rock fragments, which, if allowed, could lead to surface settlement. In rock tunnels, temporary support is often supplied by rockbolts, rockbolts with mine straps or wire mesh, or steel ribs with or without wood lagging, shotcrete, etc. Even with these types of temporary support, over time blocks of rock can become unstable and fall out, causing damage or even complete failure of the pipe. Backfill helps prevent rock loosening and movement from getting started. Also, backfilling completely envelops the pipeline, stops the flow of water around the pipe, and helps arrest corrosion of the pipe material.

Backfilling also will ensure that the pipe stays on line and grade and remains centralized within the excavated tunnel opening. This provides additional protection for the pipe from shifting ground, water infiltration, and corrosion, as well as uniform load transfer from the ground to the pipe and from the pipe to the ground. Low-strength backfill materials, such as cellular concrete, have been used in active fault crossings to allow the ground around the pipe to move without shearing the pipeline. In most cases, the strength of the grout does not need to be stronger than the in situ ground.

7.3.4   Penstocks and Other High-Pressure Pipes

Penstocks and other high-pressure pipes are usually associated with water delivery systems and hydroelectric developments. A penstock is defined as a pipe delivering water to a hydroelectric or pumped storage facility (Bishop, 2001). High pressure is considered 2715 kPa (315 psi) or more internal operating pressure, (N. Bishop, 2001). The diameter of high-pressure pipes and penstocks can vary greatly, commonly ranging from 1 m to more than 10 m (3 to 33 ft). Penstock and pipe installation within tunnels generally does not start until excavation is complete. Excavation and liner installation can sometimes take place simultaneously in tunnels when there are multiple access points to the tunnel working faces. Smaller diameter low- and high-pressure pipes are sometimes installed using microtunneling and pipe-jacking methods. In these cases, pipe is installed as the excavation is advanced. To limit the number of joints, penstocks and pipes are supplied in as long a section as practicable for shipping and handling. Penstock and pipe lengths between 18 and 24 m (60 and 80 ft) are about the longest sections commonly fabricated. The maximum length of the pipe or penstock section is controlled by the following factors:

- Overall quality of the road system(s) between the fabrication plant and the job site
- Grade and curvature of the road system(s)
- Weight of the penstock or pipe section
- Diameter of the penstock or pipe section
- Availability and capacity of rail or water transport
- State and local transportation regulations
- Capacity of the lifting equipment at the job site
- Size of the shaft and the overall job site
- Capacity of the transport system underground
- Grade and curvature of the excavated tunnel

Once in its final position within the tunnel, the penstock or pipe will be set on line and grade. Due to high internal operating pressures and/or high external hydrostatic pressures, the penstock or pipe is usually made of steel or a composite of steel and concrete (mortar). Pipe and penstock joints almost always require some type of welding method, usually full-penetration butt welding.

7.4 Backfilling Methods

Methods used to place the backfill in voids varies depending on the type of lining system, type of backfill material used, and other-site specific conditions. This section describes methods for backfilling with four types of liners.

7.4.1 Shaft Linings

Shaft backfill is almost always placed through vertical drop pipes or grout pipes, as opposed to grout ports or placement windows through the liner. In the case of conventional concrete backfill, the drop pipes are usually between 125 and 200 mm (5 and 8 in) in diameter. The concrete can be placed into the drop pipe using a conventional concrete pump connected directly to the drop pipes. The concrete backfill also can be placed into the drop pipe using a hopper attached to the top of the pipe, with the hopper filled directly from a concrete transit mix truck or concrete pipe. When conventional concrete is used it should be vibrated; vibration can be performed with internal or external vibrators or both. Because of the depth, most shaft backfilling operations do not easily allow internal vibration unless access windows are provided through the liner. With either delivery method, concrete pump or hopper, the backfill should always be discharged from the bottom of the drop pipe into fresh concrete using the tremie placement method.

When cement grouts or cellular concretes are used as the backfill material, the delivery pipe is usually between 50 and 100 mm (2 and 4 inches) in diameter. The backfill can be pumped using a standard grout pump or it can be placed by gravity using transit mix trucks. Also, like conventional concrete backfill, grout and cellular concrete backfills are placed using the tremie method. Vibration of the cement grout backfill is usually not required. Vibration of cellular concrete is not required and should not be allowed. This is because cellular concrete has a near self-leveling consistency (thus requiring no compaction), and vibration or compaction would stimulate sedimentation (collapse of the foam). Lift heights of cellular concrete can be higher than with concrete or cement grouts because of the cellular concrete's lower density, but it still must be controlled based on the structural characteristics of the liner being backfilled and the concentration of the foaming agent used.

The concrete drop pipes or grout pipes should be installed on no more than 3 m (10 ft) horizontal spacing around the perimeter of the shaft. The backfill should be placed through one pipe at a time, moving from pipe to pipe around the perimeter of the shaft. Backfill should be placed around the shaft in horizontal lifts of no more than approximately 0.6 to 1.0 m (2 to 3 ft) high. It is important to keep concrete backfill level around the liner at approximately equal height to help avoid differential loading that could displace the liner and move it off line. Cement grouts and cellular concretes will be, for the most part, self-leveling. Also, the loads imposed by the liquid head of the fluid concrete or grout prior to reaching its initial set also must be carefully monitored, because these loads can cause the pipe to go out of round or even collapse. This is especially critical with thin-wall steel, lightly reinforced precast concrete, fiberglass, and corrugated metal pipe liners. Internal bracing (stulling) should be installed in all types of pipes to help mitigate these problems.

7.4.2 Precast Concrete Segmental Tunnel Liner

Backfilling the annulus of a precast concrete segmental tunnel liner is an integral part of the tunnel excavation sequence. The typical TBM operation relies on precast segments supplied by a narrow gauge train. The number of trains depends on the tunnel length and transit times. Each train will have segment cars, grout cars, and possibly muck cars if conveyor or slurry muck removal is not used. When muck cars are used, the number and size of the cars is adjusted so each train can carry enough muck to allow the erection and backfill grouting of one segmental ring. While one train is at the TBM, a second train is at the portal or shaft bottom being loaded with backfill grout and segments while the muck cars at the portal or shaft are emptied. If the tunnel is long enough, there may be additional trains waiting on sidings inside the tunnel. All train movements are timed to the advance of the TBM. Because excavation, segment ring erection, and backfill grouting are sequential operations that all affect the tunnel advance rate, backfill grout is normally mixed on the surface and made ready for transport by the time the next empty train comes out of the tunnel. Also, unless the tunnel is a relatively large diameter, e.g., greater than 9.75 m (32 ft), there is usually not enough room on the TBM trailing gear for a grout-mixing operation in the tunnel large enough to produce the volume of backfill grout in the time allowed. Once the backfill grout enters the tunnel, transportation time and the time needed to discharge the grout car can range from minutes to hours. When the time between backfill grout batching and placement becomes too long, admixtures can be used to retard the set time or put the backfill grout "to sleep." During transportation through the tunnel, the grout railcar will experience jarring vibrations from riding on the temporary track. Often the grout probably will not be agitated between the time it was batched and the time it reaches the trailing gear of the TBM. Therefore, the backfill grout mix must be designed with this in mind. Once on the trailing gear, the grout railcar will be connected to a grout pump(s) and injected into the annulus.

Backfill can be injected through the tailshield of the TBM via grout lines (piping) integral to the tailshield (Figure 7-7). Figure 7-8 shows backfill grout piping mounted in the tailshield en route to the rear of the tailshield. Backfill also can be injected through pre-installed holes (grout ports) in the precast segmental concrete tunnel liner (Figure 7-9). Grouting through the precast liner is the older of the two methods and one that is still widely in use today. The precast liner segments are cast with threaded holes or grout ports located at specific designed locations. These grout holes also serve double duty as lifting points and as attachment points for a hitch that allows the TBM erector arm to grab, pick up, and position a segment during ring erection. Figure 7-4 shows the erector arm in the center of the photo. Once a complete ring is erected, the hitch is removed and the hole is either fitted with a plug, when grouting through the tailshield of the TBM, or used as a grouting port and then plugged. The "grouting-through-the-segment" method has the advantage of being simple and less prone to plugged grout lines, which can be a problem when the grout lines are integral to the tailshield of the TBM. Also, grout hoses and lines for grouting through the segment are easy to clean out or replace. In rock tunnels or in competent soft-ground tunnels, the grouting-through-the-segment method reduces or eliminates delays at the heading due to the grouting operation. The disadvantage of backfilling through the segment is that, in ground with little or no stand-up time, the annulus may be partly or completely filled with soil or rock fragments before backfill grouting can start. This condition may cause the backfill grout to not be uniformly placed around the liner, which can in turn increase the risk of surface settlement. Within the industry, a "rule-of-thumb" based on available working room states that if the inside diameter of the segments is 5 m (16.6 ft) or less, backfill grouting is performed through the segments. If the inside diameter of the segment is greater than 5 m (16.4 ft), backfill should be performed through the TBM tailshield.

Grouting through the tailshield is a newer method that is gaining wide acceptance. This method requires the use of grout pipes that are integral to the TBM tailshield. These grout pipes are equally spaced around the perimeter of the TBM tailshield and inject the grout at the edge of the tailshield into the annulus at the point where the precast liner exits the machine. The grout pipes can be connected via a manifold to a common grout pump(s) adjusted to maintain a set injection pressure. The trend within the industry is to have multiple pressure-controlled injection pumps, each serving only one or two grout pipes. As the TBM advances and simultaneously pushes the liner out the tailshield, the grout pump senses a drop in pressure and begins forcing grout into the annulus.

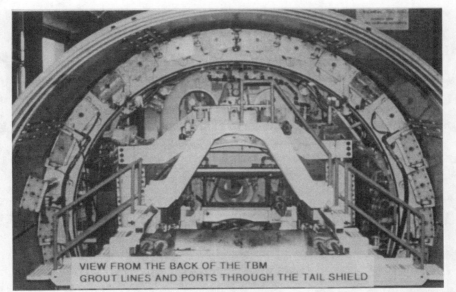

Figure 7-7. Backfill grout piping integral to tailshield of TBM, ports at 10, 11, 1 and 2 o'clock positions can be seen in the picture.

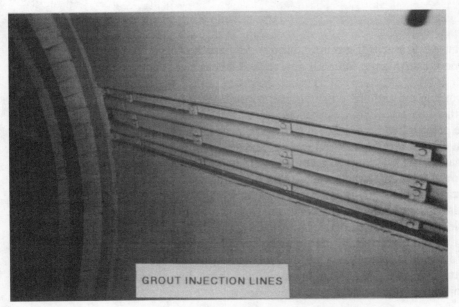

Figure 7-8. Backfill grout piping within the tailshield leading to wire brush/injection area.

GROUTING THROUGH THE SEGMENTS METHOD

Figure 7-9. Backfill grouting through pre-installed grout ports of the precast concrete segmental tunnel lining. Photo taken in the shop.

Grouting through the tailshield has advantages and disadvantages. An advantage is that it ensures grout is injected into the annulus with uniform pressure around the precast liner perimeter. The pressurized grout also prevents water from traveling through the annulus along the liner and toward the head of the TBM. A disadvantage is that the grouting-through-the-tailshield system is more complicated and requires more maintenance and attention during the TBM excavation process. If any grout backfill is allowed to set up (harden) in the tailshield pipes, it can be difficult, if not impossible, to clear out. Because of this risk, TBMs designed to backfill grout through the tailshield are often fabricated with a spare set of grout pipes. Also, the backfill grout mix design for placement through the tailshield is more critical than for pumping through segment grout ports. Backfill grout placed through the tailshield must have consistent physical properties; most important are gel time and set time.

Even when backfill grouting through the tailshield is planned, the precast segments are supplied with grout ports. These ports serve as a backup system for injecting the backfill should the tailshield piping become plugged or other system failures occur. Any problems or delays in the backfilling operations can have a direct negative effect on the tunnel excavation progress. To ensure a proper and complete filling of the annulus, grouting pressures are set at, or slightly above, the total soil and hydrostatic pressure realized at the face. Development is underway of a soft-ground tunneling system to adjust the backfill injection pressure based on recorded ground settlements (Herrenknecht Corp., 2001).

7.4.3 Pipe as Tunnel Linings

Backfilling a carrier pipe inside a low-pressure tunnel is usually done with cellular concrete. Flowable fill also is used to backfill low-pressure pipe inside tunnels. The property that makes cellular concrete especially attractive is the ability of the material to flow a long distance while maintaining a stable air content. However, cellular concrete is only stable until initial set begins. Once initial set starts, material must not be moved. The ability of the cellular concrete to flow long distances allows long sections of pipe to be placed in the tunnel before the annulus is backfilled. In most cases, all of the carrier pipe can be installed in the tunnel before backfilling is started. Because cellular concrete has a low density, the buoyancy forces on the pipe are lower than if a sand/cement grout or conventional concrete is used. The reduced buoyancy also can help reduce the amount of blocking and tie-downs used to initially hold the carrier pipe in place during backfilling. Even with cellular concrete, the rate of backfill placement must be carefully controlled to prevent overloading the liner, which could cause deformation or egging of the pipe and/or structural damage. Cellular concrete also is used in seismic areas or where the tunnel crosses fault zones. Cellular concrete may allow for some movement of the tunnel lining without causing damage to the pipe because it has a Modulus of Elasticity significantly lower than concrete. The carrier pipe also can be filled with water during backfill placement to help counteract buoyancy forces. This method can be used only when backfill is placed using slicklines located in the annulus or when the backfill is placed from the bulkhead since there is no access to grout ports inside the pipe.

Cellular concrete can be pumped long distances within the tunnel with reasonable pressures via hose or pipe delivery lines. Pumping distances up to 1,525 m (5,000 ft) have been reported; 915 m (3,000 ft) is usually the maximum allowable unless special provisions are made (P. Stephens, 2001). In very long tunnels, an intermediate pump within the tunnel can be employed to pump the slurry longer distances. The slurry foam can be added near the point of injection when the

105

point of injection is a long distance from the point of batching. The fluid nature of cellular concrete ensures the pipe can be completely encapsulated with a reasonable injection pressure. Cellular concrete also will flow around and envelop initial tunnel support, such as steel ribs and lagging. Due to its superior flow characteristics and self-leveling consistency, no vibration of cellular concrete is required. Vibration should not be allowed since it will stimulate sedimentation (flotation of foam). Also, the stable nature of the air void system (bubbles) within the mixture means the cementitious materials will not settle out during long-distance pumping or a pumping interruption, thus ensuring a consistent product and helping to eliminate grout plugs.

Cellular concrete is more flowable and wets out the surfaces so well that it will go through cracks where water will not. This requires that form and bulkhead joints be sealed (caulked) very tightly.

Backfilling with cellular concrete is usually performed by a specialty subcontractor. Although a general contractor can learn to use cellular concrete, specialty subcontractors have the experience and equipment to batch and deliver quality cellular concrete at rates up to 150 m^3/hr (200 cy/hr). The experience factor of having worked with cellular concrete is extremely important. The general contractor will usually find that buying or renting equipment, setting it up, and going through the learning curve is not economical. However, when particularly long runs of delivery pipe or hose are required inside the tunnel, the pipe/hose can be set in place by the general contractor before the specialty subcontractor comes on the job. Then, the specialty subcontractor can begin utilizing their specialty equipment and experience as soon as they arrive onsite to quickly complete the job. The general contractor also can supply tunnel labor (miners) to the specialty subcontractor to help with the more general labor requirements associated with a large cellular concreting operation.

Cellular concrete is usually mixed as a slurry grout using a portable batching plant located near the portal or at the shaft collar. For smaller cellular concrete jobs, slurry grout also can be delivered to the site in transit mix concrete trucks. A high efficiency on-site setup will have a large cement silo supplying a continuous high shear mixer for batching slurry grout. A second flyash silo also may be used when the mix contains flyash. Breaking bags of cement is too slow to provide the volume of backfill generally required. Slurry grout, consisting of cement (and possibly flyash) and water, may be foamed at the portal or at the top of the shaft, or pumped neat into the tunnel and foamed at a continuous mixer located near the point of placement. Neat grout can be foamed in batches, or foam may be continuously injected and blended with the neat grout. The older method involves mixing the neat grout in a batch and then adding foam to the mixer until the desired density is achieved. Newer equipment allows the mixing of foam on a continuous basis. Cellular concrete cannot be moved with volute type pumps because the foam will cause the pump to cavitate and break down. Cellular concrete must be moved with positive displacement pumps, such as progressing helical cavity (moyno), piston, or diaphragm pumps.

The cellular concrete is pumped underground to the injection point(s) via a hose or pipe. It is injected into the annulus through grouting ports in the carrier pipe. The number and orientation of ports depends on the size of the carrier pipe. A small carrier pipe (for example, 1.8 m (6 ft) in diameter or less), might use a single grouting port located near the tunnel crown approximately at the 12 o'clock position. Some designs call for injection ports alternating along the pipe near the crown at the 11 o'clock and 1 o'clock positions. Figure 7-10 shows this type of injection port layout. If the grade and conditions are favorable, for example, backfilling a dry tunnel at 1 grade, the entire pipe may be grouted from crown ports only. Grout ports are usually spaced along the tunnel at one per pipe joint or a maximum of 12 m (40 ft). Using low injection pressures (1 bar (15 psi)), and pumping the cellular concrete downslope is the most common placement method used. Many contractors place grout ports at 15 m (50 ft) center on center. Grout is placed at 61 to 91 m (200 to 300 ft) center on center, and interim ports are used as check holes and plugged as grout reaches them.

Backfilling smaller carrier pipes also can be performed in two stages, with the first stage filling the annulus with backfill to the top of the pipe. A second stage can be placed at a higher injection pressure of, for example, 4 bar (60 psi), to serve as a combination backfilling and contact grouting. This two-step method is usually referred to as "phase I and II" or "stage I and II" backfilling. During placement, valves are fitted to the crown grout ports approximately every 60 m (200 ft) ahead of the active grouting port where the backfill is being injected. The valves are left in the open position to bleed off air and to announce the arrival of the grout. Each valve is then closed as the cellular concrete begins to flow out of the valved port. Once the cellular concrete appears at the farthest valve of the planned placement, pumping is stopped and the delivery line is moved up to the next valved injection port. Valves from the previous days' work are removed and leapfrogged ahead.

Figure 7-10. Backfill injection ports layout at the 11 o'clock
and 1 o'clock positions in a concrete cylinder pipe.

When backfilling a large-diameter carrier pipe or a pipe in unfavorable
conditions, such as backfilling a nearly flat tunnel with extensive groundwater
inflows, a more sophisticated backfilling program will almost always be required.
Unless specially formulated mixes and specially designed placement methods are
employed, backfilling operations may not be successful. A larger carrier pipe,
e.g., greater than 1.8 m (6 ft) inside diameter, may have four injection ports: one
at the crown, two at springline, and one in the invert. Maximum spacing between
sets of grout ports is usually 12 to 15 m (40 to 50 ft). In these larger pipes, backfill
is normally placed in two or three stages. The first stage will bed the pipe in the
tunnel invert. Figure 7-11 shows an example of approximate minimum bedding of
a pipe. The second stage will bring the backfill level up to or just above
springline, and the third stage will completely fill the void above the top of the
pipe. When only two stages are used, injection of the second stage is continued
until the void above the top of the pipe is completely filled. Some projects may
require four or more stages. Even though cellular concrete has a unit weight
considerably less than conventional concrete and cement grout, the backfilling

scheme should ensure that the pipe is symmetrically loaded to avoid lateral distortion. Most pipes require internal bracing or stulling to keep the pipe from going out of round, or egging, during handling. The bracing should be left in place during backfill placement and until after the backfill has set.

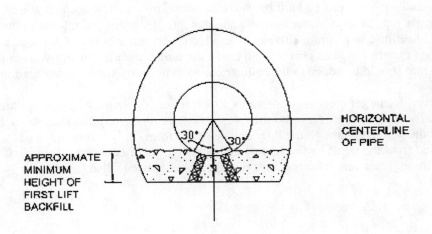

Figure 7-11. Sketch showing bedding of pipe.

The first stage is placed by injecting backfill through the springline ports and continuing until the backfill appears at the downslope invert ports. Equal amounts of backfill should be injected through both (left and right) springline ports. Each invert grout port valve is closed off as the backfill starts to appear. Depending on the viscosity of the backfill and the tunnel grade, the backfill might appear 60 to 120 m (200 to 400 ft) downslope when the backfill height at the injection point is high (deep) enough to bed the pipe. After the first stage sets, the procedure is repeated and grout is pumped until it is observed at the springline ports. This is usually about the centerline of the pipe. For the third stage, backfill is injected in the grout ports at the tunnel crown until the backfill appears at the next set of crown grout ports. The injection point is moved up to the next set of springline grout ports, where injection is again started for the first stage.

During shutdown periods, a thin layer of backfill material may set up over the crown port(s). Therefore, before backfilling resumes, drilling through the thin layer of backfill covering the crown ports should be performed. The port should first be visually inspected to determine if it is open or blocked. If drilling is

109

necessary, it should start with the first port downslope of the last injection point. The drilling should continue downslope until no void is found behind the backfill. When this grout port is found, backfill should resume using the next upslope grout port.

When annulus backfilling in pipe tunnels, special provisions should be made to control large quantities of groundwater flow. During carrier pipe installation, small sandbag dams can be built between the tunnel invert and the underside of the carrier pipe to force water from the annulus through invert grout ports to the pipe. Sheeting and panning also can be used to divert water to invert ports, as can drainage material such as gravel or piping in the tunnel invert. An anti-washout admixture should be added to the cellular concrete in heavy water flow situations.

However, for larger crown or roof voids, an air relief system may be appropriate. Typically this consists of a vent tube (plastic hose or pipe, etc.) that extends to the top of the void and through the liner or side of the form. This allows air to be expelled from the voids by the advancing backfill grout or concrete. Return of grout through the vent tube confirms that the void has been filled (see Figure 7-12).

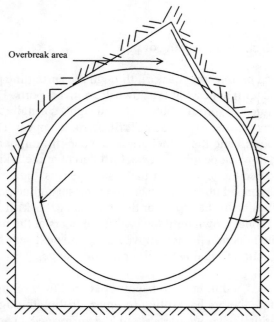

Overbreak area

Figure 7-12. Installation of air relief tube into overbreak area.

The presence of ground support can hinder flow of backfill concrete or grout; thus, it may be necessary to take special precautions to ensure all voids are filled. Where there are areas of overbreak that have been only partially filled with support (e.g., timber blocking or cribbing), extending air relief tubes into those voids as described above should be considered. However, for large voids it may be necessary to form up around the overbreak area and inject backfill material in advance of liner installation. In other circumstances, where it is safe to do so, certain support elements may be removed or holes cut into the support elements to allow greater grout or concrete penetration during backfilling and contact grouting or placement of cast-in-place liners.

In the case of short tunnels (150 m (500 ft) long) or when the designer or owner will not allow penetration in the pipe for grout ports, stay-in-place horizontal backfill delivery pipes installed in the annulus can be used. An example of the use of this backfilling method was on the South Mountain Reach 3B Tunnel Project in Phoenix, Arizona. The project consisted of a 1,850-m (6,060-ft) long, 2.4-m (8-ft) diameter TBM-excavated rock tunnel. A 1,200-mm (48-in) diameter pre-stressed concrete cylinder pipe (PCCP) was installed and backfilled with cellular concrete. The owner would not allow penetration of the pipe. Figure 7-13 shows the 75-mm (3-in) diameter steel backfill pipes installed prior to the PCCP installation. Figure 7-14 shows the backfill delivery pipe layout within the tunnel. Figure 7-15 shows the backfill delivery pipes at the tunnel bulkhead during the backfilling operation.

111

Figure 7-13. Backfill delivery pipes, 75 mm (3 in.) diameter, installed in the tunnel prior to PCCP installation.

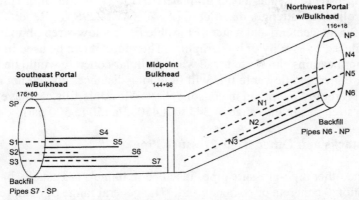

Figure 7-14. Backfill delivery pipe layout within the South Mountain tunnel.

Figure 7-15. Backfill delivery pipes at the tunnel bulkhead.

Flowable fills also are used as a backfill material. Flowable fills, more properly called "controlled low strength material (CLSM)" (ACI 229R-94 Report), are mixtures of flyash, cement, and water. Flowable fill is a low-strength material that can be placed by gravity or by pumping. Therefore, it can be used in backfilling applications similar to those where cellular concrete would be used. Like cellular concretes, flowable fills will flow long distances and do not require vibration to promote flow or aid in consolidation. Flowable fills can have 28-day compressive strengths in the range of 345 to 3,450 kPa (50 to 500 psi).

7.4.4 Penstocks and Other High-Pressure Pipe

Penstocks and other high-pressure pipes installed in tunnels are usually backfilled with conventional concrete or cement grout. The general range of compressive strengths for the backfill concretes and grouts used in these applications is 21 to 35 MPa (3,000 to 5,000 psi). The most common ways of placing backfill are with a delivery pipe (slickline) installed within the annulus to be filled or with injection ports fabricated into the liner. The drop pipe or drop hole method can be used to place concrete and grout backfills if surface access is possible and the depths from the surface to the tunnel crown are reasonable. Sometimes placement windows are fabricated into penstocks or pressure pipes to aid in placing concrete backfill. However, these windows must be welded and the welds tested after backfill is complete. Grout ports installed for backfill placement as part of the penstock or pressure pipe fabrication usually range in size from 75 to 125 mm (3 to 5 in) in diameter. However, large diameter ports, 150 to 200 mm (6 to 8 in) and larger, can be used for concrete backfill placement.

When using the delivery pipe method, the backfill delivery pipe is installed in the tunnel crown as the penstock or pressure pipe is installed. When the required length of penstock or pressure pipe is installed, a bulkhead is built at the end of the planned backfill placement. The typical length of this type of backfill placement is usually 10 to 20 m (30 to 60 ft). Longer placements are possible depending on the penstock or pressure pipe diameters, which control the volume of backfill required per linear meter (foot) of tunnel. Unless there are design requirements, controlling the length of backfill placement is the contractor's means and methods and should not be specified by the owner. The reusable backfill delivery pipe is removed during the backfill placement by pulling it out of the placement a little at a time. Care should always be taken to keep the slickline pipe end embedded in the backfill grout. The backfill delivery pipe is usually 125 to 150 mm (5 to 6 in) steel pipe with a smooth, welded joint to allow pulling it through the delivery pipe supports located at the tunnel crown.

A disadvantage of this method of backfilling is that the penstock or pressure pipe installation must be stopped, a bulkhead built, the backfill placed, and the bulkhead removed before the next length of penstock or pressure pipe can be installed. This process must then be repeated for the entire length of tunnel. The method has the inefficiency of stopping and restarting operations, the added costs of building and removing bulkheads, and the schedule impact of these operations. Stay-in-place or sacrificial expanded metal bulkheads are sometimes used to save removal costs and time.

This method has the advantage of a cost saving in the fabrication of the penstock or pipe by not requiring installation of injection ports. The method also has a labor cost saving by not requiring field welding, testing, and patching relatively large numbers of injection ports after backfilling is completed.

Backfill injection ports are normally spaced every 3 m (10 ft) along the tunnel. It is common with larger diameter penstock and pressure pipes to have four ports at each location: one port in the crown, on the vertical centerline; one port in the invert, on the vertical centerline; and two ports, one on each side, at springline. Sometimes five- and six-port layouts are used. The ports are internally threaded pipe unions welded flush with the inside surface of the penstock or pressure pipe during fabrication. The ports for backfill grout are generally approximately 75 to 125 mm (3 to 5 in) in diameter. However, larger diameter ports, 150 to 200 mm (6 to 8 in) and larger, are required when conventional concrete is used as the backfill material. A short section of pipe with a shutoff valve is temporarily screwed into the port for injection. The use of this many ports is often controversial.

When using the injection port method to backfill, backfill is placed using the springline ports first. Placement should move in an upslope (uphill) direction whenever possible. Invert ports are primarily used to allow water, which may be present in front of the advancing face of backfill, to escape. The invert ports also can be used to inject backfill depending on the backfill placement plan. As the placement advances, the port located in the crown is used last to inject backfill only when the placement has advanced at least several springline ports ahead. All ports ahead of the advancing placement should be left open to help evacuate air and water. When injection through an individual port is complete, the valve attached to the short piece of pipe screwed on to the port is closed, and the backfill delivery pipe or hose is disconnected from the valve and reattached to the next port. The valve is left closed until the backfill has achieved its initial set; then the valve and pipe stub are removed and a plug is usually screwed into the grout port. These grout port plugs have been problematic in the past and have leaked, allowing groundwater in and undesirable loss of valuable water supplies. Care should be taken in seal welding grout plugs, as the differential heat application can cause grout plugs to crack and leak.

7.5 Backfill Mix Designs

Backfill mix designs vary depending on the application, method of placement, strength requirements, placement conditions, and other project-specific properties of the in-place material. The quantities and types of ingredients used to batch the backfill must be carefully selected to meet project needs. Trial batches must be mixed for workability and contract compliance. This section describes mix designs for grout and concrete, cellular concrete, and flowable fill.

7.5.1 Mix Designs for Grout and Concrete

The re are several standard requirements for backfilling precast concrete segmental liners. The backfill grout should be workable for extended periods. The time from batching to placement may be up to several hours. The amount of time during which the grout must remain workable depends on the anticipated TBM advance rate and the anticipated delivery time from the batching location to the injection point.

The backfill grout mix must be designed to ensure that the fresh grout will resist water infiltration and washout prior to reaching initial set. The grout mix also must be designed to resist segregation and bleeding. The grout may be transported without agitation over temporary track and be subject to continuous vibration that will tend to settle out the denser grout ingredients. This may result in non-uniform grout being delivered to the point of placement and possible plugging of delivery lines and fittings. The grout must be stiff enough to remain in place behind the segments but fluid enough to flow through the pumps, hoses, piping, and fitting and into the annulus. Once in place, the grout should set and gain strength rapidly. The grout should have at least the same or greater compressive strength as the in situ strength of the surrounding soil and should remain stable under water. For rock tunnels utilizing concrete segments, backfill grout should have a compressive strength at least equal to the compressive strength of the concrete segment liner. Typical minimum backfill grout compressive strength requirements for tunnels excavated in soil are 1,380 kPa (200 psi) in 24 hr and 3,450 kPa (500 psi) in 28 days. Typical backfill grout compressive strength requirements for tunnels in rock are 4,830 kPa (700 psi) in 24 hr and 21 to 35 MPa (3,000 to 5,000 psi) in 28 days. Finally, the grout should be produced as economically as possible by maximizing ingredients such as flyash and sand, while minimizing the use of cement and admixtures.

Backfill grout for TBM precast liners is typically a combination of cement, flyash, bentonite, sand, water, and admixtures. Because the backfill is usually a unique assortment of ingredients that have never been mixed together before, a combination of analysis and trial batches is required. Even if a backfill mix has been used before for another project, geographic variation of ingredients will require retesting of the mix using trial batches. The goal is to produce a backfill that is as dense as possible, yet can be pumped and placed using the least amount of mix water. Any mix water added beyond the minimum amount required to make the backfill pumpable and flowable will increase segregation and shrinkage during curing, contribute to the porosity of the in-place backfill, and reduce the final compressive strength. In grout backfill mixes, bentonite is usually added to the mix to minimize segregation, which can cause line plugging after a pumping interruption. Bentonite also keeps the grout from losing water and stiffening up when under injection pressure.

The first step in designing a backfill grout mix is to gather information on all the possible ingredients. More than one source of each ingredient should be obtained when possible to maximize the possibility of developing an efficient grout. Type F flyash is usually favored because it is relatively inert and adds sulphate resistance. Type II cement is often used because it has a slightly slower set time than Type I and is moderately sulphate resistant. Saturation points should be determined with different ratios of flyash and cement, starting with 100-percent cement by weight and working toward 100-percent flyash by weight in 20-percent increments. Plot all the curves for each combination of cement and flyash to find the one with the least water demand. Sometimes Type II cement is not readily available and alternatives should be allowed. In many cases, Type C flyash is the only available material. The chemical makeup of both Type F and Type C varies from power plant to power plant. Sometimes the Type C is more preferable. Availability is very important, as is the availability of Type II cement.

The basic grout mixture should be determined by combining the selected cementitious materials (cement and flyash) with sand in different ratios and determining the saturation point for each ratio. Next, a 50:50 mix of sand and cementitious material should be used, varying the combination from 50-percent cementitious material by weight to 100 percent to get data points in the 10- to 40-percent range. Plotting the water demand against percent of cementitious material will show there is a point of minimum water demand and highest solids content.

The basic grout mix will be very stiff, having the maximum density possible while using the least amount of water. A more flowable grout will require additional water, which also will increase voids, segregation, bleeding, and reduced strength. To achieve good workability, bentonite can be added in the ratio of 2 percent to 4 percent by weight of cementitious material. The bentonite must be carefully proportioned to get the desired grout mixture. Bentonite for trial mixes must be premixed with water and allowed to hydrate for 24 hours. Preparing the bentonite in ratios of 20, 40, and 60 kg/1000 kg (44, 88, and 132 lbs/2,200 lbs) of water will give added flexibility when mixing trial batches. The bentonite should be added in small steps until the desired flowability and stability are achieved.

Once the desired physical characteristics of the fluid grout are achieved, the amount of cement needed to achieve design strength should be determined. Up to this point a 50:50 cement:flyash mix has been used. A series of mixes should be made, with the cement:flyash ratio varying from 80:20 to 50:50 in 10-percent increments. The grout should be tested for compressive strength using 50 mm (2-in) mortar cubes prepared and tested according to ASTM C109. Compressive strength at 24 hr and 28 days compared to cement content should be plotted to determine the cement content capable of providing the desired strength.

Once a backfill mix with the required physical characteristics and compressive strength is achieved, water-reducing admixtures and retarders (if necessary) can be tested for beneficial effects on the mix. Water-reducing admixture can be used to reduce water while maintaining the same workability.

A typical grout mix for annulus backfill around a precast segmental tunnel liner in soft ground is given in Table 7-1. This type of mix should provide compressive strengths in the range of 1,380 kPa (200 psi) in 24 hr and 3,450 kPa (500 psi) in 28 days.

Backfilling of steel pipes and penstocks for high-pressure water tunnels, usually associated with water supply and delivery, hydroelectric stations, and pumped storage development, are normally done with conventional concrete using admixtures to increase pumpability and flowability. The concrete is generally placed with a 125- to 150-mm (5- to 6-in) slickline located in the crown of the tunnel. Because of the need to develop full contact between the backfill concrete and the surrounding ground in pressure tunnels, contact grouting is almost always required after the concrete backfill has set and cured. Like backfill grouts designed for segmental liners, concrete backfill mixes also must be designed to remain workable for extended periods. The time from batching to placement may

118

be up to several hours. The amount of time during which the concrete must remain pumpable and workable depends mainly on the anticipated delivery time from the point of batching to the point of placement and the time required for the actual concrete placement.

Backfill concrete mix also may need to be designed to be pumped long distances. The mix should be designed to limit heat generation during hydration and curing. The ground surrounding the placement will limit heat loss with only the limited surface area of the liner affording heat dissipation.

The concrete backfill is pumped behind the liner using a slickline, injection ports, or windows through the liner. In all but short tunnels, e.g., approximately 305 m (1,000 ft) or less, where the concrete pump can be located at the portal or shaft bottom, the backfill concrete will need to be transported through the tunnel to the pump located within the tunnel close to the point of injection. The transport of concrete to the pump location will be by rail or rubber-tired vehicle. The concrete should be agitated during transport to prevent segregation.

A typical grout mix for annular backfill around a precast segmental tunnel liner in rock is given in Table 7-2. This type of mix should provide compressive strengths in the range of 4,830 kPa (700 psi) in 24 hr and 20.6 MPa (3,000 psi) in 28 days.

A typical concrete mix for backfill around pressure pipes and penstocks in rock is given in Table 7-3. This type of mix should provide compressive strengths in the range of 4,830 kPa (700 psi) in 24 hr and 28.2 MPa (4,000 psi) in 28 days.

Concrete mix proportions and design for backfill should be performed in accordance with ACI 211, *Standard Practice Selecting Proportions for Normal, Heavyweight and Mass Concrete.*

TABLE 7-1. – THREE TYPICAL BACKFILL GROUT MIX DESIGNS FOR PRECAST SEGMENTAL CONCRETE TUNNEL LINING IN SOFT GROUND

Material	Mix 1 Quantity		Mix 2 Quantity		Mix 3 Quantity	
	1 Cu. Yd.	1 Cu. Meter	1 Cu. Yd.	1 Cu. Meter	1 Cu. Yd.	1 Cu. Meter
Cement Type II	452 Lbs	205 kg	437 Lbs	198 kg	400 Lbs	237 kg
Fly ash Type F	452 Lbs	205 kg	357 Lbs	162 kg	400 Lbs	237 kg
Sand SSD	1,673 Lbs	759 kg	2,380 Lbs	1,080 kg	1,863 Lbs	1,105 kg
Bentonite – add as slurry	20 Lbs	9 kg	11 Lbs	5 kg	23 Lbs	14 kg
Total Water	709 Lbs	322 kg	566 Lbs	257 kg	651 Lbs	386 kg
Water Reducing Admixture					2 Oz	1 kg
Total	3,306 Lbs	1,500 kg	3,751 Lbs	1,702 kg	3,337 Lbs	1,980 kg
Grout Density	122 Pcf	1,500 kg/m^3	140 Pcf	1,702 kg/m^3	124 Pcf	1,980 kg/m^3

TABLE 7-2. – TYPICAL BACKFILL GROUT MIX DESIGN FOR PRECAST SEGMENTAL CONCRETE TUNNEL LINING IN ROCK

Material	Quantity 1 Cu. Yd.	Quantity 1 Cu. Meter
Cement Type II	400Lbs	237kg
Fly ash Type F	400Lbs	237kg
Sand SSD	1,863Lbs	1,105kg
Bentonite – add as slurry	23Lbs	14kg
Total Water	651Lbs	386kg
Water Reducing Admix.	2Oz	1kg
Total	3,337Lbs	1980kg
Grout Density	124Pcf	1,980kg/m^3

TABLE 7-3. – TYPICAL BACKFILL CONVENTIONAL CONCRETE MIX DESIGN FOR PENSTOCKS AND PRESSURE-PIPES

Material	Quantity 1 Cu. Yd.	Quantity 1 Cu. Meter
Cement Type II	500Lbs	298kg
Fly ash Type F	125Lbs	74kg
Coarse Aggregate ($^3/_8$" to ½")	1,600Lbs	951kg
Fine Aggregate	1,600Lbs	951kg
Total Water	300Lbs	178kg
High Range Water Reducer to get 188 mm +/- 50 mm (7.5 inch +/- 2 inch)		
Air 4% +/- 1%		
Total	4,125Lbs	2,453kg

7.5.2 Mix Design for Cellular Concrete (Foam Grout)

Cellular concrete or foam grout is a lightweight cementitious material that contains stable air voids distributed throughout the material. Typical densities of cellular concrete can range from 480 to 1,290 kg/m^3 (30 to 80 pcf) with a corresponding 28-day compressive strength of 345 to 8,280 kPa (50 to 1,200 psi). By contrast, neat cement grout has a density in the 1,840 kg/m^3 (115 pcf) range. Cellular concrete is made by first making a neat cement grout (slurry) and then combining the neat grout with a preformed foam, where foam is first generated before being combined with the slurry. The foam has enough physical toughness and chemical resistance to the cement that it can be blended into the neat grout without significant air loss. It has the consistency of shaving cream.

The preformed foam is made from a solution that is 96 percent water and 4 percent foaming agent. The foam generally has a density in the 48 kg/m^3 (3 pcf) range. Solution ratios and densities may be more or less, depending on the manufacturer recommendations. Foam expands to usually 30 times the foam solution volume. The foaming agent must have the ability to resist the high pH environment of Portland cement-based grout. For many years, protein-based foaming agents have been made by processing animal-based proteins. A germicide is added to the foaming agent to prevent spoilage. Once the foaming agent is diluted into a solution, the germicide also is diluted so the solution has to be used within 24 hr or it will spoil. Recently, artificially produced protein foaming agents have become available which are not susceptible to spoilage.

The neat grout portion of the cellular concrete will generally have a water:cement ratio by weight in the 0.50 range. Cement/flyash mixes also can be used to make the neat grout. Flyash reduces the overall cost of the cellular concrete and reduces the heat generated during curing. The foamed grout retains the characteristics of the cement and flyash. Sand is not used with foamed grout because it would segregate and defeat the goal of having a uniform, flowable product. Type F flyash is usually favored because it is relatively inert and adds sulphate resistance. Type II cement is often used because it has a slightly slower set than Type I, and also is moderately sulphate resistant.

Because the cellular concrete is often a unique assortment of ingredients that may never have been mixed together before, a combination of analysis and trial batches is required. The preformed foam must be compatible with all the other grout ingredients. Some foaming agents have a retarding effect on Portland cement-based grout set times. The goal is to produce a cellular concrete that is as lightweight (least dense) as possible yet can meet the compressive strength requirements of the project. However, if there is substantial groundwater present, the cellular concrete also must be dense enough to displace the water. The displaced water must be given a means to be evacuated from the void being filled. This can be an open grout port or valved drain pipe through the bulkhead. Cellular concretes for tunnel backfill are usually in the 960 to 1,120 kg/m^3 (60 to 70 pcf) range. A common requirement for cellular concrete backfill is to have a 28-day strength of 3,450 kPa (500 psi).

The 28-day compressive strength will only be achieved by having the correct combination of air void content, water:cementitious ratio, and cement:flyash ratio, if flyash is used. Some cellular concrete specialty subcontractors have only a single silo for cement. In this case, the mix design process is simplified to selecting the right air void content and water:cement ratio and not considering flyash.

To perform laboratory testing, a small-batch foam generator can be used. This typically consists of a 38-l (10-gal) pressurized pot for the premixed foaming agent and water and a small foam generator. Compressed air is used to force the foaming solution out of the pot and through a foam generator, where additional air is introduced to make the foam. The foam generator is a canister filled with inert beads designed to produce turbulence (and foam) as the solution and air are forced in from one end.

When preparing trial batches, the neat grout can be mixed in a 19-l (5-gal) pail using a heavy-duty mixer of the type used to mix plastering compound. Foam can then be added and mixed into the neat grout using the same mixer. Unit weight can be easily checked with a mud balance. The mixed cellular concrete should be placed into special 4-cylinder styrofoam molds with lids typically used for lightweight grout testing. The samples should be cured for 24 hr before stripping them from the mold. Lightweight grout cylinders are fairly delicate and are stripped from the mold by carefully breaking off the styrofoam from around each sample to avoid gouging or chipping. The samples should be cured in a curing room. Grout cylinders should be tested using sulphur end-capping compound, since neoprene end caps will cause the weak cement grout to fail prematurely.

The first step in the mix design process is to hold the water:cement ratio constant and produce cellular concrete mixes that vary in unit weight by 160 kg/m^3 (10 pcf) increments for 320 kg/m^3 (20 pcf) on either side of the assumed target unit weight. A strength versus density curve will show the minimum density required to achieve the desired compressive strength. Typically, cellular concrete densities in the 960 kg/m^3 (60 pcf) range easily exceed 3,450 kPa (500 psi) in 28 days.

However, early strengths may dictate the mix design. Once the grout density is achieved, a series of cellular concrete mixes can be made that vary the water:cement ratio from 45 percent to 60 percent in 5-percent increments. Addition of water will increase the flowability of the grout but reduce compressive strength. This series of tests will show the maximum water:cement ratio allowable to meet compressive strength requirements. If the compressive strength of the cellular concrete still far exceeds requirements, flyash can be substituted for cement. The water demand of the neat grout will drop as more and more flyash is added. Water should be removed from the mix and the consistency kept constant as more flyash is added. Neat grout of cement–flyash mixes with cement replacement ratios up to 65 percent have been successfully used. The compressive strength of cellular concrete can be approximated based on the intended wet (or fresh) density, the amount of cement used, and the material age. Thus, for 28-day compressive strength, the approximation is as follows:

$$f'_c = 1.667 \times (cc)^{0.8} \times (fcd)^{1.5}$$

where
f'_c = compressive strength at age 28 days (MPa)
cc = cement content (kg/m^3)
fcd= foam concrete density (kg/m^3)

Addition of flyash will generally result in increased compressive strength values for material ages beyond 4 weeks. A good quality (e.g., high glass content–low carbon content) Type F flyash can achieve long-term strengths that are 135 to 150 percent of the 4-week compressive strength of mixes using only cement.

Table 7-4 shows a cellular concrete mix design for a 100 percent cement mix with a unit weight of 1,121 kg/m^3 (70 pcf). This sample mix design had a 28-day strength of 8,273 kPa (1,200 psi). Trial batch mix designs should always be performed with the ingredients to be used for the specific project.

Table 7-4.- CELLULAR CONCRETE MIX DESIGN
100% CEMENT AT 1121 KG/M³ (70 PCF)
WATER:CEMENT RATIO 0.50

Material	Quantity 1 Cu. Yd.	Quantity 1 Cu. Meter
Cement Type II	1,240 Lbs	735 kg
Fly ash Type F	0 Lbs	0 kg
Water	620 Lbs	367 kg
Foam % vol	40%	40%
Wt	32 Lbs	19 Kg
Total	1892 pcf	1121 kg
Grout Density	70 Pcf	1121 kg/m3

Table 7-5 shows a cellular concrete grout mix design for a 50 percent cement–50 percent flyash mix with a unit weight of 1,121 kg/m3 (70 pcf). This sample mix design had a 28-day strength of 8,273 kPa (1,200 psi). Trial batch mix designs should always be performed with the ingredients to be used for the specific project.

Table 7-5. CELLULAR CONCRETE MIX DESIGN
50% CEMENT / 50% FLY ASH AT 1121 KG/M³ (70 PCF)
WATER:CEMENT RATIO 0.50

Material	Quantity 1 Cu. Yd.	Quantity 1 Cu. Meter
Cement Type II	621 Lbs	368 kg
Fly ash Type F	621 Lbs	368 kg
Water	621 Lbs	368 kg
Foam % vol	35%	35%
Wt	28 Lbs	17 Kg
Total	1,891 Lbs	1121 kg
Grout Density	70 Pcf	1121 kg/m3

Table 7-6 provides typical properties for foam concrete (cellular concrete).

Table 7-6. Typical properties for foam concrete (cellular concrete).

TYPICAL PROPERTIES FOR FOAM CONCRETE

	foam concrete type (density):										unit
	400	500	600	700	800	900	1000	1200	1400	1600	
density, cast	370	470	570	675	775	880	980	1180	1380	1580	kg/m³
density, cured, 28 days [1]	300	360	440	500	600	690	760	925	1100	1300	kg/m³
density, oven dry [1]											kg/m³
cube strength, 28 days, normal [2]	0.5	1.0	2.0	2.5	3.0	3.5	4.0	6.0	8.0	10.0	MPa
cube strength, 28 days, maximum [3]	1.3	2.0	3.0	3.7	4.5	5.4	6.4	10.0	12.0	16.0	MPa
tensile strength, 28 days, normal	0.05	0.1	0.2	0.25	0.3	0.35	0.4	0.6	0.8	1.0	MPa
tensile strength, 28 days, maximum	0.13	0.2	0.3	0.35	0.45	0.55	0.65	1.0	1.2	1.6	MPa
flexural strength, 28 days, normal [4]	0.1	0.15	0.35	0.45	0.5	0.6	0.7	1.1	1.45	1.85	MPa
Young's modulus E, 28 days, normal	300	650	1200	1650	2200	2900	3700	5800	8400	11500	MPa
shrinkage, 1 year, prism	0.65	0.55	0.45	0.45	0.4	0.4	0.35	0.25	0.2	0.15	%
shrinkage, 1 year, practical	0.15	0.13	0.12	0.12	0.12	0.11	0.11	0.1	0.1	0.1	%
water absorption [5]	75	50	33	22	15	10	7	5	5	5	kg/m²
diffusion resistance μ											
+ R.H. = 50 % to R.H. = 100 %	2.5	3.5	4	4.5	5.5	6	6.5	9	13	18	-
+ R.H. = 70 % to R.H. = 100 %	5	6	7	8	9	10	12	16	24	34	-
heat conductivity λ											
+ oven dry	0.09	0.10	0.12	0.14	0.17	0.20	0.23	0.30	0.40	0.50	W/m.K
+ at R.H. = 70 %	0.11	0.13	0.15	0.18	0.22	0.26	0.30	0.40	0.55	0.70	W/m.K
+ at R.H. = 95 %	0.14	0.17	0.20	0.23	0.27	0.31	0.35	0.50	0.65	0.80	W/m.K

1) density when cured to constant mass at 105 °Celsius: value depends on type of filler used (i.e. Lytag fines or sand)
2) applicable for cement amounts of 150 - 300 kg/m³
3) applicable for cement amounts of 240 kg/m³ (low densities) to 400 kg/m³ (high densities)
4) with 4 point bending test
5) total absorption in kg through 1 m² of foam concrete during 10 years exposure of that area to a constant head of 1 meter water

SvD290498

7.5.3 Mix Designs for Flowable Fill

If there is a large volume of water infiltration, cellular concrete breaks down and the volume benefit is lost. In this condition, flowable fill (cement and flyash) mixes are superior without foam. Further, the cost is better. Flowable fill is a mixture of cement, flyash, and water but no preformed foam. According to ACI 229R-94, *Controlled Low Strength Materials (CLSM),* controlled low-strength material is a self-compacted, cementitious material used primarily as a backfill in lieu of compacted fill. The ACI report also indicates that many terms are currently used to describe this material, including flowable fill, unshrinkable fill, controlled density fill, flowable mortar, flowable flyash, flyash slurry, plastic soil–cement, soil–cement slurry, K-Krete, and various other names.

An example of a flowable fill mix design is shown in Table 7-7. According to the Flo Fill Company, this mix had an average 14-day compressive strength of 538 kPa (78 psi) and an average 28-day compressive strength of 971 kPa (139 psi).

Table 7-7.- FLOWABLE FILL MIX DESIGN

Material	Quantity 1 Cu. Yd.	Quantity 1 Cu. Meter
Cement Type I	110Lbs	65kg
Fly ash Type F	1,490Lbs	884kg
Water	1,000Lbs	593kg
Total	2,600Lbs	1,542kg
Fill Density	92.8Pcf	1,542kg/m3

127

CHAPTER 8
CONTACT GROUTING

Contact grouting is the process of filling voids of unknown size and shape that were unintentionally created during a tunnel or shaft excavation. Voids that occur between the initial support system and the excavated ground, or between the excavated ground or initial support system and the final lining, need contact grouting to help prevent ground settlement, enhance effectiveness of the ground/lining interaction for load transfer, reduce groundwater flow into the excavation during construction, and seal small openings in construction joints between cast-in-place concrete liner pours.

This chapter consolidates and expands on information provided elsewhere in the guidelines, but with a focus on contact grout: reasons for contact grouting, lining systems, methods, and mix designs. It should be noted that, in shafts in which backfill or cast-in-place concrete is placed, the need for contact grout is minimal. This is because gravity works to help better distribute the backfill material, and cast-in-place concrete moves into and fills cracks, voids, and crevasses in the surrounding ground during the placement of the shaft's final liner. Pipe tunnel constructed using microtunneling sometimes require contact grouting. Contact grouting is usually performed with larger diameter (greater than 1.2 m (4 ft)) microtunneling machines. Also, as a general rule, contact grouting is not required for pipe tunnels constructed using directional drilling and various other jacked pipe tunneling methods. This is because the tunnel diameter is usually relatively small (less than 1.2 m (4 ft)) and voids formed using these methods generally are small enough (25 mm (1 in)) to not be a concern for surface settlement. They normally are filled with a lubricant (bentonite) to reduce friction and therefore the jacking forces required. The lubricant also helps keep the annulus open. In cases where the void becomes 50 mm (2 in) or more, contact grouting should be seriously considered and can be injected through these "lubrication ports" after jacking is completed.

8.1   Reasons for Contact Grouting

Some typical examples for contact grouting include the following:

- In shaft excavations in soil, filling any voids that may exist behind soldier piles and horizontal lagging, ring steel and vertical lagging, or liner plate initial support systems.

- In tunnel excavations, filling any voids that may exist behind steel rib and lagging, liner plate, or an expandable concrete segmental initial support system.

- Filling any remaining voids that may exist at the top or crown area, usually located between the 10 o'clock and 2 o'clock positions, after the cast-in-place-concrete tunnel lining has been placed and cured; or after backfilling of non-expandable precast concrete segments, various types of pipe, penstock, or other types of pre-formed tunnel linings.

- After backfill has been placed and cured, filling any skin (outer surface) voids that may exist between the final liner and the backfill of an installed pipe or penstock to account for shrinkage of the backfill material away from the liner.

- After backfilling or placing cast-in-place concrete lining has been placed and cured, filling any voids that may exist around embedments within the backfill or cast-in-place-concrete, such as stiffener rings, shear lugs, reinforcing steel, electrical conduit, small pipes, and other embedments.

- Filling voids associated with sheeting, panning, and invert gravel or piping dewatering systems installed to protect fresh backfill and cast-in-place concrete liners during placement from running water.

Table 8-1 relates contact grouting applications to the reasons they should be done and to the various lining systems involved.

Table 8.1. Summary of Contact Grout Applications

Contact Grout Application	Reason to Contact Grout	Initial Support or Final Lining System
Filling any voids that may exist between the shaft initial support system and the excavated ground.	To help mitigate surface settlement, to enhance the effectiveness of the ground/liner interaction for load transfer, and to help reduce groundwater flow into the excavation during construction.	- Soldier pile and horizontal lagging. - Soldier pile and steel plate sheathing - Ring steel and vertical lagging - Steel liner plate - Steel or CMP pipe installed as initial support or in close contact with the shaft walls
Filling any voids that may exist between the tunnel initial support system and the excavated ground.	To help mitigate surface settlement, to enhance the effectiveness of the ground/liner interaction for load transfer, and to help reduce groundwater flow into the excavation during construction.	- Expandable precast concrete segments - Steel rib and lagging - Steel liner plates - Timber supports

Contact Grout Application	Reason to Contact Grout	Initial Support or Final Lining
Filling any tunnel crown or top voids that may exist after backfill placement and cure. Voids are usually located between the 10 o'clock and 2 o'clock positions.	To help mitigate surface settlement, to enhance the effectiveness of the ground/liner interaction for load transfer, and to help reduce groundwater flow around the final liner.	- Non expandable precast concrete segments - Reinforced concrete pipe - Fiberglass pipe - Concrete cylinder pipe - Steel pipe - Steel penstock
Filling any tunnel crown voids that may exist after cast-in-place concrete placement and cure. Voids are usually located between the 10 o'clock and 2 o'clock positions.	To help mitigate surface settlement, to enhance the effectiveness of the ground/liner interaction for load transfer, and to help reduce groundwater flow around the final liner.	- Cast-in-place concrete

Table 8.1 Continued

131

Table 8.1 Continued

Contact Grout Application	Reason to Contact Grout	Initial Support or Final Lining
Filling any skin voids that may exist between a pipe or penstock liner and the backfill material. Usually only required for penstock and pipe with high internal operating pressures.	To enhance the effectiveness of the liner/backfill interaction for load transfer. Voids could be located anywhere on the circumference of the pipe or penstock	- Steel pipe - Steel penstock
Filling any voids that may exist around embedded items such as stiffener rings, shear lugs, electrical conduit, small pipes, and heavy concentrations of reinforcing steel.	To enhance the effectiveness of the liner/backfill interaction for load transfer, stabilize the embedded items, and to help reduce water flow around the final liner.	- Embedments in cast-in-place concrete liners and in the backfill of various other types of lining systems.

Contact Grout Application	Reason to Contact Grout	Initial Support or Final Lining
Filling voids associated with sheeting, panning and invert gravel or piping dewatering systems installed to protect fresh backfill and cast-in-place concrete during placement from running water.	To seal intentionally installed water passageways behind and under the final lining, and to help reduce flow around the final liner.	- Cast-in-place concrete - Can be used with any two pass lining systems that require backfilling.

Table 8.1 Continued

133

8.2   Contact Grouting of Lining Systems

Because contact grout is most often used behind the initial support system, contact grouting is generally not needed behind backfilled final shaft liners or cast-in-place concrete liners. Likewise, contact grouting is usually not required for smaller diameter microtunnels and with other types of small-diameter jacked pipe tunneling methods. The focus of this section, therefore, is contact grouting of tunnel liners.

8.2.1   Initial Support Systems

Shafts excavated (sunk) in soft-ground formations and in weak or highly fractured rock almost always require some type of initial or temporary support system. Examples of these systems include non-expandable precast concrete segments and steel liner plate. In the United States, steel liner plate is by far the more common of the two methods used. Installation methods and contact grouting of non-expandable precast concrete segmental linings would be similar to those of other initial support systems. Contact grouting also is used in conjunction with shafts excavated in soft-ground formations in which soldier piles and wood lagging, steel ring beams and vertical wood lagging, or soldier piles and steel plate sheathing, are used as initial support. Shafts with steel sheet piling do not normally require contact grouting except perhaps in the first 2 m (7 ft) near the surface. One exception would be for water inflow, particularly if the water contains solids. It is sometimes necessary to contact grout after the sheet piling is pulled (removed) at the completion of shaft construction.

In using the steel liner plate system, the initial support is brought to the temporary shaft bottom, as the shaft is being excavated, in pieces called "liner plates." Each set of liner plates is assembled at the shaft bottom to form a complete ring. Ring widths (vertical height) are typically 450 to 600 mm (18 to 24 in) deep, but no greater, to limit the amount of exposed ground during installation. The steel liner plate may be supported by steel rings typically spaced at 1.2 to 1.5 m (4 to 5 ft). As an example, the shaft could be sunk using a small excavator working at the shaft bottom with muck being hoisted to the surface in 1 to 3 m^3 (1.3 to 4 cy) buckets by a crane. The excavator digs down around the perimeter of the shaft, exposing a small amount of the ground at a time. Depending on the stand-up time of the ground, the work crew may wait until an entire ring circumference is excavated, or they may have to install each liner plate as soon as the ground is exposed. The excavator cannot avoid slightly overexcavating the ground to allow for setting the liner plate; therefore, voids of varying sizes and shapes will exist behind the liner plates that must be quickly filled with contact grout.

If the voids are allowed to remain, the ground behind the liner plate will become loose and could begin raveling. If raveling occurs, the ground will not uniformly compress the liner plate ring, and differential loading on the liner plate, with resultant distortion, could occur. A distorted liner plate ring will not carry the design loads evenly and could fail if sufficiently distorted, which could become a safety problem for structure and workers alike. Also, the ground that moves into the void will leave room for the ground above it to shift, thereby threatening the integrity of the liner plate(s) above. If the voids behind the liner plate are large enough, the ground movement can work its way to the surface and become evident as ground subsidence (surface settlement) at the shaft collar. Most likely, any ground subsidence will be uneven, which can lead to differential racking to structures on the surface and uneven work areas for equipment and workers. Since shafts under construction almost always are surrounded by heavy mobile and stationary construction equipment, materials, and people, stability of the shaft perimeter is essential.

The same ground movement and surface settlement issues also will exist with other types of initial support systems used in conjunction with shafts excavated in soils or weak rock. When a soldier pile and lagging initial support system is used, it also is necessary to overexcavate slightly to allow placement of the horizontal lagging boards. Therefore, small voids of varying shapes and sizes will exist behind the lagging. A common practice with this type of support system is to install a geofabric between the excavated ground and the lagging board, as the boards are installed, to help mitigate soil migration into the excavation through spaces and gaps in the lagging. The geofabric also will help reduce leakage of contact grout through the spaces and gaps in the lagging. When contact grouting is deemed necessary, contact grout injection tubes or hoses can be installed through the lagging into the voids as the lagging is being installed. The same method of installing geofabric and contact grout injection tubes or hoses is used for steel ring and vertical lagging initial support systems.

Contact grouting steel liner plate and steel ribs and lagging systems used as initial support in tunnels is performed for the same reasons and using the same general methods as contact grouting in shaft excavations.

8.2.2   Precast Concrete Segmental Tunnel Liner Systems

Expandable concrete segmental tunnel liners are sometimes used as initial support in both soft-ground and rock tunnels. Contact grouting, if required, is used to fill voids between the excavated ground and the segments after expansion. When

135

used, the segments are usually supplied with pre-installed grout ports. These ports are normally the same holes used for segment handling, lifting, and erection. Expandable precast concrete segments are sometimes used as the final liner system. This is not a common practice in public transportation tunnels but is sometimes used for utility, railroad, and mine haulage tunnels.

Non-expandable concrete segmental tunnel liners can be used as initial support or as the final liner or as both. In soft-ground and rock tunnel applications, the annulus between the excavated ground and the segments is first backfilled, as described in Chapter 7. Contact grouting, when required, is usually only necessary at the top or the tunnel crown area. Voids in the backfill, which do exist, are almost always located in the area between approximately 10 o'clock and the 2 o'clock positions of the tunnel crown. Contact grouting these voids is normally performed through pre-installed grout ports in the segments. These grout ports are usually the same holes used for segment lifting, handling, and erection. The same holes also may have been used to inject the backfill grout. To allow injection of the contact grout, a hole is drilled through the port and completely through the backfill material into the void. After completion of the contact grouting, the hole is filled with a non-shrink grout placed by hand. The port is then sealed with a threaded steel pipe plug, plastic plug, or other non-corrosive material plug.

In low-pressure water, stormwater, and sewer tunnels, the plug threads are first wrapped with teflon tape to help create a seal. The plug also may require welding to seal. If the grout ports are recessed in the precast concrete segment, the recess will be required to be completely filled with non-shrink grout to cover the plug and match the precast segment profile. In high-pressure water, wastewater, and sewer tunnels, the plug is nearly always welded before being patched with a non-shrink grout.

8.2.3 Pipe Liners Installed Inside an Excavated Tunnel

Contact grouting for the final liner is injected using grout ports in the same way as contact grout is injected for precast concrete segmental liners. Often, however, backfill is placed behind pipe and penstock liners using a slickline rather than grout ports. When this is the backfill method used, holes must be provided in the pipe or penstock during fabrication exclusively for contact grouting. Other types of pipe liners, especially precast concrete pipe, are sometimes supplied without pre-installed grout ports. Usually, standard precast concrete pipes used for water, stormwater, and sewer lines are manufactured by local precast suppliers. These standard pipes are often the types specified as the carrier pipe in many tunneling applications. Precast concrete pipe plants are normally set up to fabricate most standard pipe sizes in large quantities on a production line operation, which allows for an economical source of pipe for the tunnel project. However, often the pipe cannot be manufactured as quickly or as economically if grout ports must be cast in during production. Therefore, contractors may elect to omit the pre-installed grout ports in order to purchase the pipe at the lowest possible price, choosing instead to drill the contact grout holes in the field. In these cases, the contact grout holes must be drilled through the pipe after the backfill is placed and cured, and expandable packers or grouted-in pipe nipples are used at the hole collar to connect the contact grout delivery line.

Whenever possible, drilling through the line should be avoided since it requires field labor costs and construction schedule time to accomplish. It is important to remember that contact grouting is usually one of the last tasks to completing a tunnel, and the tunnel is quite often on the critical path of the construction schedule. The drilling also may cause structural damage to the pipe liner by cutting through the reinforcing steel and other embedments or causing concrete spalling around the hole.

8.2.4   Cast-In-Place Concrete Liners

Contact grouting performed in association with cast-in-place concrete liners uses basically the same methods described for precast concrete segmental liners. However, pre-installed grout ports are almost never used. Casting grout ports into the cast-in-place concrete placement is usually omitted because of field labor costs and the likelihood of displacing the embedded ports during concrete placement operations. Therefore, drilling contact grout holes through the cast-in-place concrete liner is required. Sometimes the concrete form's tapered pin (float pin) holes can be used for contact grouting injection holes. As in the case with contact grouting backfilled segmental liners, pipes, or penstocks, the voids that may require contact grouting will almost certainly be located between the 10 o'clock and 2 o'clock positions in the tunnel crown. Excessive, structurally controlled overbreak may result in voids that are located elsewhere. Detailed geological mapping of these areas should be performed prior to concrete placement to facilitate effective positioning of contact grout holes. Drilling of the contact holes is sometimes staggered on a predetermined spacing between these two positions. Care must be taken during drilling to avoid damaging reinforcing steel and any other embedments. When contact grout holes are drilled with a small rotary percussion-type drill, such as a jackleg, and reinforcing steel in encountered, the hole is abandoned. A new hole is then drilled within 150 mm (6 in) or so of the abandoned hole. However, when contact grout holes are drilled with a rotary diamond-bit-type drill and reinforcing steel is encountered, the reinforcing steel is often drilled through. Drilling completely through reinforcing steel may or may not be acceptable. The amount of reinforcing steel allowed to be cut during drilling must be addressed in the contact grouting specifications or as a note on the applicable contract drawings. Unless the volume of backfill is less than expected or there is water leakage, additional drilling should be kept to a minimum. These holes compromise the integrity of the liner and are difficult to completely seal. Other embedments, such as electrical conduit, small pipes, electrical cables, and instrumentation wiring, must never be drilled through. Giving the drilling crews accurate as-built drawings of the location of embedments will help reduce this problem.

8.3 Contact Grouting Placement Methods

Contact grouting placement methods vary to some extent with the application. Contact grout may be placed by gravity, such as when using the chute of a concrete transit mix truck to place contact grout around a shaft collar, or it can be injected under pressure. Contact grout may be placed through grout ports installed within the lining, through holes drilled through the liner directly into the void, or with pipes installed within the void itself. Figure 8-1 shows contact grout being injected under pressure through a grout port into the crown of a 1,650-mm (66-in) diameter concrete cylinder pipe. The pictured pipe had been previously backfilled with cellular concrete using the same ports. Figure 8-2 shows contact grouting behind steel ribs and steel channel lagging in a horseshoe-shaped tunnel excavated in soil. The contact grout is being injected with little, if any, pressure buildup. Figure 8-3 shows contact grouting behind steel ribs and wood lagging, with the grout being placed directly into the annulus from a delivery hose. In this case, because the void behind the initial support system is relatively large, a more viscous sanded contact grout mix was used. The use of sand in the mix helped reduce shrinkage, was more economical, and helped seal small spaces and gaps between the lagging boards. The tunnel pictured in Figure 8-3 was excavated as a horseshoe shape with a roadheader. Figure 8-4 shows contact grout being placed between the excavated shaft walls and the temporary shaft support system. In this case, the contact grout was placed from the surface directly into the voids using the chute of a concrete transit mix truck. This method was used to fill the void to a depth of approximately 2 m (7 ft) from the street surface to help limit surface settlement. Figure 8-5 shows corrugated metal pipe (CMP) liner used for temporary initial support being lowered into the shaft. The annulus between the excavated shaft walls and the CMP required contact grouting. Figure 8-6 shows the temporary support in place within the shaft with the riser pipe being installed. The annulus between the CMP and the riser pipe was later backfilled.

Figure 8-1. Pressure contact grouting through pre-installed grout ports in the crown of a concrete cylinder pipe.

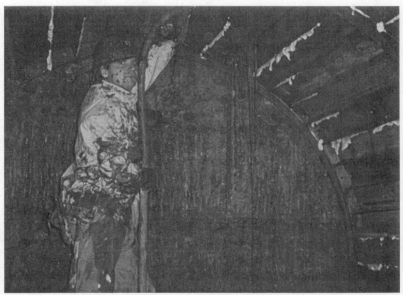

Figure 8-2. A neat cement grout being placed directly behind the initial tunnel support system of steel ribs and steel channel lagging.

Figure 8-3. Photograph shows a sanded cement contact grout being placed directly behind the initial tunnel support of steel ribs and wood lagging.

Figure 8-4. Contact grout being placed between the excavated shaft wall and the temporary shaft support using the chute of a concrete transit mix truck.

Figure 8-5. Temporary corrugated metal pipe (CMP) liner being lowered into the shaft.

Figure 8-6. Temporary CMP liner support in place within the shaft with riser pipe centered within the CMP.

For shafts (and tunnels) excavated in soil, a common initial support system is a liner plates. Liner plates are steel panels that can be supplied with or without grout ports. Usually a combination of the two types of liner plates is used, and the mixture will depend on the shaft- and tunnel-specific geology and groundwater conditions. The liner plates are assembled in a pattern with the grout ports evenly spaced around the shaft or tunnel perimeter. Maximum spacing of grout ports for shafts typically does not exceed 3 m (10 ft) horizontally and 1.2 m (4 ft) vertically. Grout port spacing for tunnel applications typically does not exceed 1.8 m (6 ft) horizontally and 1.8 m (6 ft) vertically.

Void filling behind a steel liner plate support system is a fairly simple operation. The height of the area (number of rings) in a shaft, or the length of the area (number of rings) in a tunnel to be grouted, depends on the stand-up time of the ground. Non-cohesive, water-saturated sand is likely to slough immediately and contact grouting may be necessary after only one ring of liner plate is installed. If the ground is relatively stable (good stand-up time; for example, heavy clay), then perhaps two or three rings of liner plate can be installed before contact grouting is performed. Uniform lift heights or layer of the grout should be performed unless steel ribs or other supports are used to ensure the round shape is maintained. Any deformation will cause difficulty in placing bolts and could also result in failure.

Shaft sinking in soft ground may proceed at a rate of only 0.6 to 1.8 m (2 to 6 ft) per shift. A typical cycle of excavating, installing liner plate, and contact grouting can take place once a day or every 3 days, depending on the shaft diameter, depth, and geological conditions. Because of the relatively small quantity of contact grout required to be placed during each grouting operation, combined with the start and stop nature of the operation, means a much smaller grouting equipment setup is used compared to most backfilling operations. Leakage during grouting can be an issue because most liner plate systems are not gasketed and do not allow a good seal between individual liner plates and from ring to ring. There also is the area to be sealed between the bottom of the last ring installed and the shaft bottom or the last tunnel ring and the working face. Muck can be used in shafts to make the seal. When leaks do occur, they can be sealed with okum, wooden wedges, rags, burlap, or other materials. Retarder admixtures should not be included in the grout, because the emphasis is on filling the void behind the liner plate with a contact grout mix that sets up as quickly as possible so that excavation can resume. In this regard, Type III Portland cement can be used instead of Type I or Type II.

Contact grouting of cast-in-place concrete lining and backfilled lining systems usually requires relatively small quantities of contact grout. Because of this, contact grout is usually mixed in a small, portable grout plant using bagged cement. The grout is pumped into the void using a progressing helical cavity (moyno) pump or air diaphragm pump. In shafts with sufficient depth, grout can be mixed at the surface and delivered via a drop pipe. Because there is no seal at the bottom of the liner plate in the last ring installed in a shaft, excavated material is used to dam up around the bottom of the ring. The grout may have to be placed in several lifts starting with the lowest ring to form a seal or bulkhead for the upper ring contact grout placements. The bottom lift may have to be allowed to set to provide a seal before the grouting of the upper rings can be completed. In tunnels, the opening at the face of the last ring installed is generally sealed using rags and wooden wedges.

A particular feature of contact grouting voids behind liners in a rock tunnel involves extending contact grout holes into the rock. Tunnel boring machine (TBM) tunnels excavated in soft rock, such as shale, and tunnels excavated in any type of rock by the drill and blast (D&B) method, can exhibit a zone of weakened, loose material surrounding the excavated surface. This zone can extend 50 to 300 mm (2 to 12 in) beyond the excavated surface. After the tunnel liner is placed, there is potential for subtle movements in the loosened zone over time with corresponding undesirable forces on the liner. Many designers consider this problematic and take measures to prevent it. By extending contact grout holes 150 to 300 mm (6 to 12 in) into rock, contact grout can penetrate into the weakened rock zone, see Figure 8-7. Recognizing this practice can result in larger grout takes, which may have claim potential since the contact grouting may have become a form of geotechnical grouting. Steps should be taken in the contract documents to avoid disputes over this issue. In this instance, quantities of contact grout required are no longer controlled only by the contractor's means and methods but to a large degree by geologic site conditions. Therefore, when these types of geologic conditions are known to exist, the contract documents should have payment provisions to allow for some estimated quantity of contact grout to be paid on a unit price basis. However, a weakened zone also can be created by the contractor's excavation methods, for example, a poorly designed blasting plan or poor quality control of the blast hole drilling and loading.

Regardless of how liners have been designed, backfilling and contact grouting may be the final element in determining the liner operational permeability. Generally, designers will mandate a particular criterion for infiltration, in gallons per minute (gpm) or gallons per day (gpd), relating an acceptable rate of infiltration to the tunnel length and diameter (O'Rourke, 1984). If infiltration is in excess of this level, the contact grouting program may be substantially expanded to try to reduce liner permeability. Efficient contact grouting can intercept water paths and drastically reduce potential for leakage. However, contact grouting is not a primary means of reducing the water flow through the surrounding ground. Likewise contact grouting cannot replace a poor liner system.

143

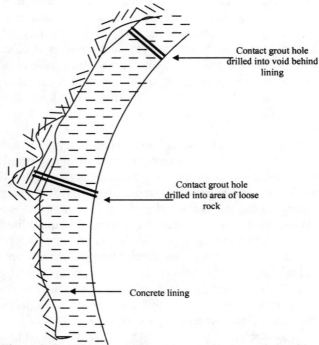

Contact grout hole
drilled into void behind
lining

Contact grout hole
drilled into area of loose
rock

Concrete lining

Figure 8-7. Drilling of contact grout holes through concrete lining into rock.

The primary means of reducing permeability of the surrounding ground is through "consolidation grouting" (a form of geotechnical grouting) and a good liner design. If the surrounding ground is too permeable for the design requirements, consolidation grouting may be performed either before or after tunneling. If grouted prior to tunneling, the tunneling progress may be more efficient. Any attempt to use contact grouting to control the water flow through the surrounding ground is very difficult and will very likely result in a claim by the contractor.

In water-scarce areas, like the American west, tunnels can unwantonly lower the water table and severely adversely affect the surface environment and water rights of landowners. Care should be taken in the design process to account for grouting to avoid adversely affecting the water table by tunneling.

There is some disagreement within the industry as to which to do first, contact grouting or consolidation grouting. One theory maintains that, unless any remaining voids between the excavation and the liner are filled with contact grout first, higher injection pressures necessary for consolidation grouting to be

144

performed properly cannot be used. The other theory is that, if there is a need for consolidation grouting, it should be done first and paid for on a unit price(s) basis, because the contractor should not be made responsible for grouting the ground surrounding the excavation without additional compensation. This theory claims that, unless the consolidation grouting is done first, contact grout will travel beyond filling the void and permeate the ground surrounding the tunnel, thus also performing geotechnical grouting. These issues should receive special attention during design and when drafting contract documents since they can be the subject of disputes.

Weeping cracks and construction joints in a concrete liner should be caulked and sealed prior to start of contact grouting operations to prevent grout leakage. When contact grouting also is designed to mitigate leakage through cracks in the concrete liner and construction joints, as well as to fill voids, the size of the voids and seepage paths to be grouted needs to be considered. Sometimes voids intended for grouting can be too small to accommodate Portland cement particles, and ultrafine cement or chemical grout may be needed. However, the cost of such programs must be evaluated for benefit gained and monitored for quality and efficiency. If ultrafine cement or chemical grouts are intended to be used for any type of contact grouting, this fact must be clearly specified in the contract documents.

Tunnels and shafts constructed in rock under very wet conditions may require additional measures to control and ultimately eliminate water inflows. If water is running down the walls of a tunnel or shaft or from the crown of the tunnel of the excavation, the quality of a cast-in-place concrete liner or backfill material will be severely compromised. The flowing water may cause washouts of cement paste and fines, resulting in an inferior concrete liner or backfill. To combat this, the water should be trained directly away from the cast-in-place concrete and backfill. One method of controlling the water is with thin steel or fiberglass sheets (called panning) affixed to the tunnel walls or tunnel crown wherever water is running. The panning is extended to the tunnel invert or shaft bottom and connected to a conduit leading out of the pour. This conduit may be a pipe or a gravel layer (French drain). The edges of the panning are sealed with caulk or some other material. The cast-in-place concrete or backfill is then placed against the panning, which allows the water to continue to flow but not come in contact with the fresh concrete or backfill material. After the cast-in-place concrete or backfill has reached design strength, holes are drilled to access behind the panning and contact grout is injected. To stop the flow of water, the contact grout injection pressure will need to be higher than the in situ water pressure. If a pipe and/or gravel layer is used, holes may have to be drilled into the liner invert to inject contact grout into the drain pipe and gravel. By this process, water is first contained and then sealed off (see Figure 8-8).

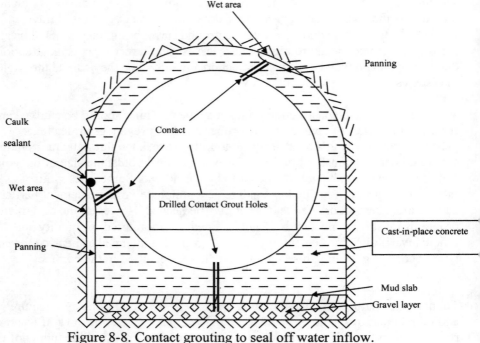

Figure 8-8. Contact grouting to seal off water inflow.

Groundwater inflows are less of a problem with sealed pipeline systems or watertight segmental liners. For these systems, it may be acceptable and less costly to allow the water to run freely within the annulus to a collection point and then to direct it through the bulkhead. As the final liner material is presumably designed to resist full hydrostatic head, the backfill material can be placed at a corresponding pressure. The only part of the system that should need upgrading will be the bulkhead. This will need to be fitted with a means to close off the water flow (e.g., a valve) and will have to be capable of withstanding full hydrostatic pressure. When backfill is placed behind the liner, it must eventually be pressured up to balance the groundwater pressure, thereby eliminating inflow. Later, the injection ports in the pipe or segments will be opened up and contact grouted, at which point any residual flow should be eliminated.

146

8.4 Contact Grout Mix Designs

Contact grout mixes are usually kept simple because of the normally small quantities of grout involved. Contact grout is usually batched using a small portable, skid-mounted grout plant and bagged cement. The primary requirement of the contact grout mix is that it fill the void completely and set quickly. Since most contact grouting is used to fill relatively small voids distributed over long distances along the tunnel alignment, a neat cement grout (only cement and water) is used. Examples of these types of voids are the ones normally located in the crown area of tunnels following the placement and curing of backfilled or cast-in-place concrete liners, and voids behind steel liner plates. The water:cement ratio of these neat cement grouts is usually 1:1 by volume. When somewhat larger voids are known to exist, such as voids that might exist behind a steel rib and lagging initial support system in an overexcavated/overbroken D&B-excavated tunnel (and even TBM tunnels), a contact grout mix composed of cement, sand, bentonite, and water should be utilized. When larger quantities of contact grout are required, it can be supplied to the job site from an offsite batch plant via transit mix concrete trucks. Sand is added to the mix to reduce the overall cost for larger volumes of grout per running meter of tunnel involved with this type of contact grouting. Bentonite is added to help keep the sand in suspension and increase pumpability. Flyash is generally not used in the neat cement grout mix in order to keep the mixes simple for field batching. A typical cement- and water-only contact grouting mix design is given in Table 8-2. A cement, sand, and water contact grout mix is given in Table 8-3.

Table 8-2. – NEAT CEMENT CONTACT GROUT MIX DESIGN

WATER:CEMENT RATIO (BY VOLUME) 1:1

Material	Quantity 1 Cu. Yd.	Quantity 1 Cu. Meter
		Kg
Cement Type II	1,692 lbs	1,004
Water	1,123 lbs	666 Kg
Total	2,815 lbs	1,670 kg
Grout Density	104 pcf	1,670 kg/m3

147

Table 8-3. – SANDED CONTACT GROUT MIX DESIGN
WATER:CEMENT RATIO (BY VOLUME) 1:1

Material	Quantity 1 Cu. Yd.	Quantity 1 Cu. Meter
Cement Type II	1,015 lbs	606 Kg
Sand	1,140 lbs	676 Kg
Water	674 lbs	400 Kg
Bentonite	2-4%	2-4%
Total	2,859 lbs	1699 kg
Grout Density	106 pcf	1699 kg/m3

CHAPTER 9
EQUIPMENT

The equipment used to mix, store, pump, and monitor cement-based grouts must be compatible with the characteristics of the grouts themselves, as well as with the project-specific parameters, such as anticipated volumes, maximum permissible injection pressures, total batch-to-injection time, and access and space restrictions. This chapter describes equipment used in backfilling and contact grouting operations.

9.1   Mixing

The two basic principles for mixing backfill and contact grout are by agitation and mixing by creating high shear. These are described below.

9.1.1   Mixing by Agitation

This group includes the simple paddle mixer (Figure 9-1), and the continuous screw mixer (Figure 9-2). The mix components are stirred or blended together until they slowly intermix. However, the shearing forces are very small, and unmixed cementitious lumps are typically indicative of an unstable, heterogeneous product. Such lumps are sometimes orders of magnitude larger than the void openings they are intended to fill; the grout instability also is reflected in blockages in grout hoses, pumps, and valves. This is usually somewhat less important with backfilling and contact grouting since most voids associated with these two methods are usually larger than voids associated with geotechnical grouting. However, keeping unmixed cementitious lumps to a minimum is still quite important to help prevent plugging of grout lines, valves, and other injection equipment. This is especially important when backfilling through the tailshield of a tunnel boring machine (TBM). An unstable mix also is susceptible to dilution with groundwater. The paddle mixer is a "batch" mixer wherein the water–cement ratio can be closely controlled. In contrast, the continuous mixer is subject to grout variation due to fluctuations in the pressure of the water and/or the flow of cement. From both mixers the grout must be gravity fed into a holding tank or agitator, which can be mounted below or beside the mixer (Figure 9-3).

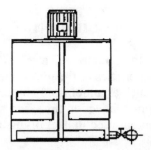

Figure 9-1. Schematic of a paddle mixer.

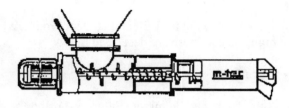

Figure 9-2. Schematic of a continuous screw mixer.

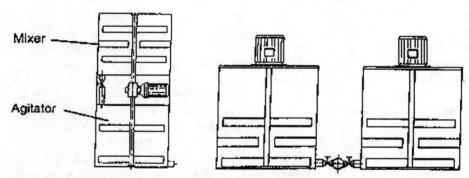

Figure 9-3. Schematics of a paddle mixer and agitator setups for continuous grouting.

9.1.2 Mixing by Creating High Shear

High-speed, high-shear mixers are often referred to as "colloidal" type mixers in recognition of the nature of the suspension created, although the suspension more correctly remains "mechanical" rather than "colloidal." These mixers most commonly comprise a mixing tank and a mixing/circulation pump. Figure 9-4 shows a sketch of a high-shear mixer; Figure 9-5 shows a picture of a Hany

Model HCM 500 mixer. The pump circulates water from the bottom to the top of the tank while the other mix components are added and prewetted. The cement particles are then individually mixed by the high shearing action of the pump, thus preventing coagulations or lumps, ensuring the homogeneity and enhancing the stability of the grout. Contemporary high-shear mixers have the following features:

- Mixing pump speed of 1,400 to 2,000 rpm. (Most contemporary electric motors run at 1,450 rpm at 50 Hz and are directly connected.)

- Mixing pump capacity such that the whole tank content is circulated a minimum of three times per minute. The pressure generated by the pump is of little importance but is typically up to 0.2 MPa (30 psi).

- The mixing pump should create high shear either through close tolerances between impeller and casing (e.g., Figure 9-6), or by creating high turbulence in the pump housing (Figure 9-7). The latter must have recessed vortex-type impellers to ensure adequate turbulence. High-turbulence pumps have much less wear than those of the close-tolerance types and are less prone to damage by larger grout particles. They also are suitable for mixing sanded grouts without the need for a separate sand-mixing drum (Figure 9-8). Sand for backfill grouting is typically specified to have 100 percent finer particles than the No. 8 sieve.

- The shape of the mixing tank should be such that the grout vortex in the tank is broken up, near the base, to avoid the intake of air. Peripheral baffles are not suitable as they lead to a buildup of grout and are difficult to keep clean.

Close-tolerance high-shear mixers can produce neat cement grouts of water/cement ratio as low as 0.32 (by weight) and even lower when dispersing admixtures are employed. Only 45 to 60 sec are needed for complete mixing after the addition of the last portion of Portland cements, although up to 4 min may be required to properly disperse and hydrate ultrafine cements. Longer circulation is unnecessary and may be deleterious to the grout properties due to excessive heat generation resulting from the very efficient mixing action. The mix should,

151

therefore, be transferred as quickly as possible to the agitator/holding tank, using the natural pump pressure.

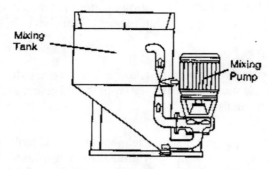

Figure 9-4. Schematic of a high shear mixer.

Figure 9-5. Hany Model HCM 500 colloidal type mixer.

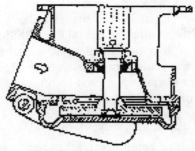

Figure 9-6. Schematic of an Atlas Copco Craelius system mixer.

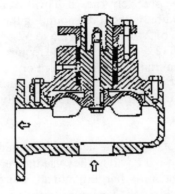

Figure 9-7. Schematic of a Hany system mixer.

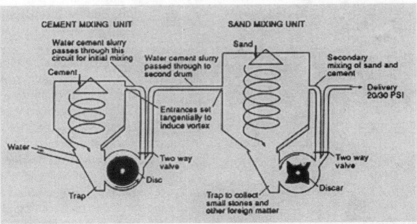

Figure 9-8. Schematic of a Colcrete double drum mixer for sanded grouts (Weaver, 1991).

Such mixers are batch mixers, which means a full mixing cycle has to be completed before the mix can be used. This makes use of a holding tank (also called an "agitator") or a second mixer essential if a continuous pumping operation is required. This arrangement does, however, allow the water–cement ratio and the various filler and admixture portions to be precisely controlled. In this regard, water is monitored via a calibrated holding tank, or a water flow meter, usually equipped with a preset cutoff control. Other components are measured by discrete premeasured volumes (e.g., bags of cement; packets of admixture) or by bulk delivery systems (e.g., bulk delivered materials and screw feed, weight or volume batching equipment). It has been found that, if the mixers themselves are mounted on load cells, the weight of all components *actually placed in the mixer* can be precisely known. This feature also saves space and allows for easy transportation without dismounting the scale. Most mixers have rated outputs in the range of 2 to 40 m³/hr (2.5 to 52 cy/hr), with usable drum volumes of 100 to 2,500 l (3.5 to 88 ft³). These require electric motors of 3 to 52 kW (4 to 70 Hp). A typical range of mixers from one manufacturer (Hany) is shown in Table 9-1. Most contact grouting specifications call for a mixer capacity of at least 400 l (14 ft³). Backfilling operations usually require much larger capacities.

It should also be noted that high-shear action also could be provided by "jet mixers," which have no moving parts. They use the venturi principle to make a vacuum; a strong jet of water discharging into an enlarged chamber accomplishes this. The cement is sucked into the vacuum and then mixes with the water jet. Such mixers are best suited to high-volume outputs of relatively fluid mixes. The water–cement ratio can be controlled by varying the rate of water flow in response to readings from a nuclear density meter mounted on the discharge line (Houlsby, 1990).

Special equipment will be required for generating foamed grouts. Such grouts may be multicomponent, including water, cement, flyash, foaming agents, and admixtures. Foam generators are used to produce a predetermined quantity of pre-formed foam (concentrate, water, and compressed air) into the mixer or the slurry discharge line for blending with the cement slurry. This can be done on a continuous or on a batch basis. The best systems employ bulk materials, automatic batching (accurate to less than 2 percent) and a continuous production of up to 75 to 150 m³/hr (100 to 200 cy/hr), regulated by the pump output. Figure 9-9 shows a typical foam generator. For both types, a foam-refining column or nozzle calibration should be employed to ensure the correct foam quality and discharge rate.

Table 9-1. Details of Hany high shear mixers.

Model	Units	HRW 100	HRW 300	HRW 300	HRW 600	HRW 800	HRW 2500
Production approx. (w:c ratio = 1)	m³/hr	2	5	5	8	20	40
Circulation capacity	l/min	540	1100	1400	1400	2400	4800
Usable volume	Liter	100	260	260	550	800	2500
Max. particle size	mm	5	8	8	8	3	-
Electric motor 50 Hz	kW	3	5.5	9	9	22	45
60 Hz	kW	3.6	-	11	11	25	52
Water connection		¾"	1"	1"	1½"	-	-
Length	mm	800	1150	1150	1360	1650	2600
Width	mm	640	820	820	1010	1400	2220
Total height	mm	1075	1140	1140	1500	2000	2040
Batching height	mm	870	1000	1000	1360	2000	1900
Weight	kg	115	250	275	320	1150	2350

Figure 9-9. A foam generator (Courtesy of AJ Voton LLC).

155

9.2.   Agitators/Holding Tanks

Batch mixers, either paddle or high shear, must be complemented by a holding tank to allow uninterrupted pumping and injection. Such tanks should have a capacity at least 30 percent larger than the usable capacity of the mixer to prevent the pump from running dry. A slowly revolving agitator paddle, usually mounted at an angle to the axis of the tank prevents the mix from tending to segregate and releases any air bubbles that may have been entrained during the high-shear mixing and grout transfer processes. Figure 9-10 shows an example of an agitator with an angled paddle. A sieve located at the inlet intercepts any large particles or debris when necessary. Agitators can be equipped with level probes to control automatic mixing cycles based on consumption rates.

As is the case for all grouting equipment reviewed in these guidelines, the actual power source can be varied to suit local conditions. Thus, although electric drive is most common (either directly or electrohydraulic), diesel engines or compressed air also are common choices. Per regulations, gasoline-powered equipment should never be operated underground.

Agitators are typically of useful capacity (160 to 3,000 l (5.7 to 106 ft^3)), requiring electric motors of 0.75 to 3.6 kW (1 to 4.8 Hp). Table 9-2 provides some detail on various sizes of agitators.

Figure 9-10. Agitator tank with angled paddle.

156

Table 9-2. Details of Hany agitators.

Model	Units	HRW 160	HRW 350	HRW 800	HRW 1200	HRW 3000
Usable volume	Liter	160	350	800	1050	3000
Electric motor						
50 Hz	kW	0.75	0.55	0.55	1.5	3
60 Hz	kW	0.90	0.66	0.66	1.8	3.6
Paddle speed						
50 Hz	min^{-1}	36	47	47	34	32
60 Hz	min^{-1}	43	56	56	40	38
Length	mm	1100	810	1000	1200	2000
Width	mm	1100	810	1000	1200	1950
Height	mm	1280	1230	1550	2300	2350
Weight	kg	150	155	230	450	1025

9.3. Water Measuring Devices

Grout mixers should be provided with resettable water meters with large, easily read dials. Meters that can be preset to shut off when the desired volume of water is discharged are available and should be used on projects where errors in proportioning are potentially critical. Flow rates up to 378 L/min (100 gpm) can be accommodated through 38-mm (1.5-in) diameter water delivery lines. Water meters should be located in an easy-to-read and direct view of the mixer operator and should be calibrated in units appropriate to the proportioning method used. For volumetric batching in the United States, meters are typically calibrated in cubic feet (ft^3) with a reading accuracy of 0.1 ft^3. However, as noted by Weaver (1991), calibration in Imperial gallons is appropriate for weight-batching operations in the United Kingdom and Commonwealth countries, as one Imperial gallon (4.5 L) of water weighs 4.5 kg (10 lbs)—an easy figure with which to work (Note: Canada and South Africa use metric). Elsewhere, weight-batching is simplified if the meter is calibrated in liters. Use of other methods for measuring the volume of water placed in the mixer, such as by use of buckets or a "fill line" painted on the mixer drum, are unsatisfactory and should not be allowed. Additionally, although the calibrated tank method is very precise, it also is very slow and is a potential source of delays. Electronic meters and recording systems are available that create a record of all important pumping and measuring parameters.

9.4. Pumps

9.4.1 Basic Considerations

The key choices to be made in selecting a pump relate to the required flow rates and injection pressures required. Flow rates must be compatible with the nature of the mix and the annulus or void being filled, the purpose of the injection program, as well as logistical and economic factors. Even more important is the selection and control of grouting pressures; excessive pressures may distress or damage the final lining system, whereas insufficient pressure may lead to inefficient backfill or contact grout placement. For backfilling and contact grouting applications, the maximum grout pressure can be readily calculated, based on structural strength parameters of the initial and final liner and the surrounding ground.

A somewhat controversial point within the grouting industry is whether the injection pressure should be at a constant pressure or whether fluctuations can be accommodated. While it is obvious that any pressure peaks cannot exceed the maximum allowable injection pressure (see Figure 9-11), many grouting engineers and practitioners believe that short pressure drops within the specified pressure range may not only be acceptable, but also may actually help move grout particles into finer fissures and voids. The opinion is that short and frequent pressure relaxation allows grout particles to reorient and adapt to constraints of smaller voids, whereas constant pressure will cause bridging and initiate pressure filtration (Figure 9-12). This latter phenomenon is only acerbated by raising the constant pressure. Therefore, many grouting engineers and practitioners consider it advantageous to use plunger or piston pumps, as long as they are equipped with precise pressure control valves. Such pumps also allow the use of single line grouting and permit holding a specified maximum pressure to encourage proper refusal, assuming appropriately formulated grouts are being injected.

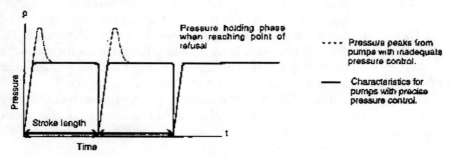

Figure 9-11. Output pressure characteristics of piston and plunger pumps.

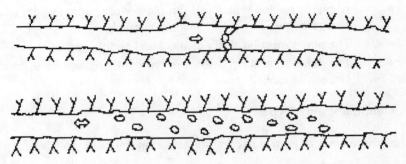

Figure 9-12. Void grouting showing particle bridging effect at constant pressure (above), and reorientation of particles under short pressure fluctuations (below).

Conversely, traditional grouting specifications typically state that "the pump shall be capable of developing in a continuous uniform manner the design pressure at the grout hole connection, up to the maximum pressure required." Specifications typically require bypass values necessary to avoid sudden excessive pressure development, or they permit piston pumps operating at fast stroke rates over 100/min, combined with certain minimum hose lengths ≥ 30 m (100 ft) to further reduce pressure fluctuations. Pressure accumulators or other "dampening" devices also are commonly required. As argued above, however, all these provisions may actually not be in the best interests of the project. Overall, backfilling and contact grouting pressures rarely exceed 0.35 MPa (50 psi) above in situ hydrostatic pressure.

9.4.2 Pump Selection Criteria

Attention should be paid to the following factors when selecting a pump:

- The maximum injection pressure should be adjustable on the pump. All the controls must be on the drive ("dry") side and not on the grout ("wet") side where valves do not function as reliably or as long. The control valves should allow a predetermined maximum pressure to be held over a preset period of time. Pressure control devices with an ON-OFF function should be avoided as they cause the pump to cut in and out very frequently, and no pressure holding effect can be achieved near refusal.
- Output should be fully adjustable.
- Piston or plunger pumps do not allow pressure and flow to be controlled adequately.

159

- Abrasive sanded grouts call for a low-wear pump system (e.g., plunger).
- The pump must be easily cleaned and maintained.
- The pump should have nonclog-type, full area valves to handle viscous or sanded grouts.

9.4.3 Common Pump Types

There are three types of pumps in common contemporary use worldwide:

1. **Progressive Cavity Pumps (Figure 9-13).** These also are known as helical screw, progressive helical cavity, worm, Mono, or Moyno pumps and are widely used in rock grouting and other types of geotechnical grouting. Although they are relatively inexpensive to purchase and mechanically simple, their maintenance costs may be higher due to high wear rates on the rubber stator and the steel rotor, especially when sanded grouts are used. Maximum pressure is moderate 2 MPa (284 psi) for a 4-stage pump, although injection rates can be high, exceeding 90 m^3/hr (120 cy/hr). Some of the larger size progressive cavity pumps can pump 50 mm (1/2 in) and larger aggregates. Pressure and output controls may not be closely adjustable for some models; therefore, a valve system at the injection point is required, in conjunction with a return line system. Such pumps provide an essentially constant pressure output.

2. **Piston Pumps (Figure 9-14).** Most are double-acting reciprocating pumps and have a higher initial capital cost but lower maintenance costs. They tend to be less bulky than plunger pumps. High pressure, more than 7 MPa (1,015 psi), and moderate flow characteristics are allied to close pressure and flow rate controls especially on electrohydraulic units. Grouts with fine sands can be accommodated readily, although the tight fit between piston seal and lining results in increased wear. Another potential disadvantage is that gravity-type valves may clog when pumping more viscous grouts over prolonged periods. Piston pumps are available and are regularly used to pump concrete mixes with 150-mm (1.5-in) aggregates.

3. **Plunger Pumps (Figures 9-15, 9-16 and 9-17).** These are very versatile and are used worldwide. Initial costs are similar to or slightly higher than piston pumps, while the pressure and flow ranges cover all usual grouting requirements. Some manufacturers provide very precise pressure and flow control features on their hydraulic or pneumatic drive systems. They have low wear characteristics and, by virtue of being able to quickly change

160

plungers, can significantly reduce the number of pump sizes that have to be carried by the contractor faced with a wide range of applications. The fast suction stroke creates a high grout velocity, which flushes the suction valve on every stroke, thus helping to eliminate clogging or " floating" of the valves when injecting at high pressure or low flow rates. Heavily sanded grouts, with particle sizes up to 8 mm (5/16 in) can be pumped without the risk of blockage, whereas other types can pump particles of sizes up to 5 mm (3/16 in). Rates of injection of 1 to 13 m³/hr (1.3 to 17 cy/hr) can be provided at pressures up to 10 MPa (1,420 psi).

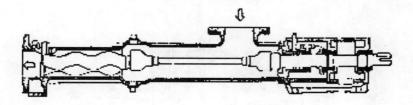

Figure 9-13. Schematic of a progressive cavity pump.

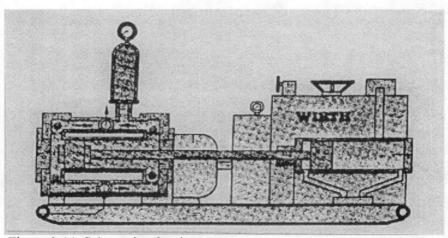

Figure 9-14. Schematic of a piston pump.

161

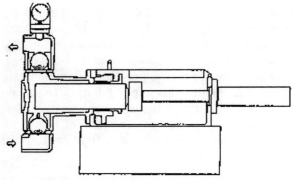
Figure 9-15. Schematic of a plunger pump.

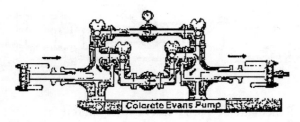
Figure 9-16. Schematic of a double acting, reciprocating plunger pump.

Figure 9-17. Photo of a double acting plunger pump ("side by side").

9.5   Pressure Gauges and Gauge Savers

Where traditional pressure gauges are used, there should be at least two in any injection system: one at the pump, the other at the grout injection point. The sensitivity of the latter gauge in particular must always be appropriate to the range of pressures anticipated so pressures can be closely and accurately read to at least 0.3 bar (5 psi) and carefully controlled. Gauges must be accessible and easy to read. It is a good idea to protect the gauges by installing a metal grille to prevent accidental and inevitable mechanical damage. A high-precision master gauge should be maintained at every site so that all operating gauges can be regularly calibrated against it.

The backfill and contact grout materials should never be allowed to come into direct contact with the pressure gauge (Henn, 1996). Therefore, a protective medium must be used to separate the backfill and contact grout material from the gauge. A gauge saver is used to provide this separation. Within the body of the gauge saver, the upper portion is isolated from the backfill and contact grout by a diaphragm. The area between the top of the diaphragm and the pressure gauge is completely filled with a suitable fluid, usually oil. Displacement of the fluid through movement of the diaphragm transmits pressure changes to the pressure gauge. Figure 9-18 shows a gauge saver installed at discharge of pump.

Figure 9-18. Gauge saver installed at discharge of pump.

9.6   Packers

As summarized by Weaver (1991), packers are devices designed to isolate a section of a borehole for the purpose of performing permeability tests or injecting grout. Packers are used when backfilling or contact grouting holes are field-drilled through the liner or when smooth (no threaded inserts installed) pre-installed holes are supplied in segments. Backfilling and contact grouting packers commonly consist of an expandable element that forms a seal at the collar of the hole and through which the grout is injected. The expandable element usually consists of stiff, fiber-reinforced synthetic rubber. Depending on the design, it may be expanded mechanically or inflated either pneumatically or hydraulically. Figure 9-19 shows a mechanical packer. Compressed nitrogen, supplied in bottles (small tanks), is sometimes used to inflate pneumatic packers, when the inflation pressure required is greater than that of the construction compressed air available at the site. However, some contractors use hand pumps with equal success. The inflation pressure typically must exceed the grout injection pressure.

Figure 9-19. A mechanical packer.

164

The effectiveness of the packer in sealing the collar of the hole depends on the diameter of the hole, the regularity or irregularity of the hole wall the length of the expansible element, and the flexibility of the expandable element. The expandable element for backfilling and contact grouting commonly is 100 to 200 mm (4 to 8 in) long and is fiber-reinforced.

Cup-leather packers, rather than expansible packers, have been used in small-diameter holes in relatively fresh crystalline rock or concrete. The sealing action of this type of packer is dependent on the return flow of grout forcing the leather cups into contact with the hole wall. However, short, mechanically expanded packers are the most common type of packer used to contact grout through cast-in-place concrete liners and precast concrete pipes when no pre-installed grout ports are supplied.

9.7   Nipples

Nipples are short pieces of pipe that are screwed into the pre-installed grout port. The other end of the nipple is connected to the grout header or directly to the contact grout delivery line. Nipples also can be installed into the field-drilled grout holes. When a field-drilled hole is used, the nipple is caulked or "dry packed" into place within the drill hole. After the "dry pack" has set, the threaded end of the nipple is connected to the grout header or directly to the contact grout delivery line.

9.8   Delivery and Distribution System

Specifications typically call for the grout lines to be of sufficient type and size to safely withstand the maximum water and grout pressures at the anticipated injection rates. Depending on the types of pumps used, the system may be arranged as a circulation line method (e.g., as shown in Figure 9-20) or a single line method, which is becoming more common with the increasing use of "new" materials and variable output pumps. Provision should be made for periodic flushing of the lines to evacuate buildup while in no way interfering with the hole injection process.

Space is usually restricted in underground backfilling and contact grouting operations, but certain basic principles can be stated (Weaver, 1991). The location of batching and pumping operations should minimize delays due to interference with other construction operations and allow grout delivery from the mixer(s) to the portable agitator(s) to take place by gravity flow whenever possible. Good access should be provided for materials delivery, and ample room should be provided for protected materials storage. If batching is done above ground or at the bottom of the shaft, the location should be sufficiently large and flat so that a protective structure can be erected over the equipment.

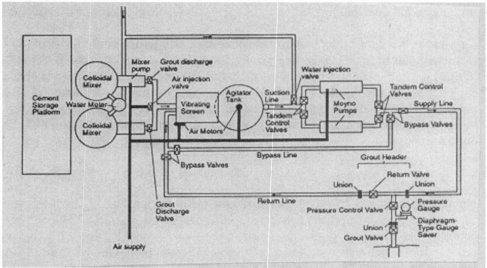

Figure 9-20. Schematic diagram of typical grout layout specified for use on California Department of Water Resources projects (Weaver, 1991).

The grout plant, which may be in the shaft or above ground, should be provided with radio or telephone communications to the agitator(s)/pumps. The agitator(s)/pump should be located within approximately 30 m (100 ft) of the hole(s) being backfilled or contact grouted. Keeping the agitator(s)/pumps in close proximity to the injection location accomplishes a number of purposes, among which are the following:

- The grout crew and the inspector are able to keep maximum control of the operation, concurrently monitoring injection rate, injection pressure, leakage along the tunnel, and any nearby drilling operations.

- Sedimentation of grout in the grout lines is minimized.

- Heating of the grout due to line friction or when grout lines are exposed to direct sunlight, if mixing is performed above ground, can be minimized.

- Opportunity is provided to flush the lines frequently, reducing the tendency for grout scale to form and to flake off into the grout lines.

- The volume of waste grout during cleanout is reduced.

For small operations, such as contact grouting of crown voids associated with a cast-in-place concrete or backfilled tunnel liner, one or two portable grout plants may be placed at conveniently accessible locations near the area being grouted. These plants will be moved from time to time as the work proceeds.

Contractors tend to favor using integrated skid-mounted or trailer-mounted plants in which the mixer, agitator(s), and pumps are all together as a unit. Figure 9-21 shows a rail-mounted portable grout plant for tunnel use. Although these plants may reduce grout crew size, as compared to using remote agitator(s)/pumps, they may be somewhat cumbersome to mobilize or move underground. Replacement of damaged or worn parts and equipment also may be difficult due to the limited working space. The costs to move utilities, materials, and support equipment, including air, water, and electrical supply, when the area being grouted moves out of reach must be considered. Also, the plant location may interfere with other construction operations, exacerbating the inconvenience involved in moving integrated plants on some underground projects. Moreover, supplying materials to integrated plants with limited working room can lead to interruptions in grout injection. Therefore, the grouting engineer or grouting inspector should exercise some degree of control over grout plant layout. This will allow personnel involved to verify that grouting of a hole will not be interrupted due to material supply problems and help ensure that excessive delays to the grouting operations or other construction operations are avoided. However, the smaller skid-mounted integrated plants are usually the best choice for smaller volume contact grouting jobs, such as filling the crown voids of a cast-in-place concrete or backfilled tunnel liner. When larger volumes of material are required, such as backfilling behind a precast segmental liner, the backfill should be batched at an area remote to the placement. The backfill can be transported to the placement area by pipeline or railcar or rubber-tired vehicle. Once at the point of placement, pumps are used to inject the backfill.

Figure 9-21. Portable rail mounted grout plant for tunnel use.

Torres Engineering and Pumps, Ltd. Introduced a compact, modular equipment system developed to mix, pump, deliver and control required grout pressure(s) and catalyst levels for backfill grout, Figure 9-22.

Initiated on the Channel Tunnel project (M.F. Annet & J. Stewart, 1991), six TBM's were equipped with the hydraulic powered modular components, consisting of a hydraulic Variable Control Module, Catalyst Pump Module and Grout Pump Module. The hand held Grout Gun completes the system and is fitted with a grout line connection and two fittings with check valves to receive liquid catalyst (sodium silicate) and water to flush the gun and the inline static mixing element, upon completion of individual segment grouting operations.

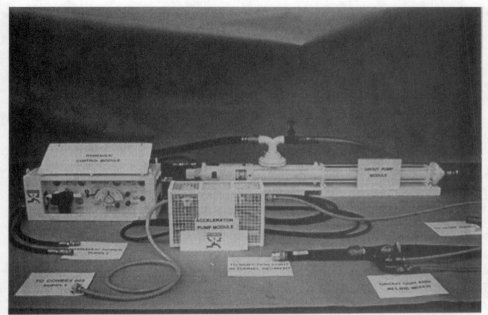

Figure 9-22. An example of a compact, modular equipment system developed to mix, pump, deliver, and control grout pressures and catalyst levels for backfill grout.

9.9   Injection Parameter Recording

Accurate recording and informative presentation of all mixing and injection parameters are essential elements in backfilling and contact grouting quality assurance/quality control (QA/QC) and verification processes. In particular, such data can be used in real time to allow the grouting engineer or grouting inspector to make informed decisions regarding progress and efficiency of the injection of each hole. There are various steps in this process, as described below.

- **Mix Batching Verification.** The accuracy of mix batching when manually conducted is dependent on the skill and care of the operators. It is verified by systematic testing of the mix, in its fluid state, by the quality control inspectors. Typical testing includes specific gravity, bleed, flow time, and setting and stiffening times. When an automatic mixing plant is used, computer-generated records of the weight of the components in each batch constitute the prime record, supported as with manual batching, by fluid mix test data. In the simplest cases, data from a totalizing water meter

169

and a count of cement bags used forms the most basic batching records.

- **Data Acquisition of Pressure and Flow Rates.** Pressure transducers should be located close to the point of injection to minimize friction loss implications. Such transducers must be separated physically from the backfill and contact grout by a diaphragm. It is now common to have the output directly transferred to the grouting engineer's or grouting inspector's computer display via telemetry or hardwire. Flow rates are preferably recorded by an inductive flow meter, which has no obstructed passage or moving parts. Sensitivities should reflect the full range of flow rates anticipated, but should typically be in the range of 1 to 5 l/min (0.21 to 1.1 gal/min). The meter also must be able to accommodate quick velocity changes, especially important when piston or plunger pumps are being used. Generally, the accuracy should be within 1 percent for flow rates down to 5 percent of the full scale, and at 1 percent of full scale, the accuracy should still be within 5 percent. Grout composition has no influence on the measurement accuracy provided the grout has a minimum conductivity of about 5μs. Chemical additives or admixtures are generally compatible with the use of these meters. Recent developments have made it possible to record flow rates and quantities by stroke impulses from piston or plunger pumps. The value of an impulse can be calibrated to within 5 percent, although at high flows and pressures the accuracy will be in the range of 7 to 10 percent. Prime advantages of stroke recording are the simplicity of the system and its low costs relative to inductive flow meters.

- **Recording, Display, and Analysis Equipment.** The most commonly used recorders incorporate electromagnetic (inductive) flow meters and electronic pressure transducers. Pressure and flow rate are continuously recorded and displayed on a chart recorder (Figure 9-23), the total quantities being accumulated by a resettable counter. Water test data and grout location injection information can be provided, although these are generally not required for backfilling and contact grouting. Contemporary computer technology permits an almost unlimited variety of data output to be displayed and processed, and, when used by knowledgeable grouting engineers or grouting inspectors, it can be a very powerful tool for significantly improving the quality and efficiency of the grouting program (Wilson and Dreese, 1998). In addition, such records constitute an invaluable source of data when planning a similar program in comparable conditions. All monitoring equipment must be designed to cope with typical site conditions and must be operated and maintained by skilled operators as opposed to computer specialists. New units are capable of recording pressure and flow data from up to eight grout lines simultaneously. Signals from flow meters and/or stroke impulses are collected, and limits on grout volume, pressure, and flow rate can be preset for each group pump. Data is recorded on standard memory cards and can be processed later under a Windows-based program or be processed and displayed in real time.

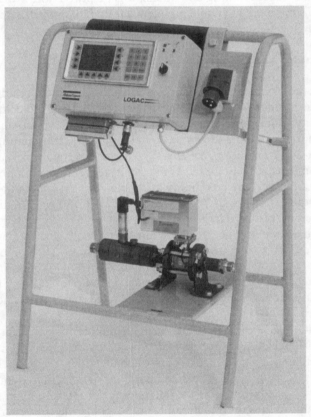

Figure 9-23. Simple pressure and flow recording unit.

171

Weaver (1991) described proprietary automated injection systems wherein the outputs from drilling parameter recorders are "married" to automated plants to cause "the proper grout mix to be injected at the proper pressure for a given soil condition." Similar electronic recording and analytical equipment also can:

- Obtain, record, and interpret in situ permeability tests
- Design grout patterns and quantities
- Identify anomalies and produce various tables, graphs, and documents
- Record and display structural movement data in relation to the grouting progress

While this level of equipment sophistication generally is not needed for backfilling and contact grouting operations, it is helpful to know the types and capabilities of equipment available, in the event that the project requires or can obtain labor-saving efficiencies by using this technology.

9.10 Automated and Combined Units

Depending on the contact grouting application and the project requirements and constraints, it is often useful that all equipment components are combined into one portable unit. Thus, for contact grouting, compact integrated units are available, comprising a high-shear mixer, holding tank, grout pump, and power pack (Figure 9-24). In addition, a water flow meter or grout injection parameter instrumentation is usually mounted on the same steel frame. Outputs of 1 to 8 m^3/hr (1.3 to 10.5 cy/hr) are commonly available. Pumps are available with injection pressure capacities of 2 to 10 MPa (290 to 1,450 psi). In the case of backfilling operations where large volumes of materials may be required, larger containerized units are produced. These units are usually fed by screw conveyors. Figure 9-25 provides a view of a typical two-pump setup. Such plants can produce 12 to 45 m^3/hr (16 to 60 cy/hr) depending on mix type and composition, have a weight-batch accuracy of ±3 percent, and can weigh up to 8,500 kg (18,750 lb) of material. Volumetric batching also can be conducted, but it is less accurate.

Automated batch plants offer potential savings in material and labor costs for large projects. The batching process is controlled by the injection rate. For example, the Hany system features a control panel with a large schematic diagram that facilitates programming the desired quantities of each ingredient in the grout. Interlocks in the system minimize the potential for proportioning errors by starting a vibrator in the silo if material is not reaching the conveyor, shutting

172

down, and sounding an alarm. Comparable or larger equipment is available from other grouting equipment manufacturers and suppliers.

Figure 9-24. Integrated grout plant.

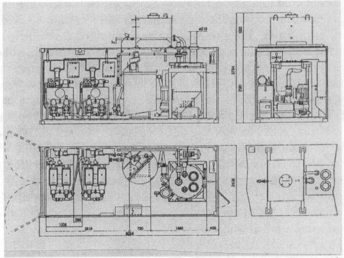

Figure 9-25. Plan of a typical containerized combined unit.

9.11   Underground Transport

As previously explained in the guidelines, most contact grouting requires small-enough quantities of materials per length of tunnel or depth of shaft to allow batching of the mix underground and in close proximity to the point(s) of injection. This type of arrangement has the advantages of allowing the batch plant operator to be in visual contact, and maybe even voice contact, with the rest of the contact grouting crew. The contact grout ingredients are brought underground to the batch plant, which is usually a skid-mounted setup, before any batching starts. The water, air, and wastewater discharge lines are piped to the plant while the bagged cement and any other ingredients are transported by rail or rubber-tired vehicle to the batch plant locations.

For most backfilling operations, and when the quantities of contact grout required are large, the batching of the various mix ingredients is usually done on the surface. Batching backfill material and contact grout can be done onsite utilizing a temporary batch plant, or the mixes can be supplied from a local conventional concrete batch plant. Once batched, the backfill material or contact grout can be transported to the point(s) of placement or injection in a number of ways. For example, using a concrete transit mix truck, or other similar type of vehicle, the mixes can be delivered to a predrilled drop hole and discharged directly to the tunnel level or shaft bottom via the drop hole near the location where the backfill will be placed or injected. The mixes also can be pumped from the top of the shaft or from the portal to the point of placement using a conventional concrete pump or grout pump. Depending on the mix design and the distance pumped, mixes may require remixing and secondary pumping at the point of placement. Additionally, mixes can be transported into the tunnel using railcars or rubber-tired vehicles. In larger tunnels and underground chambers, conventional concrete transit mix trucks can often be driven into the tunnel to transport the batched material as close as possible to the point of placement. Figure 9-26 shows an example of a rubber-tired, low-profile vehicle for underground delivery of concrete or grout. This type of vehicle can be supplied with or without the discharge chutes. Figures 9-27, 9-28a, and 9-28b show examples of rail-mounted, low-profile concrete or grout delivery vehicles. Figure 9-29 shows an example of a low-profile concrete remix surge hopper.

Figure 9-26. Example of a rubber tired low profile concrete or grout delivery vehicle.

Figure 9-27. Example of a rail mounted low profile concrete or grout delivery vehicle.

Figure 9-28a. Another example of a rail mounted, low profile grout delivery vehicle (transfer car).

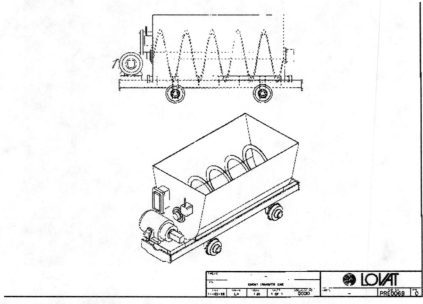

Figure 9-28b. Drawing of transfer car pictured in 9-28a

176

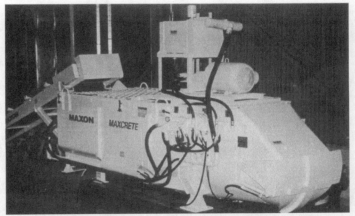

Figure 9-29. Example of a low profile concrete remix surge hopper.

Like other types of backfill, flowable fill can be batched onsite or at an offsite facility. Figure 9-30 shows an example of onsite flowable fill batching equipment. Figure 9-31 shows flowable fill being discharged directly from the onsite batch plant as shaft backfill. When flowable fill is not delivered and discharged directly into the placement via a drop pipe or is not delivered directly from the batch plant into a shaft from the top of the shaft, flowable fills can be transported underground using the same types of equipment used to transport other types of backfills and grouts.

Figure 9-30. Example of on site flowable fill batching equipment.

Figure 9-31. Flowable fill being placed from a batch plant directly in shaft as backfill.

9.12   Backfill Placement through the TBM Tailshield

When utilizing a precast concrete segmental tunnel lining system in conjunction with an earth pressure balance (EPB) or a slurry shield (SS) TBM, the state of the practice is to place the annulus backfill through a piping system installed integral to the TBM tailshield. Figures 7-7 and 7-8 (see Chapter 7) show this tailshield piping. Figure 9-32 shows a drawing of a backfill grouting system through the tailshield of a TBM, utilizing two pumps to supply two grout pipes each. Figure 9-33 shows a backfill grouting system through the tailshield of a TBM utilizing an onboard grout pump located on the grout car. The system shown utilizes a "rotary distributor" to supply the grout pipes. While the placement of annulus backfill behind a segmental lining system also can be performed through pre-installed grout ports cast into the segment, this method of backfill placement is becoming somewhat less common in poor ground conditions. The question of whether to inject the backfill through the tailshield of the TBM or through grout ports in the segments is a very controversial issue within the underground industry. Figure 7-9 shows segmental grout ports with fittings installed. Figure 9-34 shows backfill grouting through the segments utilizing two pumps to supply two grout ports each. Figure 9-35 shows backfill grouting through the segments utilizing an onboard grout pump located on the grout car. The system utilizes a "grout manifold" to supply the four grout ports. However, the pre-installed grout ports, which also are used as segment lifting and handling points, are a necessary backup means of backfill injection should the TBM tailshield backfill piping system become plugged or otherwise inoperable.

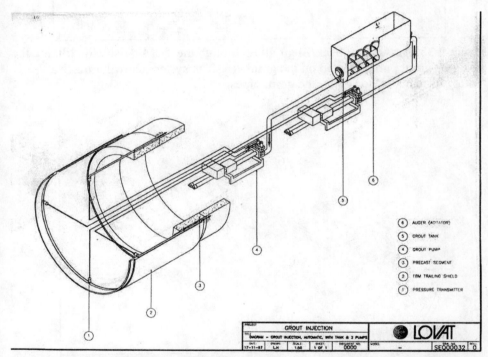

Figure 9-32. Drawing of backfill grouting through the TBM tailshield utilizing two pumps supplying two grout pipes each.

179

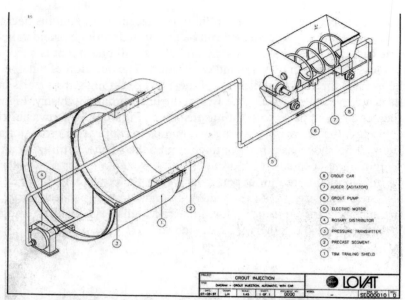

Figure 9-33. Drawing of backfill grouting through the TBM tailshield utilizing the on-board grout pump located on the grout car. The system shown utilizes a "rotary distributor" to supply the grout pipes.

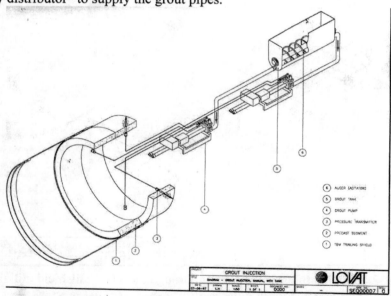

Figure 9-34. Drawing of backfill grouting through the segments utilizing two pumps to supply two grout ports each.

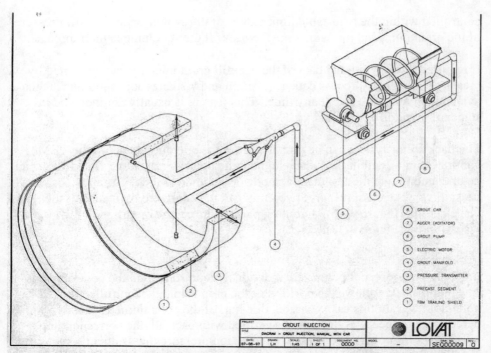

PROJECT							
TITLE	GROUT INJECTION						
	DIAGRAM - GROUT INJECTION, MANUAL, WITH CAR						
DATE: 07-08-97	DRAWN LH	SCALE: 1:45	SHEET: 1 OF 1	DOCUMENT NO. 0000	MODEL —	DWG. NO. SE000009	REV. 0

Figure 9-35. Drawing of backfill grouting through the segments utilizing on-board grout pump located on the grout car. The system utilizes a "grout manifold" to supply the four grout ports.

When utilizing the tailshield piping system to place backfill, the injection pressure must be sufficient to guarantee complete filling of the annulus, but should not exceed the structural capabilities of the segment ring or lead to damage to the tailshield seals. To achieve the goals of maximum control pressure and backfill quantity, the current practice is to supply backfill to each injection pipe with an individual pump. This method also helps ensure equal injection pressure and backfill material distribution around the tunnel circumference.

Injection points in the tailshield are equipped with pressure cells that register the pressures in the individual grout lines. The injected volume can be determined by means of level measurement in the backfill grout tank or by weighing the grout cars (wagons). Information about the injected volume and the injection pressures at individual injection points can be taken from monitors or gauges in the TBM control cabin. These monitors and gauges are referred to as "visualization." If the system is operated correctly, the pressure in the annulus can be permanently controlled within the adjustable limit values of the switch-on/switch-off pressure of the grout pumps at the same time the backfill grout volume is monitored.

If required, the operational data of the backfill grout injection can be stored by means of so-called "process data acquisition and visualization," and this is thus available in real time and at any time. This feature is usually not included in standard monitoring systems.

The backfilling system can be operated from the operating panel in the TBM control cabin or within the tailshield, near the point of injection. Backfilling can be operated in two modes: manual mode or automatic mode. Instantaneous backfill values (pressures, grout volume) can be monitored by means of the visualization (Figure 9-36). Grouting parameters can be modified in the visualization (Figure 9-37).

In manual mode, grout pumps are individually controlled via the control panel. The pump speed follows the position of the proportionally controlled potentiometer. In this case position, one-half of the potentiometer means 50 percent of the speed. If the annulus is filled with backfill, the corresponding injection point is switched off via the injection pressure that is directly measured in front of the injection pipe.

In automatic mode, all grout pumps are switched on and off together via the control panel. The control is the same as for the manual operation. However, the injection points are switched on differently. If backfilling is restarted, the injection point must be switched on manually. During operations, switch-on and switch-off is automatic via the adjusted injection pressures. Figure 9-38 shows a schematic diagram of the backfill delivery system in the area of the TBM's trailing gear (backup area) and the tailshield injection points. Figures 9-39 through 9-42 show pictures of the actual equipment depicted in Figure 9-38.

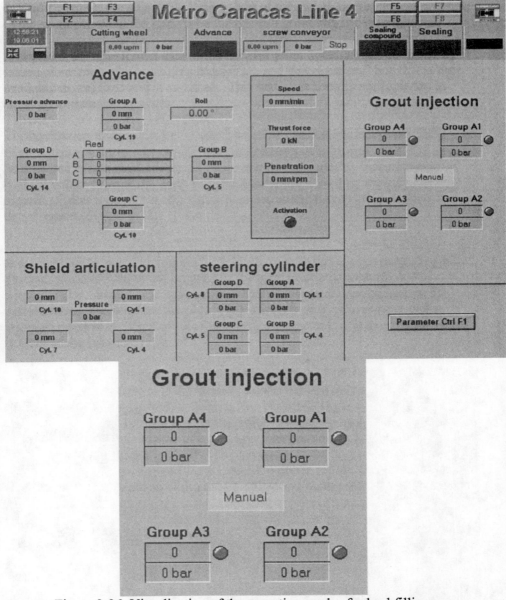

Figure 9-36. Visualization of the operation modes for backfilling.

183

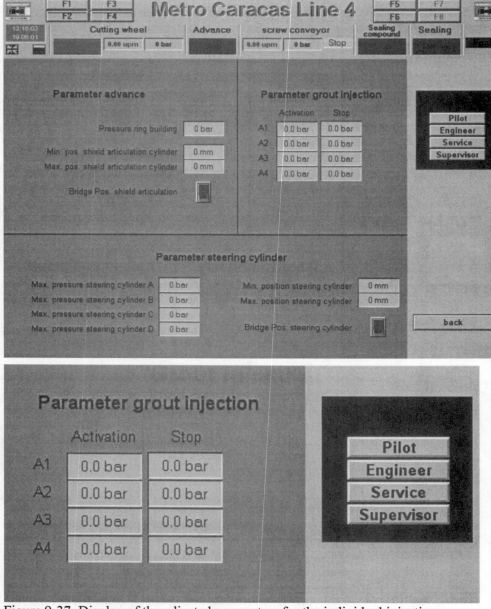

Figure 9-37. Display of the adjusted parameters for the individual injection pumps.

184

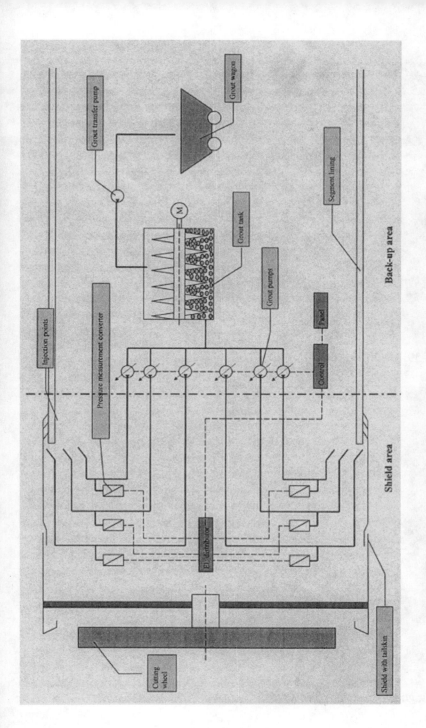

Figure 9-38. Schematic of a TBM backfill delivery system

185

Figure 9-39. Backfill grout transfer car (grout wagon).

Figure 9-40. Transfer car (grout wagon) connected to grout injection system on trailing gear (gantry) of TBM.

Figure 9-41. Backfill grout injection system located on trailing gear (gantry) of TBM.

Figure 9-42. Longitudinal view of TBM, trailing gear (gantry).

9.13   Cellular Concrete

The batching, transportation, and placement of cellular concrete is similar to other types of backfill material placement operations. There is, however, some specialized equipment used in conjunction with cellular concrete placement operations. For example, a typical cellular concrete mobile plant will consist of the following:

- Silo(s) for cement and flyash
- Suitable slurry grout mixer
- Foam generator (integral or separate)
- Suitable cellular concrete pump

Figure 9-43 shows a picture of an AJ Voton LLC dry mix foam concrete plant with a cement silo and a flyash silo in the background. Figure 9-44, a close-up picture of the plant shown in Figure 9-43, shows slurry mixers. Figure 9-45 shows a picture of a Pacific International Grout cellular concrete continuous mixer unit.

Figure 9-43. An AJ Voton LLC dry mix foam concrete plant showing a cement silo and a flyash silo in the background.

188

Figure 9-44. Close-up of plant shown in Figure 9-43 showing computer controlled slurry mixers.

Figure 9-45. Pacific International Grout's cellular concrete continuous mixer.

Figure 9-46 shows a picture of Pacific International Grout cellular concrete dosing equipment used for adding/blending chemicals for acceleration of high water inflow areas.

All pumps suitable for grouts also can be used for cellular concrete, provided the foam is injected at the pump discharge. If cellular concrete travels through the pump, only positive displacement type pumps are advised, such as the following:

- Peristaltic or hose pumps
- Progressing cavity pumps
- Rotary positive displacement pumps
- Diaphragm pumps

While high-shear mixing of the cement and water slurry is necessary, high-shear mixing does not necessarily include a pump for recirculation. Also, high-speed tube mixers and high-speed pan mixers can achieve the same result: a lump free grout. An example is a pan mixer with 250 liter (8.9-cf) neat slurry volume with 5.5 kW/ 60 Hz drive, giving mixer action of 1,000 rpm and output of 20 m^3/hr (26 cy/hr).

Figure 9-46. Pacific International Grout's cellular concrete dosing equipment used for adding/blending chemicals for acceleration of high water inflow areas.

State-of-the-art foam equipment is composed of a controller to input the required amount of foam, an air control valve combined with an air-flow meter that measures actual air flow coming from a compressor (an oil well cementing nitrogen is used instead of air because nitrogen creates smaller air bubbles). Equipment also would include a water pump (slave) and a foaming agent pump (slave), both directed by the air-flow meter (master). All flows combine into a static mixer or the liquids are combined and sent through a nozzle to be dispersed in the air flow. There is virtually no limit to the capacity of foam generators (compare fire-fighting equipment at airports), but in foam concrete practice capacities range from 20 m^3/hr (26 cy/hr) to 160 m^3/hr (209 cy/hr).

Typical cement slurry manufacturing capacities for mobile equipment ranges from 5 m^3/hr (6.5 cy/hr) to 60 m^3/hr (78.5 cy/hr). Thus, combined with foam this will give practical foam concrete manufacturing capacities of up to 200 m^3/hr (262 cy/hr).

CHAPTER 10
RECORD KEEPING

Detailed drilling and backfilling and contact grouting placement records must be kept at the same time that the work is being performed. This is accomplished using preprinted, custom-designed daily inspection report forms. The grouting engineer or grouting inspector—who is normally employed by the design engineer, owner, or construction manager—will keep the project's official backfilling and contact grouting records. Additionally, the contractor's drilling/grouting supervisor usually keeps an independent set of records.

The minimum required information to be recorded on official drilling, and backfilling and contact grouting placement daily inspection report forms should be determined during the design phase of the project. The information requirement should later be refined in the constructability review phase of the project's backfilling and contact grouting programs through a thorough review of the drilling and grouting specifications and drawings. The inspection report forms should be project-specific documents based on known geology and groundwater conditions, anticipated construction means and methods, requirements of the contract documents, and any other requirements of the completed facility. During the design phase of the project, the engineer should identify the initial data requirements based primarily on information gathered during the geological site investigation and from issues addressed in the project Geotechnical Baseline Report (GBR). Expectations for the drilling, backfilling, and contact grouting inspections report forms should be clearly defined. During final design, constructability, and bidability reviews, the design team should reexamine the data-capturing capability and expectations for drilling, backfilling, and contact grouting forms. Also during the constructability and bidability reviews, these needs should be reconciled with the contractor's reporting requirements found in the contract documents. If, during the constructability and bidability reviews, the inspector's or contractor's drilling and grouting record keeping is unclear or imprecise, the drilling and grouting specifications should be revised with more specific documentation requirements, including sample forms if necessary. Within the drilling and grouting specification, it is recommended that the contractor be required to submit detailed drilling and grouting work plans for approval by the grouting engineer and/or the construction manager's quality assurance/quality control (QA/QC) manager.

Just prior to the start of work, the inspection forms should be reviewed and modified as necessary based on the contractor's proposed means and methods and any design modifications. The daily inspection report forms should be modified as necessary after the drilling and backfilling and contact grouting starts to match the information required on the inspection forms with the actual field conditions and construction methods being used. Once work starts, it is absolutely necessary that, at the end of each shift, the grouting engineer or inspector and the contractor's drilling/grouting supervisor agree on measured drilling and backfill and contact grout quantities and all other issues relating to the work, note their disagreement, and give detailed specifics. Just as other pay quantities should be tabulated and reconciled daily to avoid disputes in advance of the contractor's monthly pay applications, the grouting inspector's daily inspection reports should be reconciled daily with those prepared by the contractor's drilling/grouting supervisor. When backfilling or contact grouting operations are working more than one shift per day, the oncoming shift grouting engineer or inspector and the contractor's drilling/grouting supervisor should meet with the off-going counterpart and read the previous shift or shifts inspection reports at the start of the shift.

The daily drilling and backfilling and contact grouting inspection report forms should be designed to allow ample space to record comments and observations as well as space for field sketches. Additionally, the grouting engineer or inspector and the contractor's drilling/grouting supervisor both should keep separate waterproof field notebooks. The field notebook should be used to record additional information, which may not have been included in the daily inspection report form. The field notebook should be kept with the philosophy that no entry is too meaningless, too silly, or too unimportant to be written down. Unless various details and observations are recorded as they happen, they will most likely be lost forever. It is always much better to have the information and not need it than to need it and not have it.

Only one field notebook should be kept by each party at a time: one by the grouting engineer or inspector, and one by the contractor's drilling/grouting supervisor. The first field notebook should be labeled "Field Notebook Number One" and should be completely filled before starting the second notebook. This same method needs to be carried out for all subsequent field notebooks. The field notebook should be passed on from shift to shift when the project is working more than one shift per day. The grouting engineer or inspector and the contractor's drilling/grouting supervisor receiving the notebook should read the entries from the previous shift or shifts at the start of the shift. At the end of each shift, a horizontal line should be drawn across the page below the last entry, indicating the last entry for that shift. The grouting engineer or inspector and the contractor's drilling/grouting supervisor should enter the shift (first, second, or third), shift start time and end time (as this could change through the course of the project), and the date, and then print and sign their name on the line. Even if there were no entries made into the field notebook on the shift, the words "no entries this shift" should be written above the horizontal line and the line should show the shift, times, day and date, and person's name and be signed. Care must be taken to make all entries legible so others can the read the entries and so there is no mistake about what was meant by the entries.

A critical requirement is that every backfill and contact grout hole must have a unique and unambiguous identification number. A numbering system should be established before drilling for the first backfill or contact grout hole starts. The numbering system must be agreed on by both the contractor and the person responsible for the owner's inspection program. There must be only one backfilling and contact grouting hole numbering system for the project.

An example of a unique numbering system for a contact grout hole along a tunnel alignment might be "Hole #C-2 @ 14+55." This hole is located at tunnel station 14+55, it is a contact grout hole (note the "C"), and it is the number two contact grout hole at that location. In circular-, horseshoe-, rectangular-, and other-shaped tunnels, hole numbering should always increase in a clockwise direction, looking "upstation" (looking in the direction of increasing total stationing: 8+25, 8+30, 8+35, etc.). Only the project stationing shown in the contract documents and used for all other inspection records. The tunnel may have been excavated in the "upstation" or in the "downstation" direction. The direction of the tunnel excavation advance does not matter, nor does the direction of the drilling and backfilling or contact grouting operation advance matter when locating and numbering backfill and contact grout holes. Only the project tunnel stationing looking "upstation" should be used. In tunnels, the "No. 1" hole should be the hole at the 12 o'clock position, at the top of the vertical centerline of the tunnel, or the first hole to the right of centerline if a hole is not located directly on the vertical centerline. Figures 10-1 and 10-2 show examples of these types of numbering systems. Backfill and contact grout holes should always radiate outward on a plane perpendicular to the tunnel alignment.

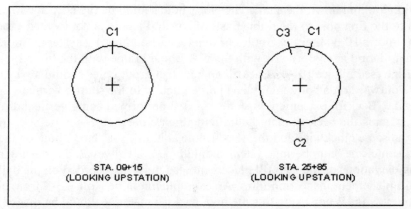

Figure 10-1. Example of hole numbering system for tunnel contact grouting operation.

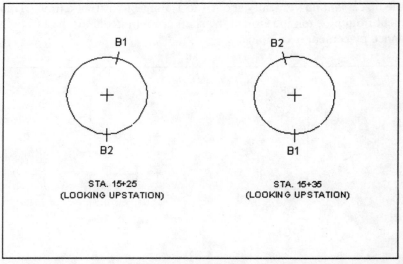

Figure 10-2. Example of hole numbering system for tunnel backfilling.

An example of a unique numbering system for a backfill grout hole in a shaft might be "Hole #B-7 @ elev. +379 (62 ft bgs)." This hole is located in the shaft at elevation positive 379 ft. As a crosscheck, the vertical distance below ground surface (62 ft bgs) should also be recorded. It is a backfill grout hole (note the "B") and it is the No. 7 hole at that elevation. For circular-, square-, rectangular-, and other-shaped shafts, hole numbering should always increase in a clockwise

195

direction looking down the shaft. The No. 1 hole should be the hole at compass North or the first hole to the right (East) of North if a hole is not located exactly at North. Figure 10-3 shows examples of this type of numbering system. Sometimes hole numbering in shafts starts with the No. 1 hole in line with the tunnel centerline (see Figure 10-4). Backfill and contact grout holes should always radiate outward on a horizontal plane perpendicular to the shaft's vertical centerline. Backfill placement in shafts is often performed using vertical drop pipes, placing the backfill material utilizing the tremie placement method. In this case, the same clockwise and the "No. 1 hole at North" or "No. 1 hole on the tunnel centerline" numbering system should be used. However, the starting and ending elevations of the backfill placement also must be recorded on the daily backfill placement inspection form. An example might be Hole #B-4 from elev. +5 to elev. +15. When using this method, backfill material should be placed using all the backfill drop pipes within a given elevation interval during a single backfill grouting operation. The placement should move from pipe to pipe around the perimeter of the shaft, placing approximately equal amounts of backfill through each pipe. The amount of material injected into each of the backfill pipes should bring the placement up vertically about 1 to 1.5 m (3 to 5 ft) at a time. This movement from pipe to pipe around the shaft is continued until the full height of the planned placement is completed.

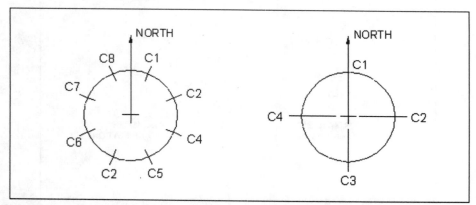

Figure 10-3. Example of hole numbering system for shaft contact grouting.

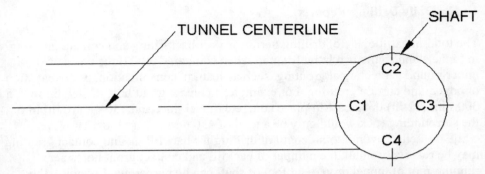

Figure 10-4. Shaft contact grout numbering system where the #1 hole is located on the tunnel centerline.

It is important to note that in shafts, contact grouting voids between the ground and the initial support system is sometimes required. However, in shafts as a general rule contact grouting behind backfill material or cast-in-place concrete liners is not required. Contact grouting is usually not required behind backfill material or cast-in-place concrete shaft liners because, unlike in tunnels where gravity is acting on the backfill material or cast-in-place concrete to pull the material downward and away from the tunnel crown, thus creating a void, in a shaft gravity is acting to help the backfill material or cast-in-place concrete to fill voids. However, contact grouting may still be desirable behind shaft liners to restrict flows of surface water or near-surface groundwater from accessing drinking water aquifers by percolating downward through the slightly disturbed ground surrounding the excavation. This condition could lead to regulatory problems or a public health hazard. The additional water entering the excavation also could increase the contractor's pumping and water treatment expenses. This is particularly true if the surface water carries contaminants or near-surface groundwater movement advanced a migrating contaminate plume that then could advance further and faster by short-circuiting to deeper groundwater lenses through project excavations. Possibilities of these conditions developing are very real when the project is located in older, highly urbanized areas. Failure to take appropriate steps to stem the flow of contaminated surface or near-surface groundwater could unnecessarily expose project participants to state and federal environmental protection action along with the added cost and scheduling impacts.

10.1 Daily Drilling Reports

The total linear footage of drilling performed for backfilling and contact grouting in tunnels and shafts is relatively small when compared to various types of underground geotechnical grouting, such as feature, consolidation, pre-excavation or cover, and curtain grouting. For example, a contact grout hole drilled through a 300-mm (12-in) thick cast-in-place concrete tunnel liner and 150 mm (6 in) into the surrounding rock would only be a total of 450 mm (18 in) long. However, while the actual overall total length of drilling for backfilling and contact grouting may be relatively small, the number of backfill and contact grout holes per running foot of tunnel or vertical foot of shaft can be numerous. Likewise, the number of drill rig "setups" and "hole hookup" for injection can be quite large.

As discussed in previous chapters, backfill materials can be injected into the annulus behind tunnel and shaft liners (1) through the tailshield of earth pressure balance (EPB) or slurry shield (SS) tunnel boring machines (TBMs) (tunnels only); (2) through pre-installed injection holes in precast/prefabricated liners, or (3) with slicklines or grout pipes installed longitudinally within the ground/liner annulus along the tunnel alignment or vertically within the ground/liner annulus for shafts. Of these three backfill placement methods, the only one that requires field drilling is the backfill grout injection "through the liner" method. However, even with this method, the current industry practice is to manufacture the liner system with pre-installed backfill holes or ports, therefore eliminating the need for and avoiding the cost of field drilling through the liner. Because the need to field drill for backfill grouting holes is uncommon, this discussion and the examples given of daily drilling inspection report forms are limited to drilling for contact grouting holes through the liner. Contact grout holes are normally drilled directly through cast-in-place concrete liners or through the backfill material utilizing pre-installed grout ports for pipe and penstock liners. If drilling, and therefore records, is required for a backfilling operation, the contact grouting drilling daily inspection form formats can usually be used with only slight modifications to accommodate backfill drilling forms.

Drilling for contact grouting is performed after placement and curing of the backfill material behind final lining systems (e.g., non-expandable precast concrete segments, precast concrete or fabricated pipe systems, liner plates, steel liners, penstocks). Drilling for contact grouting also is performed after installation of expandable precast concrete segmental liner systems and placement and curing of the cast-in-place concrete final liners. Drilling and contact grouting also may be performed to fill voids behind an initial support system prior to backfill material placement or a cast-in-place liner system. Likewise, drilling and contact grouting of voids created by the installation of sheeting, panning, and invert gravel or pipe dewatering systems may need to be performed.

As described in Chapter 8, contact grouting is first performed to fill voids between the ground and the initial support system and is later performed (as a separate operation) to fill the voids between the initial support system and the backfill material or cast-in-place concrete liner system. This two-step process is often referred to as "phase I or II" or "stage I or II" contact grouting. However, some designs allow contact grouting of voids between the ground and the initial support system, and the voids between the initial support system and the backfill material or cast-in-place lining, to be filled at the same time in a one-step process. The requirement for a one-step versus a two-step contact grouting process is usually based on site-specific geology and groundwater conditions and on how these conditions affect issues such as potential settlement of surface and underground utilities, initial support system loading, ground/liner interaction requirements, and operational requirements of the completed facilities. When a one-step contact grouting program is specified, it is often advisable to drill some test contact grout holes and attempt to inject grout. If there is a meaningful grout take, it may be in the project's best interest to initiate a full two-step contact grouting program. If during the design phase a one-step grouting program is contemplated followed by a contact grout hole test program, then the project's delivery strategy, contracting plan, bid form, plans, and specifications must anticipate the possible need for a full two-step contact grouting program. Otherwise, the project could be faced with costly change orders and delays.

As stated above, the daily drilling inspection report forms should be project specific based on geology, groundwater conditions, and the drilling equipment and methods actually used. The information recorded on the drilling inspection report form also must document contract specification and drawing-specific requirements. Examples of information that should be recorded includes, but is not limited to, the following:

- Date, times, and shift
- Driller's name, foreman's name, and drilling inspector's name
- Crew size and makeup
- Unique hole identification number for each hole
- Type of drilling equipment (model, power source, etc.)
- Hole diameter
- Length of hole drilled

- Any loss of drilling fluids or drilling fluids appearing in other holes, cracks, etc.
- Hole depth at which groundwater is encountered in the hole or a statement that no groundwater was encountered
- Volume of groundwater, if any, produced by the hole
- Thickness of backfill material or cast-in-place concrete penetrated before encountering the void or surrounding ground
- Voids depths, if any, found during drilling behind the initial support, backfill, or cast-in-place concrete
- Start and completion time for drilling each hole

As noted above, for contact grout holes drilled through backfill material and cast-in-place concrete liners, the backfill and concrete thicknesses, as well as the depth of any void found behind the backfill or concrete liner, should be recorded. Also, the inspection forms should have an area for general comments; during contact grout hole drilling, for example, if reinforcing steel or other embedments were encountered, the action taken should be described. Encountering and/or drilling through reinforcing steel has been the basis for claims on projects in the past, so it would serve the project well to track such encounters. An example of a daily drilling inspection report for contact grouting is shown in Figure 10-5. The example given is for contact grouting a cast-in-place concrete tunnel liner that was placed in a tunnel excavated by the drill and blast (D&B) method.

Contract 379 Menahan Springs Water Delivery Project
Tunnel Contact Grout Holes-Daily Drilling Report

Date: 08-05-01	Shift: 2 ND	Shift Start: 1730 HRS	Shift End: 0330 HRS

Drilling Performed By: GLENLOE DRILLING, WENATCHEE, WASH.

Drilling Foreman: F. MORGAN	Driller(s): S. SEDLER, M. DOUCETTE	Inspector: E. DONEGAN

Station Number	Hole Number	Time Start Complete	Total Depth Drilled (in.)	Concrete Drilled	Void Depth (in.)	Rock Drilled	Loss of Drill Water Yes/No	Water Inflow Yes/No	Water Inflow Amount (gal)	Comments
7+82	C-2	1810 1814	20	13	1	6	No	No	N/A	
7+92	C-3	1826 1830	21	15	Ø	6	No	No	N/A	
8+02	C-1	1855 1900	25	12	7	6	No	No	N/A	
8+12	C-2	1915 191B	18	11	1	6	No	No	N/A	
8+22	C-3	1932 1937	20	13	1	6	No	No	N/A	
8+32	C-1	1952 1958	24	9	9	6	No	No	N/A	
8+42	C-2	2012 2016	20	10	4	6	No	No	N/A	
8+52	C-3	2029 2033	21	9	6	6	No	No	N/A	
8+62	C-1	2049 2057	27	8 1/2	12 1/2	6	No	No	N/A	
8+72	C-2	2110 2114	18	12	Ø	6	No	No	N/A	

Drill Method and Bits Used:

JACKLEG; BIT 1 3/4" DIA.

General Hole Layout:

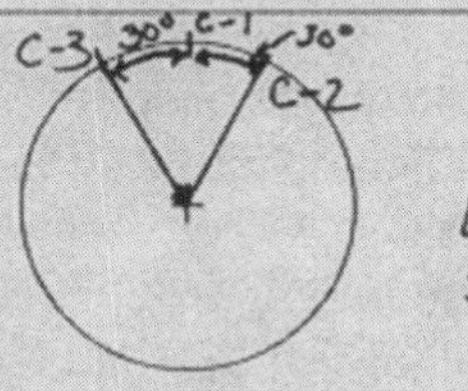

LOOK UP
STATIONING

General Comments:

Inspector: EDWARD DONEGAN (Print Name)	Signature:

Figure 10-5. Example of a daily inspection report for drilling contact grout holes.

10.2   Daily Contact Grouting Reports

Information required to be recorded on daily contact grouting inspection report forms is similar to grouting information required for most other above- and below-ground structural and geotechnical grouting methods. Examples of typical information that should be recorded includes, but is not limited to, the following:

- Date, times, and shift
- Foreman's and grouting inspector's names
- Crew size and makeup
- Type of grouting equipment used
- Weather and ambient temperature above ground
- Ambient temperature underground
- Unique hole identification number for each hole
- Number of times connections are made to each grout hole
- Water:cement ratio of the grout mix
- Quantity and type of additive(s)/admixture(s), if used
- Time grout is mixed (cement added)
- Grout mix temperature after mixing is complete
- Starting and stopping times of grout injection for each hole
- Grout injection pressure
- Quantity of grout injected into each hole
- Communication of grout to other holes, cracks in the liner, etc.
- Time and approximate quantity of grout that is wasted if age exceeds specification or grouting was stopped for any reason

However, in recording the quantity of grout injected into each hole, there is one noticeable difference between backfilling and contact grouting. With backfilling, the takes (quantity) of backfill material injected into a void is usually relatively constant and predictable. This is unlike contact grouting and geotechnical grouting, where grout takes can vary greatly due to the variations in void size and in geology and groundwater conditions. The estimated quantity of backfill material required, based on the theoretical volume of the annulus or void space to be filled, can normally be calculated fairly closely. Estimating the quantity of backfill material required for underground applications is similar to estimating the quantity of concrete required to be placed between an outside wall concrete pour and the excavated ground to complete an above-ground, open-cut excavation. In this outside wall pour example, the concrete pour is usually made utilizing a one-sided form, where the concrete is being placed directly against an excavated surface; thus, the quantity of concrete required can vary but can still be estimated. When relatively large variations between the calculated and actual quantity of backfill required per lineal meter of tunnel or vertical meter of shaft do occur, the differences are usually caused by variations in the amount of overbreak or overexcavation in rock, or as a result of overexcavation or ground loss in soil. Generally, in underground soft-ground excavations, very little backfill material, such as conventional concrete or sanded grouts, is lost to the surrounding ground since these materials are normally too viscous to permeate any significant distance into the surrounding soils. In underground rock excavations, large open joints and cracks in the rocks could potentially become passageways for backfill material and contact grout, thus increasing the quantity of material injected. These larger open joints and cracks can be sealed or backfilled separately before mass backfilling and contact grouting starts. Likewise, smaller open joints and cracks in rock can act as solution channels for surface water or groundwater and lead to unwanted piping. These smaller open joints and cracks can usually be sealed with backfilling or contact grouting with only a slight increase in take.

The material takes associated with contact grouting will almost always vary more than the material takes associated with backfilling, since the voids being filled by the contact grouting can vary considerably in thickness, shape, and overall size per length of tunnel or depth of shaft. Grout used for contact grouting is usually significantly more than that used for backfill. An example of where the quantity of contact grout injected might vary considerably over a relatively short distance is when performing contact grouting of the void in the crown region of a tunnel. The presence of crown voids, generally located between approximately the 10 o'clock and the 2 o'clock positions, is a common occurrence associated with cast-in-place concrete tunnel liner and backfill tunnel lining placements. As a result of the affect of gravity alone on the cast-in-place concrete or backfill materials, it is common for the size of the crown voids and therefore the contact grout takes to be the greatest at the uphill end of the cast-in-place concrete pour or backfill placement. Conversely, because of gravity, there is generally a reduction in the size of the crown voids and therefore less of a contact grout take at the downhill end of a cast-in-place concrete pour or backfill placement. In the length of an individual tunnel concrete pour or a backfill placement, of, for example, 60 m (200 ft), the quantity of contact grout injected into tunnel crown voids at one end of the cast-in-place concrete pour or backfill placement (the downhill or downslope end) can be very small or there may be no recordable grout take at all. However, the quantity of contact grout injected into the tunnel crown voids at the opposite end of the same cast-in-place concrete pour or backfill placement (the uphill or upslope end) can be fairly large. The reduction of the contact grout takes per unit length of tunnel between the uphill end and the downhill end of the cast-in-place concrete pour or backfill placement are not necessarily linear or predictable within an individual cast-in-place concrete pour or backfill placement. The size, shape, and extent of tunnel crown voids, and therefore quantity of the contact grout take, will almost certainly vary from cast-in-place concrete pour to cast-in-place concrete pour and from backfill placement to backfill placement within the same tunnel. In addition to the affect of gravity, the size, shape, and extent of these voids also depends on factors such as the consistency of the concrete and backfill mixes, injection pressures, and workmanship during the individual pours and placements. Equipment breakdowns during concrete pours or backfill placements, delays in concrete and backfill material deliveries to the job site, leakage of concrete or backfill material through the formwork, a bulkhead failure, running water within the placement—all these events can have a significant affect on the size and distribution of tunnel crown voids.

It is important to remember that, while the most common location of voids between cast-in-place concrete pours or backfill material placements and the surrounding ground is in the tunnel crown, voids can exist anywhere around the perimeter of the placement. Except for gravity, the same causes of crown voids noted above can cause non-crown voids in sidewalls and the tunnel invert. Non-crown voids also can be caused by a high-density of closely spaced reinforcing steel and embedded items, such as shear lug attachments, electrical conduits, small piping, and initial support systems; these can all cause blockage to the flow of the cast-in-place concrete or the backfill material during placement. An example of a daily contact grouting injection inspection report is shown in Figure 10-6. The example given is for contact grouting crown voids in a cast-in-place concrete tunnel liner that was placed in a drill and blast tunnel.

Contract 379 Menahan Springs Water Delivery Project
Tunnel Contact Grout Injection-Daily Grouting Report

Date: 08-14-01   Shift: 1 ST   Shift Start: 0700   Shift End: 1730

Grouting Performed By: Buck-Buck UNDERGROUND, INC.   SEATTLE, WASH.

Grouting Foreman: R. BURNS   Batch Plant Opr: R. POND   Inspector: T. FARRELL

Above Ground Temp-Start Shift: 62°F   End Shift: 84° F

Station Number	Hole Number	W/C Ratio	Time Start Injection	Time Complete Injection	Grout Temp °F	Injection Pressure (Psig)	Quantity of Grout Injected (CF)	Comments
3+22	C-3	1:1	0810	0825	75°	15	1 ½	
3+32	C-1	1:1	0830	0845	75°	15	2	
3+42	C-2	1:1	0853	0910	75°	15	∅	
3+52	C-3	1:1	0914	0923	75°	15	½	
3+62	C-1	1:1	0928	0943	75°	15	4	
3+72	C-2	1:1	0949	1017	77°	15	½	HOSE FITTING Broke
3+82	C-3	1:1	1022	1038	77°	15	∅	
3+92	C-1	0.75:1	1043	1112	77°	15	13	
4+02	C-2	0.75:1	1116	1137	77°	15	7	
4+12	C-3	0.75:1	1143	1204	77°	15	2	

Grouting Equipment: HANY PLANT

General Hole Layout:

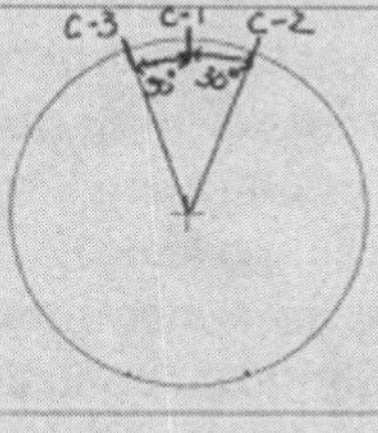

C-3 C-1 C-2

30° 30°

LOOK UP STATIONING

General Comments:

Inspector: THOMAS FARRELL
(Print Name)   Signature:

Figure 10-6. An example of a daily inspection report for contact grout injection.

10.3   As-builts

As-built backfill and contact grout hole drilling and material placement data should be compiled and presented in a summary form as the work is in progress. The data should be presented on a predetermined scheduled basis, for example, daily or weekly. The schedule of when to update and present the data should be established based on the grouting program's complexity and the actual field progress being achieved. The data should be compiled and presented for the entire length of a tunnel or the complete depth of a shaft, even when the data appears to be consistent and may seem to be repetitive. By presenting the data on a regular basis, development of trends (good and bad) or anomalies can be detected and dealt with quickly. Trending can be used to create "estimates to complete" and "estimated costs at completion" of the drilling and grouting program, which can assist the contractor or owner to understand that he may need more money to complete the contract program or have money left over after the program is complete. Presenting real-time feedback also will allow for a modification of the grouting program to address the actual field conditions. In presenting the data in this "up-front way," the as-built information can help save the contractor, as well as the owner, time and money, and help improve the quality of the backfilling and contact grouting programs.

In addition to being instrumental in optimizing the placement program during construction, the as-built records can be an important source of information during the startup phase of a project. Examples might be where a pressurized water delivery tunnel fails to hold pressure during testing, or where the surrounding groundwater levels rise more than allowable during tunnel filling. By reviewing the drilling and backfill and contact grout placement as-built data, it may be possible to identify a potential leakage area within the tunnel or shaft. The potential leakage area may show up in the as-built data as a hole or group of holes that made high volumes of water or lost drilling fluid during the drilling operations. It also could be an area of unusually large backfill or contact grout takes or erratic injection pressure readings during the placement operations. It might show up as dampness or dripping water through the tunnel or shaft liner even after completion of the backfilling and contact grouting operations.

A well-documented as-built record also can be useful months or even years after the facility has been put into service. For example, many times in areas of high groundwater inflows, fractured and faulted ground, overbreak, or ground loss, large backfill or contact grout takes that were encountered during the drilling and placement operations may show up as a maintenance problem years later. Good as-built records can often help maintenance personnel and engineers identify the possible cause of the problem as well as the potential extent of the area that may be causing the problem. A good as-built record also can be critical in supporting or defending against a claim for differing site conditions or extra work made by the contractor, as well as be helpful in settling less-formalized, day-to-day disagreements and disputes.

As-built records can take many forms; however, one of its main advantages is that it can be used to improve the overall drilling and placement operations as work progresses. Therefore, the as-built records should be easy and fast to create and use. The challenge is to make as much useful information available in an easy-to-use format very quickly so it can be put to use while the work is being performed. A multicolored graphical presentation of the data with supporting text as required can be the most "user-friendly" way of presenting the information. The graphical representation and the coloring can be done by hand or with the aid of a computer. The data should be entered at the job site, only by field personnel who have been working directly with the drilling and placement operations, so that errors in data interpretation or entry can be avoided. Additional and more detailed information should be added to update the as-built records as the work progresses and as more information becomes available.

One very helpful addition to an as-built record is to superimpose geologic investigation data (boring logs) and any "as-excavated" geologic tunnel or shaft mapping information onto the as-built records. This can make it easier to correlate the drilling and placement results with the geology and groundwater conditions. Also, it is very helpful to superimpose any groundwater or ground movement instrument readings onto the as-built. The as-built records should be finalized immediately after the backfilling and contact grouting have been completed, while the details are still fresh in everyone's mind. Submittal of the completed as-built records within a specified time after completion of the backfill and contact grout placements should be required in the contract documents. Any delay in completing the as-built increases the risk that individuals who need to supply information or answer questions will have left the job site. Sometimes these people can be hard or almost impossible to contact once they have left the site. Also, nothing can completely replace the person-to-person exchange of information. An example of a very simple as-built record is shown in Figure 10-7. The as-built information is for the drilling and contact grouting of a cast-in-place concrete liner placed in a drill and blast tunnel.

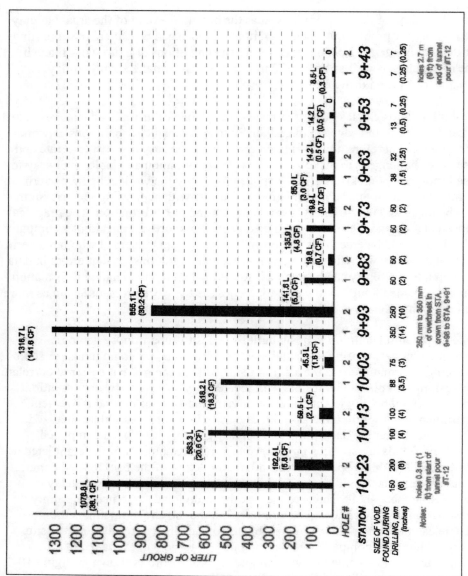

Figure 10-7. Example of simple as-built for the drilling and contact grouting of cast-in-place concrete liner placed in a tunnel which was excavated by the drill and blast method.

208

CHAPTER 11
QUALITY CONTROL

The goals of a quality control (or quality assurance) program for backfilling and contact grouting work are to assure that mixes are properly designed; that appropriate equipment and injection procedures are used; that complete void filling is achieved; and that detailed records are maintained for all drilling, backfilling, and contact grouting operations. This chapter establishes requirements for assuring a high-quality backfilling and contact grouting program.

To assure the propriety of backfill and contact grout mixes, the quality, proper proportioning, and mixing of individual constituents must be assured. Standard, established tests are available to evaluate individual mix ingredients, and careful batching and testing of the final mix properties will assure that the appropriate backfill and contact grout mixes are being used.

Assurance of complete void filling is less straightforward. Backfilling can be generally assured for voids with consistent cross-sections, such as the annulus between a precast concrete segmental lining or a pipe liner system and the ground. However, neither the volume nor the configuration of the voids to be filled is commonly known prior to contact grout injection. In these situations, complete void filling requires careful monitoring of both the contact grout mixture and the contact grout's behavior during injection, as well as continuous observation of both the pressure and rate of contact grout injection. Additionally, all aspects of contact grout hole drilling, including the results of any pre-injection hole inspection, water testing, or other evaluation data, should be consulted prior to injection.

11.1 Injection Holes

Prior to starting any work, a layout and numbering system to identify all backfill and contact grout injection hole locations should be established (see Chapter 10). Each injection hold location should be accurately marked with a unique identification number. Because it is very easy to become confused and misidentify injection holes underground, special attention to hold identification is required. Hole identification markings can become obscured by drilling circulation flush and during backfilling and contact grouting. They should be marked with spray paint initially, visually checked occasionally, and re-marked as required. It is useful to color code different types of holes, for example, one paint color for backfill holes, and a different paint color for contact grout holes. Any geotechnical grouting holes should have a separate and unique identification numbering system and a different color code. Prior to making connection to individual injection holes, they should be visually inspected to ensure they are open. For contact grout holes, the drilling logs should be reviewed and any anomalies found during drilling, the presence of groundwater, the size of the voids found should be noted. Holes should be probed to assure they are open to their original depth as shown on the drilling inspection reports. Water testing of contact grouting holes is sometimes required, in which the rate of water take and the pressure of injection are recorded. Even where this is not a project requirement, it is advisable to run water into the holes to assure they are open and amenable to receiving contact grout.

11.2 Material Testing Standards

To evaluate or qualify the properties of mix ingredients, common tests, such as ASTM C150, *Standard Specification for Portland Cement*, or ASTM C33, *Specification for Concrete Aggregates,* can be used. It is important, however, to always consider carefully the requirements for in-place backfill and contact grout, because these common standards are not always appropriate. The standards were generally developed for applicability to concrete or mortar mixes, so strength is therefore the primary focus. Strength is the main controller of materials that would go into a common concrete mix, but backfill and contact grouts must be much more flowable than normal concrete or mortar. Thus, they will often contain significantly greater amounts of water. Modern water reducing and plasticizing admixtures can greatly reduce the amount of water required while maintaining the backfill and contact grout's pumpability and flowability. Sand used in backfill or contact grout mix is often much finer than that used for concrete, and, although this will generally result in lower strengths, it is nonetheless adequate for most backfill and contact grouting applications.

The most important properties of backfilling materials and contact grouts are consistency, pumpability, penetrability, set time, cohesion, resistance to bleed and pressure filtration, and durability; strength is often of somewhat less importance. Therefore, the requirements of many well-established standard tests are not always warranted for some backfills and contact grouts, and their indiscriminate use should be avoided. Higher compressive strengths are more in line with conventional concretes and sanded grouts, however, and are often an important property of backfill material and contact grout when working with pressure tunnels and shafts.

11.3   Batching

Within the confines of many underground workings, coupled with the normal pace of backfilling and contact grouting work, extensive mix testing is not always practicable. The best assurance of uniform contact grout is to use pre-blended grout mixes to which only water is added. A pre-blended grout mix is especially useful when relatively small quantities of contact grouting are required. Although such a mix is more expensive than would be the individual ingredients which it contains, its use can simplify logistics and handling within underground workings, and may thus actually result in less cost. Where a pre-blended mix is not used, uniformity of contact grout can be greatly facilitated by providing all the ingredients in batch size containers to which only water must be added. When backfilling and when relatively large quantities of contact grouting are required, the backfill and contact grout should in most cases be mixed on the surface and transported, completely mixed, to the point of injection.

Batching accuracy of mix water is especially important in all types of concreting and grouting work. Maintaining the correct water amount in the mix and, thus, the water:cement ratio, is of the utmost importance, especially when utilizing smaller skid-mounted batch plants. These are common in small-quantity contact grouting applications, where water is added by the operator using a water meter. Only digital or dial-type water meters, which can be easily read, should be used. Water batch tanks are available that can be set to fill to the precise amount of water required for a single batch of grout; these can be quite useful, especially where water supply is limited. Water meters and other measuring devices must be kept clean and in good condition. The readout of water meters must be plainly visible, especially underground where lighting conditions may not be the best.

Even when proposed backfill and contact grout mixes and mix constituents have previously been used successfully on other projects, and their properties are well known, it is important to require a design and perform trial batching prior to starting work. Mix designs that were successful previously can have quite different properties depending on the source of water, cement, flyash, admixtures, etc. For example, a mix that worked well on one project may not behave the same way or as well as it did on another project located at a different part of the same state. Material properties can vary considerably from state to state or even within a state or region of the country. The shape of the cement, sand, and other constituent particles, and the condition of their surface, is of immense importance in backfilling and contact grouting. Rough, angular particles are far more likely to form blockages within very small voids and inhibit the grout flow than are smooth, round particles. Experience has repeatedly shown that cementitious grouts containing large amounts of pozzolanic materials, such as flyash or silica fume, are more penetrable than those grouts containing only cement. This is no doubt due to the near spherical shape of most pozzolans. Round-shaped grains tend to roll past and over each other, rather than bind together as would rough angular shapes. Water chemistry also can vary from one geographic location to another; the source of mixing water (for example, well versus municipal water supply) also will vary the water chemistry.

All mix constituents used during production should come from the same sources as those used in the original design mix and trial batching. Although it is not widely understood, the manufacturing requirements of Portland cement allow for wide variability. In fact, there are no standards that regulate the actual grain size distribution for common cements. Curves are shown in Figure 11-1, for Types I and III cement that was produced in one particular batch at a given plant. ASTM C150, *Standard Specification for Portland Cement,* specifies only the Blane fineness, which is a measure of the specific surface area of all of the grains in a given volume of cement. Type III Portland cement is required to be finer than Type I or II; however, the maximum grain size, or grain size distribution, is not specified.

Ultrafine cement also can be quite variable, as shown on Figure 11-1. There are two main types: those derived from slag, and those derived from Portland cement. Ultrafine cements also are supplied as a blend of Portland cement and slag or other pozzolanic material. Although they all are comparable in many respects, there can be a fundamental difference in the span of hydration and thus the resulting setting time. Because of the very high specific surface area of ultrafine cements of Portland cement origin, hydration activity is high, resulting in rapid set and strength gain. For this reason, retarders such as citric acid are sometimes included. Portland cement–citric acid combinations are extremely sensitive to temperature changes, so the proportions of the additive must be matched to the temperature of both the working environment and the medium being injected. Problems with flash set, and difficulties with both setting time and rate of strength gain, have been reported. Ultrafine cements based on slag, however, tend to set and gain strength much slower than their Portland cement cousins. Thus, retardation is seldom a problem; in fact, accelerating admixtures may be required in some instances. Well-established accelerators are available and their behavior is quite predictable, so set times are not much of a problem with the slag-based ultrafine cements.

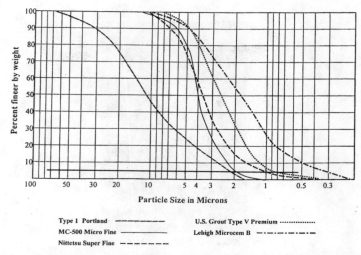

Figure 11-1. Grain size distribution of Portland and ultrafine cements.

11.4 Tests for Evaluating Grouts

11.4.1 Flow Cones

Several configurations of funnel devices have been proposed and/or used to evaluate the flow properties of grout. Two of these have become somewhat commonly used. The "flow cone" (Figure 11-2), originally developed in the early 1940s, has been used for many years by the U.S. Army Corps of Engineers under the designation CRD-C611, for both research and field quality assurance. In 1981, it was adopted by the ASTM for ASTM C939, *Standard Test Method for Flow of Grout for Preplaced Concrete Aggregate*. The "Marsh Funnel" (Figure 11-3), long used to evaluate the flow properties of drilling fluids, is now also used for pourable grouts.

Figure 11-2. ASTM C939 Flow Cone.

213

Figure 11-3. Marsh funnel.

Flow evaluations are made by filling the funnel while holding a finger over the outlet. The finger is then released, allowing the funnel to empty. The time is recorded to the nearest second, providing the number of seconds required until a break in the grout flow occurs. Should any grout remain in the cone after the first break of flow, the test is not considered appropriate for the particular grout. The time required for the cone to empty is known as the "efflux" time. The ASTM-C939–specified cone is typically made of cast aluminum, whereas the Marsh funnel is usually made of plastic. Neither funnel material can have wetability properties at all similar to the wide variety of geologic formations and void surfaces into which a grout might be injected. The reason is that backfill material and contact grout can be injected into voids between various types of soil and rock and a wide variety of materials such as concrete, steel, wood, plastic, fiberglass, and cast iron. The funnels do, however, provide for easy confirmation of the uniformity of different batches of grout and are widely used in quality assurance testing.

11.4.2 Specific Gravity

Another testing device originally developed for evaluation of drilling fluids is the Baroid Mud Balance (see Figure 11-4). It is a simple and very rugged device for determining the density of drilling mud or grout. In application, the cup and beam are removed from the fulcrum, and the cup is dipped into the grout mixer or holding tank until it is completely filled. The cup is capped, and any excess grout that has come in contact with the beam, or outside of the cup, is removed. The beam and filled cup are then placed on the fulcrum, and the weight is slid along the beam until the bubble of an attached spirit level is centered. The density is then read directly from a scale on the beam. The Baroid Mud Balance is a particularly useful device for quality assurance testing of cement–water suspensions because the water:cement ratio can be easily and accurately determined. Control of density also is very important where low-density cellular concrete (foamed grout) is being used for backfilling. Since cellular concrete is often batched using a continuous batching plant and mixer, the mud balance is the primary tool used to verify mix proportioning.

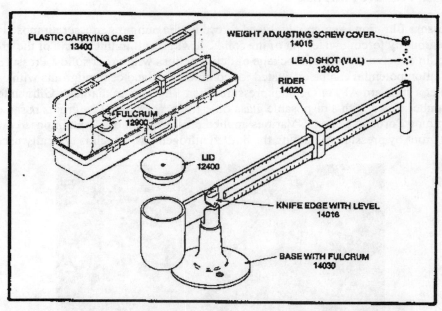

Figure 11-4. Baroid Mud Balance test for specific gravity of grout.

11.4.3 Evaluation of Bleed

"Bleed" refers to the propensity of grout solids to fall out of suspension, resulting in excess water gathering on top of the settled solids. The water evaporates and the space previously occupied by the water fills with air over time, resulting in voids at the top of the hardened grout. Controlling bleed of suspension grouts is thus important, especially when slow pumping rates are used or large voids are being filled. The bleed potential of a suspension grout can change quite markedly with changes of the water:cement ratio, shear mixing energy, cement properties, or other grout constituents. Bleed evaluation is easily accomplished by filling a transparent tube or jar with grout and observing the amount of clear water that collects on the top after about 2 hr. Where accurate determinations are desired, 1,000-ml graduated cylinders, as shown in Figure 11-5, can be employed. These are used in a manner similar to that provided in ASTM C940, *Standard Test Method for Expansion and Bleeding of Freshly Mixed Grouts for Preplaced-Aggregate Concrete in the Laboratory*. Whereas this procedure is useful for laboratory evaluations, the required settlement time often renders it impractical for control of field injection parameters.

11.4.4 Pressure Filtration

Pressure filtration is essentially bleed forced by the pumping pressure imposed on the grout by forcing water out of the solids. It will result in thickening of the grout and, in extreme instances, blockage of delivery lines with grout solids. Pressure filtration potential can be evaluated for common Portland cement grouts with either a standard API or Gelman pressure filter. The 47-mm diameter Gilman test chamber, fitted with a disposable glass fiber filter, works well on grouts based on common Portland cements. Various applied pressures can easily be imposed on the grout by pressure regulating the bottled nitrogen gas, which is typically used.

Figure 11-5. Test for bleed using 1000 ml graduated cylinders.

11.4.5 Slump

The slump test, ASTM C143, *Standard Test Method for Slump of Hydraulic-Cement Concretes*, was originally developed for evaluating the consistency and workability of concrete that includes both clean sands and large aggregate in its composition. Even for use with that material, for which the test was developed,

216

ASTM states in their document, ASTM Special Technical Publication 169C, *Significance of Tests and Properties of Concrete and Concrete-Making Materials*:

> Slump Test--The slump test (see Fig. 1) [sic] is the most commonly used method of measuring consistency or wetness of concrete. It is not suitable for very wet or very dry concrete. It does not measure all factors contributing to workability, nor is it always representative of the placeability of the concrete.

The slump test is widely used for evaluation of the consistency of concrete used for backfilling large voids since this concrete usually is not "very wet or very dry." The C143 test utilizes a mold, the form of which is the frustum of a cone, with the base 8 in. in diameter, the top 4 in. in diameter, and a height of 12 in. The test should not be specified or used for pourable grouts, which are nearly always void of large aggregate and of a "very wet" consistency.

11.4.6 Compressive Strength Tests

In most applications of backfill and contact grouting, the cured materials 28-day compressive strength usually is not required to be as high as strengths normally associated with concrete structures or structural grouts. As a general rule, the 28-day compressive strength of backfills and contact grouts should be at least as much as that of the adjacent formation when the work is being performed in soil. However, early strengths, 24-hour and 7-day, may be more important to support the excavation and liner erection schedule or where surface settlement is an issue. Backfill and contact grout compressive strength requirements for non-pressure tunnels and shafts in rock can generally be much less than the rock strengths. The actual compressive strength requirements will be specific, on a project-to-project basis. The exception would be applications in pressure tunnels and shafts in rock or where geologic or structural requirements of the completed structure require the backfill and contact grout to be of a higher, 28-day strength. Low bleed and high resistance to pressure filtration also are important because they can affect the compressive strength and continuity of the in-place backfill and contact grout. A frequent error made by designers is specifying backfills and contact grout strengths based on typical concrete or mortar standards. Specifying unnecessarily high 28-day compressive strength for backfill and contact grout is, in most cases, of little benefit, can present difficulties in pumping and injection, and almost always results in increased costs.

To help ensure 28-day compressive strength requirements have been met, either standard concrete cylinders or grout cubes are used. Other times, such as 24 hr, 3 day, and 7 day, also may be of equal or greater importance to a specific project. Cylinders should be prepared and cured in accordance with ASTM C31, *Practice for Making and Curing Concrete Test Specimens in the Field,* and tested in accordance with ASTM C39, *Test Method for Compressive Strength of Cylindrical Concrete Specimens.* Whereas test specimens for concrete are commonly 150 mm in diameter by 300 mm high (6 by 12 in), those used for grout are usually smaller; 50 mm in diameter by 100 mm high (2 by 4 in) and 75 mm in diameter by 150 mm high (3 by 6 in) are the most common. The ASTM C39 is limited to material having a minimum unit weight in excess of 801 kgs/m^3 (50 pcf). Therefore, strength evaluation of lightweight mixes, which are often used for backfill grouting, should be in accordance with ASTM C495, *Test Method for Compressive Strength of Lightweight Insulating Concrete.*

An alternate for cylindrical test specimens is the use of 50-mm (2-in) test cubes for grouts. These should be prepared and tested in accordance with ASTM C109, *Test Method for Compressive Strength of Hydraulic Cement Mortars (using 2 in. or 50 mm Cube Specimens).* Molds for these cubes are readily available and are generally cast out of aluminum or brass with three cubes per mold.

11.4.7 Grout Injection Monitoring

In contact grouting, where size, volume, and configuration of the void usually are unknown, careful monitoring and injection control is required to establish the pre-grouting conditions and confirm the grout injection is complete and adequate. While much attention has traditionally been given to the maximum grouting pressure allowed or attained, such values are of little worth unless the rate of material injection also is known. Thus, continuous records should be maintained that include both pressure and rate of injection.

11.4.7.1 Injection Pressure

Setting the maximum injection pressure is perhaps one of the most contentious issues in geotechnical grouting, especially in the United States. Likewise, opinions on setting maximum injection pressures for backfilling and contact grouting can vary considerably. A widely recognized rule of thumb for geotechnical grouting says the maximum injection pressure in pounds per square inch should not exceed the injection depth in feet for rock and half that for soil. However, well-documented experience in the United States as well as abroad has proven this idea to be faulty. According to a basic law of hydraulics, the pressure level obtained is directly proportional to the rate of injection. If the pumping rate is increased, the pressure level also will increase; conversely, as the rate of flow is decreased, the required pumping pressure also will be lower. For reasons of economics, use of the highest *safe* injection rate and thus highest pressure is desirable for virtually all types of grouting. Maximum allowable pressure levels for backfilling and contact grouting will be variable and are dependent on many factors. These factors include the type and rheology of the backfill material or contact grout being used, geology and groundwater conditions, the purpose of the injection, particulars of the individual site, depth of the structure below ground, proximity of other structures and utilities, liner type, and the liner's structural characteristics.

The pressure used in all types of grouting can be divided into two distinct modes: (1) pressure that is needed to overcome friction and any restriction within the delivery system (from the pump discharge to point of injection), and (2) pressure that results from resistance within the void or formation into which the backfill material or contact grout is being placed. Where grout delivery is through a system of uniform cross-sections, such as a pipe or injection hose, the total pumping pressure will be dependent on the length of the system and will be the product of unit length resistance times the number of units of length. Added to this is the resistance of bends in the line, couplings, fittings, valves, etc. Unless a void is filled with water, or isolated such that air cannot escape, pressure at the leading edge of the backfill or contact grout will always be zero. Where backfill or contact grout injection is made against a porous mass, such as soil or fractured rock or voids of varying size and configuration, the pressure distribution within the grout mass will be ever variable. The pressure will, however, always be greatest at the point of injection, typically the discharge end of the injection port, packer, nipple, or slickline. The pressure will decrease with distance from that injection point.

Because the effective pressure on the shaft or tunnel liner and the surrounding ground will invariably start at the discharge point, it is important to consider the pressure differential between that point and the top of the hole or hole collar where pressure readings are typically observed. This value may be either positive or negative, depending on the particulars of both the backfill material or contact grout and the delivery system. It is important to remember that most backfilling and contact grouting performed in tunnels is injected overhead or in an upward direction. Therefore, the pressure at the hole collar must be greater than when injecting in a downward direction to overcome the affect of gravity on the grout column which is overhead (above springline).

With the above in mind, it is possible, through experimentation and calculation, to determine the *approximate* pressure differential between the pressure gauge at the point of injection and the discharge point, where the backfill or contact grout makes first contact with the void. The word "approximate" is used because some variation will occur within a delivery line depending on the smoothness of its interior, number and sharpness of bends, and any restrictions at couplings or other fittings. Because it is the injection pressure at the discharge point that is pertinent, gauges for pressure evaluation should always be located as close as possible to the grout port through the liner or the end of the slickline, or at the collar of the hole when a packer is used. The injection pressure must be corrected for any loss or gain due to gravity.

Many factors contribute to the total pump pressure required for injection. Major contributors to that pressure are frictional resistance within the total delivery system, backfill and contact grout rheology of the material being pumped, pumping rate, delivery line size and resulting material velocity, and the frictional resistance at the interface between the backfill or contact grout and the delivery line wall. The frictional resistance is a function of the wall smoothness and its affinity for the particular backfill or contact grout being used. Once the material is in the void being filled, both the size and shape of the individual void, as well as the surface conditions of the liner and the surrounding ground, are major factors. Obviously, the rheology of the material and its affinity for the liner and surrounding ground also are significant contributors.

11.4.7.2　　　Pumping Rate

As noted for injection pressure, the pumping rate and developed pressure are directly related. An increase in pumping rate will *always* result in an increase in pressure, as will a pumping rate reduction result in lower pressure. This is well illustrated in Figure 11-6, which is an actual printout of a computer-generated record of pressure behavior on a recent project where the grout pump malfunctioned. In this case, the pump's piston speed varied such that one piston was traveling nearly twice as rapidly as the other. The actual pump strokes can be observed by their pressure differentials, and the pressure on the short stroke (higher pumping rate) was more than 6.9 bars (100 psi) greater than that on the slower long stroke. Also in this figure, the pressure raised slightly during each of the short strokes, which is indicative of a generally optimal pumping rate; whereas there was a slight pressure decay during the long strokes, which indicates a slower than optimal rate.

220

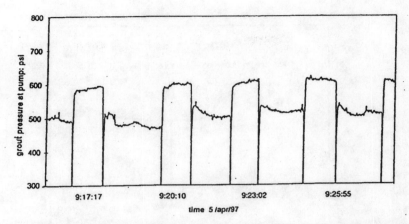

Figure 11-6. Pressure differential resulting from varying pumping rate

Because development of resistance within the void being filled is beyond control, the injection rate selected must be limited to prevent excessive pressure. Wide variation of void resistance is common, especially with contact grouting; flexibility in pump output capacity, then, is usually required. This is probably why circulating grout injection systems were in widespread use in the past. In such systems, the grout is continuously circulated in a route from the pump, past the grout hole, and back to the agitator, as shown on Figure 11-7. A connection to the grout hole is made with a "T" fitting in the line. A valve is located on the return side of the "T" fitting, and a valve and pressure gauge are located between the "T" fitting and the injection hole collar. The amount of grout that is allowed to go into the hole, and thus the injection rate, can be varied by "throttling" the valves. Because economy dictates use of the highest practical injection rate, the valves are adjusted to allow the maximum amount of flow possible, without exceeding the maximum allowable pressure.

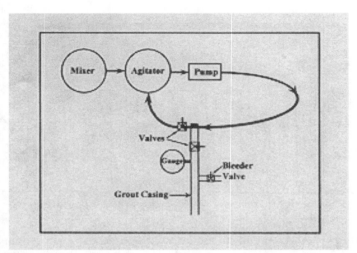

Figure 11-7. Circulating grout injection system.

Single-line direct delivery systems, in which the grout flows directly from the pump to the grout hole (Figure 11-8), should be used only with variable output pumps. Pump speed, and thus the rate of grout output, is regulated to maintain injection rates without exceeding the allowable pressure. Varying the rate in discrete increments provides the advantage of observation of even slight changes of pressure, facilitating optimum evaluation of grout movement within the void. Most backfilling operations are performed using a single-line direct delivery system, often employing a conventional concrete pump, grout pump, or the specialty equipment required when cellular concrete is the backfill material.

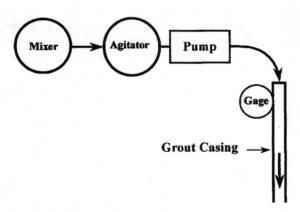

Figure 11-8. Direct grout injection system

222

Concrete and grout pumps, and the associated delivery systems, should be sized for reasonable injection rates to prevent development of excessive pressures during injection. All other things being equal, system pressures will usually diminish as the delivery pipe or hose diameter increases. However, the diameter should not be so large that the delivery system is completely emptied before additional material is mixed and delivered to the pump. In this regard, the set time of the backfill and contact grout must be considered so that it is not allowed to begin to set within the delivery system. Many backfill and contact grout materials, and especially rich cementitious mixes (high cement–content mixes), will tend to build up on the walls of the delivery system if sufficient line velocity is not maintained. Build-up causes an ever-decreasing opening size through which the backfill and contact grout can travel, increasing both the material's velocity and the indicated resulting pressure.

The importance of the relationship of injection pressure to pumping rate cannot be overemphasized and warrants special attention. Many practitioners *erroneously* believe that the maximum grout pressure level alone indicates the degree of void filling obtained. The specifying or recording of injection pressure is of absolutely *no usefulness*, unless the injection rate at which the pressure level occurred also is specified and recorded.

11.4.7.3 Pressure Behavior

A basic law of physics states that an increase in pressure *always* indicates greater resistance to flow, whereas a reduction in pressure indicates less resistance. Although somewhat subjective, knowing the value and nature of the pressure variation allows the experienced practitioner to make an informed prediction as to the cause. As an example, assuming a pressure of 690 kPa (100 psi) was required to pump a grout material through a given length of hose, and a connection located in the middle of the length became broken, the pressure would sharply drop to approximately half of its original value. Similarly, were a restriction placed on the hose's outlet end, a sudden increase in pressure would result. In reality, it is widely recognized that a sudden reduction in pressure indicates a likely disruption in the interior of the soil or rock mass surrounding the excavation or the void opening being grouted (Houlsby, 1990; Warner and Brown, 1974).

Experience has shown that sudden changes in pressure, or increases of injection rate at a constant pressure, *always* indicate the occurrence of a significant event, such as bulkhead failure, a break in the delivery line, large leaks, or loss of a gasket seal in a segmented liner system. The damage caused by such events can be greatly minimized and in many cases completely averted through quick response, usually by immediately lowering the pumping rate or completely stopping the injection.

Additional typical events that are accompanied by a loss of pressure include the following:

- Hydraulic fracturing of the soil or rock surrounding the excavation
- Displacement or heaving of the ground
- Backfill or contact grout loss into a subsurface pipe or other utilities or substructure
- Outward displacement of a downslope or retaining wall
- Grout entering a much larger fracture or void in the surrounding ground or encountering a much more permeable geologic formation
- Thinning of the grout or other change in the grout rheology which increases its mobility
- Malfunction of a pump

Events that are preceded by an increase in pressure include plugging or restriction in the injection system, thickening or lowering the mobility of the backfill material or contact grout, or completing the filling of a void. Another event is the chemical reaction of cement and water (hydration). Even though there is movement and agitation, along with retardant admixtures, some initial set takes place. Obviously, this requires greater pressures to fracture grout.

Whereas major events can be detected by substantial pressure fluctuations or changes of injection rate, those that are more subtle often result in only minor changes. Such minor changes cannot easily be observed in circulating injection systems, or with systems that are subject to heavy pulsations from pump stroking. Thus, where detection of minor events is important, it is recommended that a constant output pump that is free of any significant pulsation, combined with careful and continuous pressure monitoring, be used. Piston pumps operating at rates greater than about 100 strokes per minute, combined with a minimum hose length of about 30.5 m (100 ft), are advantageous since, at high rates, the stroking results in only a flutter of the pressure gauge needle, and dampening occurs in the flexible hose. Pressure pulsations resulting from stroking of piston or diaphragm-type pumps, also can be lessened through use of a hydraulic accumulator near the pump outlet, and/or an increase of at least 50 percent in the diameter of the injection hose, for a distance of about 7 m (25 ft). Starting at the pump outlet, the actual pressure of individual pump strokes can be observed in the case of piston pumps operating at very slow stroke rates.

For an effective QA/QC grout program, the grout engineer/inspector must be aware of the pressure behaviors of grout, flow rate, and pumps and accurately document compliance or noncompliance with specifications. Also, the constructability review of the drilling and grouting specifications should address acceptable expected pressure behavior and consequential action for unacceptable behavior.

Pressure behavior information can be recorded by taking continuous readings of a pressure gauge and writing entries onto an inspection form, or with fully automated equipment employing either a continuous disk or strip chart recorder or computer processing. Regardless of the recording method, the actual time of each entry should be included and, when feasible, continuous real-time data should be included in the record. When manual monitoring is performed, it is good practice to record entries at predetermined uniform increments of pressure. Alternatively, entries can be made at regular time intervals. The magnitude of pressure increments or time intervals employed will vary according to the individual application and type of grout being used, but should be of sufficient frequency to allow plotting of a curve that accurately displays all significant pressure movements.

Although disk recorders are commonly used with automated systems, especially in Europe, continuous strip chart recorders provide records that are easier to interpret, especially when they include many different parameters. The ability to record multiple parameters allows a favorable way to compare and interpret them. Regardless of the method used, the records produced must include real time and facilitate immediate interpretation on the job site, as well as provide a permanent record for later reference.

Computer monitoring systems are now readily available that provide for instantaneous readout of all injection parameters. These systems have the advantages of storing a permanent record on disk and printing hard copies as desired. When performing contact grouting, the constant changing of injection rate (grout takes) due to variation in sizes and shapes of the voids being filled makes accurate manual recording very demanding on the grout engineer/inspector. The use of real-time, continuous computer monitoring is thus especially beneficial in such cases. Accordingly, the drilling, backfilling, and contact grouting specification needs to reflect the requirement that the contractor must supply equipment compatible with, or including, computer monitoring, unless it is expected the grout engineer/inspector will supply the computer monitoring.

11.4.7.4 Pressure–Volume Relationship

The quantity of backfill material or contact grout injected at any one location, and the size and shape of the material's mass that is formed, has a significant effect upon the loads applied to the lining system, initial support system, and the surrounding ground. A given pressure on a very large mass of backfill or contact grout will effect a greater area and thus exert a much larger *total* force on the initial support system, surrounding ground, and liner system, than will a small grout mass. Depending on the specifics of the individual backfill or contact grout injection, this might affect the pressure level that can be safely used. Where large quantities of materials are placed, as is common in backfilling operations, the pressure used for initial injection may be too high once a significant mass of backfill has been placed. Therefore, reduction of the pumping rate and, thus, pressure, is often required during injection as the injected quantity of backfill or contact grout grows.

The shape of the injected material mass also is important. As an example, if the backfill or contact grout were to form an essentially horizontal lens, as is common with backfilling and contact grouting, a large surface area would be affected and the likelihood of displacing the surface upward or inward would be increased. The likelihood of upward displacement (heave) is of special concern where the backfilling or contact grouting is being performed at relatively shallow depths. Unintended backfill and contact grout jacking of both the surrounding ground and adjacent structures has unfortunately occurred in the past. Much damage has been done as a result of such *uncontrolled* jacking, stemming from too great a pumping rate and associated excessive pressure, especially when combined with a large or adversely shaped backfill or contact grout mass. Unintended grout jacking can lead to third-party claims against the entire project team. Thus, the grouting engineer/inspector's first advocacy will be honest observations and accurate documentation so any assessment of entitlement can be made.

11.5 Surface Surveillance

Virtually all backfilling and contact grouting imparts elevated pressures into the surrounding ground. When the backfilling and contact grouting operations are near the ground surface, there is a continual risk of ground movement from possible hydraulic fracturing of the soil or rock, surface heaving, and lateral spreading. Such deformations can continue into surface improvements, substructures, or underground utilities, resulting in their damage. It is thus imperative that the ground surface, and all improvements, substructures, and utilities located within the area influenced by the backfilling and contact grouting operations, be continuously monitored during material injection. Likewise, underground structures, and especially sewer, water, drainage pipelines, manholes, and electrical duct banks, must be monitored to assure that they have not been displaced or that grout has not entered the utility. Most damaging movements of the ground or surrounding structures are immediately proceeded by a significant loss of injection pressure, as has previously been discussed. It is imperative that field personnel be particularly observant of the areas surrounding the backfilling and contact grouting work site, both above and below ground, of any such sudden drops of injection pressure.

Many methods are available to monitor movement of ground surface as well as surface and subsurface structures. To be effective in backfilling and contact grouting, however, the selected methods must able to survey very large areas and immediately give notice about any movements. Thus, conventional surveying may not be satisfactory for the primary surveillance. Rotating laser instruments (Figure 11-9), combined with multiple targets mounted on stands distributed throughout the work area, as shown in Figure 11-10, are quite effective.

Figure 11-9. Rotating laser instrument can monitor many targets at different locations.

Figure 11-10. Typical laser target.

Another widely used method is the multi-station manometer, which is simply a fluid reservoir with virtually any number of individual tubes attached. Typically, 9.5-mm (3/8-in) clear plastic tubing is used. Because the surface of the fluid, usually water, will always achieve the same level, the level in the individual tubes will always be that of the reservoir. With this method, one or more reservoirs can be used, as illustrated in Figure 11-11. Any number of tubes can be connected to a single reservoir, with the terminal end fixed to the ground surface or on structures as desired. The precise water level is marked on the tube or adjacent mount prior to start of backfill or contact grout injection. Any vertical movement that occurs will cause a change that is readily observable. To enhance the visibility of the water in the reservoir, it can be colored with a few drops of food coloring.

Figure 11-11. Manometer reservoirs mounted on fence posts.

Multi-station manometers are extremely flexible, as is the manner in which they are used. Figure 11-12 shows tubes from several different reservoir locations attached to a common terminal board, enabling surveillance of an extended area from one location. In Figure 11-13, the terminal end of a tube is simply fixed with duct tape to the wall of a structure. Note the ruler affixed to it, enabling easy reading of the exact magnitude of any movement.

Figure 11-12. Several manometer tubes terminate at a single location.

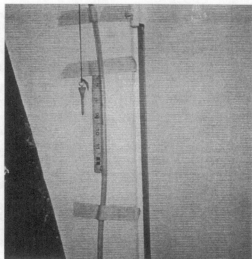

Figure 11-13. Manometer tube taped to wall with ruler.

Although conventional survey instruments do not necessarily provide continuous information about surface movement, they can scan large areas. Figure 11-14 shows part of a large prism array, which has been set into the slope of a dam. They are constantly being swept to detect any movement of the slope by a total station located in the small protective shelter (see Figure 11-15). Movement and displacement of the liner being backfilled or contact grouted must also be monitored.

Figure 11-14. Large array of survey prisms on face of dam.

Figure 11-15. Total Station in protective shelter constantly monitors prisms to detect any surface displacement.

Buoyancy forces imposed during backfilling can cause floating of a pipe or penstock—a common concern. To help prevent floating, tie-downs are installed and/or blocking (sidewall and crown) is used. The tie-downs and blocking are installed for each individual section of pipe/penstock after the individual section has been set in place to line and grade. Additionally, internal bracing, called "stulling," is often required, especially for larger diameter steel pipes and penstocks, to help keep the section round by resisting buoyancy forces. Also, loading of the lining system by forces applied by the liquid head of the backfill or contact grout needs to be monitored. These loads and buoyancy loading can cause steel ribs to bend or be displaced, circular shaped lining to go out-of-round ("egg shaped"), precast concrete linings to crack, and lining to go off line and grade. During backfilling placement operations, the pipe/penstock should be continuously monitored for line and grade and for roundness. This monitoring is usually performed using a stationary laser set on the tunnel centerline and a ruler or other type of measuring device.

11.6 Verification of Grouting Effectiveness

Verification of the effectiveness of grouting has been the topic of many papers and discussions; among them are the American Society of Civil Engineers (ASCE) Geo-Institute's Committee on Grouting, which held an entire session on the subject at their 1995 meeting (Byle and Borden, 1995). From a practical and economic standpoint, the most meaningful verification of the results of any backfilling or contact grouting operations occurs as the material is being injected. This is through continuous observation and control of the various injection parameters, especially the rate of injection and pressure behavior. No amount of post-injection investigation or testing can duplicate the benefit of careful monitoring and control during the actual material injection. There is, however, a variety of post-material placement tests that can, to a varying degree, confirm the completeness and the general quality of the backfilled or contact-grouted void.

One common pre-injection verification method is to visibly or mechanically measure the void (Henn, 1996). Pre-grouting verification is most common with contact grouting, where the void measurement is done after drilling through the cast-in-place concrete liner or the backfill material. When drilling through cast-in-place concrete liners, the thickness of the concrete also can be verified at the same time. The most common post-injection verification method for backfill and contact grouting is to drill a hole through the lining and the backfill and/or contact grout into the surrounding ground. Drilling methods that recover core specimens are most often used to verify post-placement results. Noncore-recovery drilling methods can be used with visual inspection of the drill hole, but these are not as effective as having a core sample that also can be used to test unconfined compressive strength. Regardless of the thickness of the cast-in-place liner or the backfill behind the liner, the hole diameter will need to be large enough to allow visual inspection. Mechanical measurement, such as a "steel washer on an all-tread rod" method, also can be used (Henn, 1996).

A variety of geophysical methods have been promoted and successfully used for verifying all types of grouting. The most commonly used methods involve evaluation of stress-wave velocities traveling through the works. This is commonly referred to as "seismic tomography," in which sound waves travel faster through a hard medium than a soft one. Thus, a grouted void will provide a higher velocity than an adjacent void or formation that has not been grouted. By analysis and interpretation of the velocity and attenuation of a large number of sound waves driven at different inclinations through a profile, the relative density or stiffness of the various components of that profile can be determined.

Stress-wave velocities are usually determined with direct paths between two boreholes (cross-borehole survey), or by analysis of reflective rays, sometimes referred to as "impact echo." In backfilling and contact grouting, impact echo has a substantial advantage in that it can be performed on the interior surface of the liner without the need for any drilling.

Ground-probing radar is another process that has been considered; however with present technology, the accuracy and precision of its output are not as good as with the previously described seismic methods. In radar evaluation, an electromagnetic pulse is generated on the surface. It is then reflected from the various interfaces at depth to a retrieval instrument on the surface. Equipment is available that can traverse the surface, radiating and receiving repetitive electromagnetic pulses, to obtain a continuous record of the subsurface interfaces along the route traversed.

Ground-probing radar instruments basically measure variations in the electromagnetic velocity of the different formation materials encountered. The procedure is especially useful for identifying clear interfaces, such as those of the liner and grout, or ungrouted areas if they exist. Likewise, where the velocities of different materials of a composite vary greatly or have clearly different water content and/or chemistry, identification of the boundaries may be practicable. As with advanced monitoring in general, the process is in constant development and advancement. It may become more applicable to the verification of grouting work in the future.

It is important to note that, except for post-injection inspection hole drilling with visual or core removal, most of these verification methods are not routinely used for most backfill and contact grouting programs. The methods are available, however, to be used in those rare cases where questions arise as to the backfill or contact grout quality or completeness.

CHAPTER 12
CONTRACT DOCUMENTS

The contract documents for a backfilling or contact grouting program will be just one component of a larger underground civil works contract. The documents must address all the issues described in previous chapters of the guidelines that are pertinent to the project. The aim is to develop the most useful, clear, and easy-to-bid contract documents possible for use in dealing with requirements reasonably and cost effectively.

This chapter describes the need for and use of contract documents in a backfilling and contact grouting project, and illustrates how documentation supports the project through each phase of development. Writing down and costing out all requirements that need to be met *before* a project starts ensures that all parties understand the scope of work to be performed. Documents also specify planning, design, materials, construction approach, testing, quality control, and operation and maintenance steps that will be taken to assure a quality project. This information can be helpful in resolving potential disputes or claims, such as against a contractor based on contractor errors, or when unanticipated problems arise if the site geology does not match specified conditions.

12.1   The Need for Contract Documents

A successful project delivery strategy depends on a very thorough understanding of the contracting plan and the types of grouting likely to be employed on the project. Contract documents meet that need. Technical and project-specific requirements should be completely understood by the design engineers and specification writers so the design intent can be met by field application. It is recommended that an individual most familiar with the project scope and with drilling and grouting be charged with the responsibility for preparing the drilling, backfilling, and contact grouting documents to make sure the field application is clearly communicated in the terminology used. Moreover, the project's engineers, contract administrators, construction managers, and field inspectors all need to have a thorough understanding of the design intent and the full content of the contract documents, because they will enforce the documentation. If these project participants do not have what they need to do their jobs, then all that follows may be problematic or of questionable value. Moreover, the project, and all those connected with it, are likely to have a very difficult time achieving the desired end results without disputes, cost overruns, or delays.

During the design phase, individuals with extensive experience in drilling, backfilling and contact grouting, and contract document preparation should be made part of the constructability and bidability review team. The contractor should accept the risk of the adequacy of his cost estimates for factors he controls. The factors include, but are not limited to, means and methods, labor productivity and workmanship, the excavated dimension of the tunnel versus the final lining dimensions, and sequencing and scheduling of the work. The owner should accept the risk of the adequacy and accuracy of the geotechnical data presented. The owner should also accept the risk and assume the responsibility should the actual geotechnical conditions differ from those presented.

With a clear understanding of the technical requirements of the backfilling and contact grouting to be employed and the various related aspects of the project, the next critical point deals with allocation of risk and cost control. These two issues determine whether the backfill material and contact grout should be paid as a "unit-price item" or as incidental to the tunnel or shaft liner installation on a "lump sum basis." In allocation of risk for backfill and contact grout projects, the engineers and designers must consider that backfilling behind a liner is generally viewed as incidental to the final liner installation. This philosophy comes from the fact the quantity of backfill required is in major part dependent on the contractor's selection of excavation methods, workmanship of the crews, liner type, and the means and methods used to install the liner. An example of this would be a tunnel requiring a finished diameter of 3.4 m (11 ft) with a 600-mm (12-in) thick precast concrete segmental liner system used as the final liner. If the contractor selects a tunnel boring machine (TBM) with a diameter of 4.7 m (15.5 ft), then the resulting annulus of 675 mm (15 in) behind the liner would require backfilling. Following a unit-priced formula (price per linear meter of tunnel excavation and final liner), this would not be an owner-compensated issue; rather, since the contractor's machine selection dictated the relatively large volume of backfill material required, no additional compensation for backfill is due the contractor. In this example, all reimbursement to the contractor for backfill is incidental to final liner installation: if the contractor had used a TBM that excavated the diameter of the tunnel to about 4.1 to 4.3 m (13.5 to 14.0 ft), the result would have been a smaller annulus that required less backfill (75 to 150 mm (3 to 6 in)). The contractor may have already owned the larger diameter TBM or purchased it at a good price on the used equipment market. Therefore, there is no logical reason for the owner to pay extra for the increased quantity of backfill material because the contractor selected a larger-than-necessary TBM. In reality, however, the owner does pay, since the extra cost of backfill already would be included in the contractor's bid price.

The same would be true if the contractor decided to perform a conventional drill-and-blast (D&B) excavation. The annulus between, for example, a steel pipe lining system and the irregularly and possibly overbroken and/or overexcavated surface of the surrounding ground would be backfilled by the contractor incidental to the final liner installation. In this case, the total quantity of backfill required would be a result of the contractor's selected (and documented) means and methods, quality control, and the workmanship of the D&B crew(s). The same case can be made for contact grouting, since the amount of contact grouting required also will be influenced by the contractor's means and methods, quality control, and skill and workmanship of personnel placing the cast-in-place concrete liner or backfill material. Generally, the contractor's backfilling and contact grouting requirements flow from contractor actions. They are incidental to related work and can be priced on a lump-sum basis or be made incidental to the unit price for tunnel excavation and lining bid price.

Geotechnical grouting requirements—pre-excavation grouting, consolidation grouting, installation of a grout curtain, or feature grouting—are unrelated to contractor's means and methods. Because they are dependent on geology and groundwater conditions, they are typically specified and paid for as unit-specific priced items per the contract documents. In this way, geotechnical grouting becomes the owner's risk. Items such as length of hole drilled, number of hole hookups for injection, and the amount of grout placed into each hole or section of hole are competitively bid and typically paid for as unit priced items.

A reasonable argument can be made that contact grouting quantities are sometimes controlled to a larger degree by the geological conditions surrounding the excavation than by the contractor's means and methods and are, therefore, not incidental to the line placement. For example, the soil surrounding the excavation is quite porous, such as coarse sand or gravel, allowing the contact grout to permeate the soil. The argument would be that the contractor was performing geotechnical grouting rather than contact grouting and, therefore, should be paid by the owner for the contact grouting. The same type of argument for payment is often made by contractors when contact grouting in rock containing open joints, fissures, and other defects. Both of these examples also could apply to backfill material entering into the surrounding ground.

When geological conditions are known to exist that could affect the quantity of the backfill material or contact grout required, these conditions should be clearly stated in the contract documents. Also, when geologic conditions warrant, provisions should be included in the contract documents to address and pay for items such as sealing open joints and fissures in the rock prior to starting the backfilling and contact grouting operations. Because of the geologic conditions surrounding the tunnel, there may be cases in which the designer may elect to make contact grouting a unit-priced item. Support for this could come in the form of a complete Geotechnical Baseline Report (GBR) as one of the contract documents. The GBR could report on the porosity of the soil surrounding the project and the results of any design phase permeability or grout take tests. If the project soils tests indicate some potential for grout take, the contractor can be alerted through the bid documents and bid the project accordingly, thus eliminating a potential dispute.

12.2   Contractor-Affected Grout Programs

Contractor-affected grout programs are technically those that follow "but-for" logic. This means that, but-for the contractor's means and methods or equipment selection, the backfill volume would not have been as great. Therefore, the contractor is responsible for those items and they can be priced incidental to the attendant work, such as in the case of backfilling the annulus behind the final liner. Likewise, contact grouting can be viewed as a necessary item that is influenced to a great degree by the contractor's cast-in-place concrete or backfill placement methods, techniques, and workmanship. However, contractors have been known to argue this point by stating, for example, that the need for contact grouting is a result of soil behavior after excavating the tunnel and, but-for the owner's interest in having the project built, the settlement would not have taken place and the contact grouting would not have been necessary. This argument often fails on merit when the time interval between the liner installation and the subsequent backfilling and contact grouting has not been as precise as necessary to minimize settlement issues. In any case, the issue is rendered moot by the fact that owners know they are going to pay for some backfilling and contact grouting in the contractor's bid. They are just transferring the risk of quantity overrun to the contractor because the contractor controls the means, methods, workmanship, timeliness, and precision of the backfill and contact grouting installation. Any claim or dispute that fails on merit or entitlement should never be studied for monetary damages. Thus, the record keeping procedures suggested in Chapter 10 should be fully understood and followed in order to make fair and honest assessments of contractor or third-party claims, such as grout jacking or heave that results in damage to nearby structures.

12.3   Geology Dictates Other Types of Grouting

Geotechnical grouting, although not covered in these guidelines, is dictated by the site specific geological conditions. It is generally the owner's responsibility since the owner selects the location and chooses to build the underground facility at the site.

A site-specific geotechnical grouting program must be custom designed and developed based on a comprehensive geotechnical field exploration and testing program. These should be performed only after the final vertical and horizontal limits of the project have been agreed upon.

While the site's geology, groundwater conditions, surface structures, underground utilities, other existing underground facilities, or the new facility's operational requirements are critical for designing and implementing the project's geotechnical grouting program, the same conditions and requirements also play an important role in designing and implementing the backfilling and contact grouting programs and contract terms. Some obvious examples of how geological conditions can have an influence on backfilling and contact grouting are listed below:

- When the permeability of a soil is high enough to allow backfill and/or contact grout to permeate the surrounding ground beyond the limits of the void(s) being filled
- When backfill material and contact grout have the potential to permeate into joints, cracks, and other defects in the rock surrounding the void(s) being filled
- When running groundwater can make standard backfill or contact grout placement impractical or too costly
- When geologic conditions or structures might cause overexcavation that subsequently requires additional backfilling or contact grouting
- When changing geology or groundwater conditions along a tunnel alignment might make different backfilling and contact grouting methods necessary at different locations

These examples, if not adequately addressed in the contract documents, could lead to misunderstandings and claims. Using the philosophy stated earlier—that backfilling and contact grouting are incidental to liner placement because the contractor dictates the means and methods of excavation and liner installation—it must be determined who is responsible for the costs of the extra backfill material and contact grout that enters the surrounding ground: (a) the owner, who is responsible for project siting and therefore the in situ ground condition? Or (b) the contractor, who had knowledge during bidding of the project's geology and groundwater conditions and subsequently designed the methods and mixes? Questions, misunderstandings, and disagreements can arise once construction begins, if the designer and the other drafters of the contract document do not address issues of responsibility during the engineering and design phases of the project.

One way to mitigate some misunderstandings and potential for claims is to specify the order or sequence of performing the various backfilling, contact grouting, and geotechnical grouting operations. Two examples for the order in which geotechnical grouting, backfilling, and contact grouting could be performed are shown below:

Example 1:
- Pre-excavation grouting
- Backfilling
- Contact grouting
- Feature grouting
- Consolidating grouting
- Curtain grouting

Example 2:
- Pre-excavation grouting
- Backfilling
- Consolidation grouting
- Feature grouting
- Contact grouting
- Curtain grouting

In these two examples, the difference in performance sequencing could be influenced by site-specific geological conditions. In Example 2, the contact grouting is the next-to-last operation to be performed. In this case there is a strong possibility that any void, which may have existed and were specified as needing to be filled with contact grout might already have been filled by one of the previous geotechnical grouting operations. Therefore, the owner is paying for most, if not all, the contact grouting as a unit priced geotechnical grouting pay item.

The placement within the contract documents of the sequence listing is also important because geotechnical grouting may very likely be in a different specification section than the backfilling and contact grouting. Therefore, the sequence listing should appear in all specification sections to which it applies. However, if the order of grouting precedence changes in one location in the specifications, it must be changed equally in all locations or the specifications will be in conflict.

12.4   Backfilling and Contact Grouting Contract Documents

The following should be included in the drawings and specifications portion of the contract documents:

- **Scope/Description.** A definition of the work that is expected to be performed and the contractor's responsibilities regarding this work. It should provide what is included in and excluded from the contractor's scope of work.

- **Requirements.** The purpose of the backfilling or contact grouting, the required performance of the contractor, a description of the areas to be backfilled and contact grouted, and a list of the related specification sections.

- **Definitions and Abbreviations.** A list of definitions and abbreviations to ensure that all parties understand what is being stated and what various terminologies mean.

- **Qualifications.** The necessary minimum previous experience and qualifications required of the contractor and subcontractors. Experience requirements generally apply to both the company and the personnel that will be assigned to the backfilling and contact grouting.

- **Ground Conditions.** Specifies that the work will be performed in subsurface conditions as reported in the geotechnical investigation reports and baseline reports.

- **Referenced Standards.** These are typically references to ASTM, ACI, AWS, API, and other standards. Additionally, these may include local, state, or federal codes and regulations.

- **Submittals.** A description of what is required to be submitted by the contractor. These may include bid, pre-construction, work plans, and detailed procedures, as well as post-construction (as-built) information.

- **Equipment.** A list of the equipment expected to be required for the project, as well as specific requirements for each piece of equipment. Requirements may include drilling, testing, controls and instrumentation (monitoring), mixers, agitators, pumps, transport equipment, hoses, pipe fittings, packers, and valves.

- **Materials.** A list of the materials expected to be required for the project and specific requirements for each item. The requirements for the materials are typically based on ASTM standards and may include cement, water, flyash, admixtures, bentonite, and sand.

- **Quality Control.** A description of the records, documentation, testing, and procedures the contractor must employ to ensure the work is being performed in compliance with the contract documents.

This list is not all inclusive and must be tailored to the specific project. It is very important that drawings and specifications from one project never be used for another project without a complete review of every aspect of what is presented, even when the projects have the same basic design, geology, and groundwater conditions.

REFERENCES

Aberle, P.P. 1976. Pressure grouting foundation on Teton Dam; rock engineering for foundations and slopes. In *Proceedings of the Specialty Conference of the Geotechnical Engineering Division,* 1. New York: American Society of Civil Engineers, pp. 245-263.

AJ Voton, LLC 2001. Personal communications between Raymond W. Henn and Steven E. La Vallee of AJ Voton, LLC.

Barton, N., R. Lien, and J. Lunde. 1974. Engineering classification of rock masses for the design of tunnel supports. *Rock Mechanics* 6(4), pp. 189-236.

Bickel, J.O. 1982. Tunnel characteristics. In *Tunnel Engineering Handbook*, J.O. Bickel and T.R. Kuesel, eds. New York: Van Nostrand Reinhold Co.

Bickel, J.O., T.R. Kuessel, and E.H. King. 1996. *Tunnel Engineering Handbook, 2nd ed.* New York: Chapman & Hall, 544 pp.

Bishop, N. 2001. Personal communications between Raymond W. Henn and Norman Bishop of Montgomery Watson Harza.

Brady, G.S., and H.R. Clauser. 1986. *Materials Handbook, 12th ed.* New York: McGraw Hill.

Brekke, T.L. and Ripley, B.D. 1987. Design guidelines for pressure tunnels and shafts. EPRI AP-5273.

Bruce, D.A., G.S. Littlejohn, and A. Naudts. 1997. Grouting materials for ground treatment: a practitioner's guide. In *Grouting: Compaction, Remediation, and Testing*, C. Vipulanandan, ed. Proceedings of Sessions Sponsored by the Grouting Committee of the ASCE Geo-Institute, Logan, UT, July 16-18. Geotechnical Special Publication No. 66. Reston, VA: ASCE, pp. 306-334.

Byle, M.J., and R.H. Borden. 1995. Verification of geotechnical grouting. Proceedings, Grouting Sessions held at the ASCE National Convention, San Diego, CA: New York: ASCE.

Deere, D.U. 1964. Technical description of rock cores for engineering purposes. *Rock Mechanics and Engineering Geology* 1(1), pp. 17-22.

Eskilsson, J.N. 1999. Design of pressure tunnels. In ASCE Geotechnical Special Publication No. 90. Reston, VA: ASCE.

Ewert, F.K. 1985. *Rock Grouting with Emphasis on Dam Sites*. Berlin: Springer-Verlag.

Gause, C.C., and D.A. Bruce. 1997. Control of fluid properties of particulate grouts: part 1, general concepts. In *Grouting: Compaction, Remediation, and Testing*, C. Vipulanandan, ed. Proceedings of Sessions Sponsored by the Grouting Committee of the ASCE Geo-Institute, Logan, UT, July 16-18. Geotechnical Special Publication No. 66. Reston, VA: ASCE, pp. 212-229.

Hansmire, W.H., B. Schmidt, and J.E. Monsees. 1989. Perspectives on soft ground tunnel lining design. In *The Art and Science of Geotechnical Engineering at the Dawn of the Twenty-First Century*. Englewood Cliffs, NJ: Prentice Hall, pp. 437-459.

Harris, Robin R.W. 1982. Pre-stress grouting of high pressure waterways. In *Grouting in Geotechnical Engineering*. Proceedings of the conference sponsored by the ASCE Geotechnical Engineering Division, New Orleans, LA, February 10-12. New York: ASCE.

Henn, R.W. 1996. *Practical Guide to Grouting of Underground Structures*. Reston, VA: ASCE Press, 191 pp.

Herrenknecht Corp. 2001. Personal communications between Raymond W. Henn and Jack Brockway of the Herrenknecht Corporation.

Heuer, R.E., and D.L. Virgens. 1987. Anticipated behavior of silty sands in tunneling. In *Rapid Excavation and Tunneling Conference Proceedings*. American Institute of Mining, Metallurgical, and Petroleum Engineers and American Society of Civil Engineers, New Orleans, LA. Baltimore, MD: Port City Press, Inc, Vol. I, pp.221-237.

Hoek, E., and E.T. Brown. 1980. *Underground Excavations in Rock*. London: The Institution of Mining and Metallurgy.

Houlsby, A.C. 1990. *Construction and Design of Cement Grouting*. New York: John Wiley & Sons, 442 pp..

243

Jefferis, S. 1982. Effect of mixing on bentonite slurries and grouts. In *Grouting in Geotechnical Engineering.* Proceedings of the conference sponsored by the ASCE Geotechnical Engineering Division, New Orleans, LA, February 10-12, pp. 62-76.

Keusel, T.R., J.O. Bickel, and E.H. King. 1996. *Tunnel Engineering Handbook.* Chapman and Hall, 544 pp.

Kosmatka, S.H., and W.C. Panarese. 1988. *Design and Control of Concrete Mixtures.* Portland Cement Association.

Littlejohn, G.S. 1982. Design of cement based grouts. In *Grouting in Geotechnical Engineering.* Proceedings of the conference sponsored by the ASCE Geotechnical Engineering Division, New Orleans, LA, February 10-12. New York: ASCE, pp. 35-48.

Lombardi, G. 1985. The role of cohesion in cement grouting of rock. *Fifteenth Congress on Large Dams,* Vol. 3. Lausanne, Switzerland: International Commission on Large Dams, pp. 235-261.

McCusker, T.G. 1982. Soft ground tunneling. In *Tunnel Engineering Handbook,* J.O. Bickel and T.R. Kuesel, eds. New York: Van Nostrand Reinhold Co.

Mehta, P.K., and P.J. Monteiro. 1993. *Concrete Structure, Properties, and Materials, 2nd ed.* Englewood Cliffs, NJ: Prentice Hall.

Merritt, A. 1999. Geologic and geotechnical considerations for pressure tunnel design. In ASCE Geotechnical Special Publication No. 90. Reston, VA: ASCE.

Merritt, A.H. 2001. Personal communications between Raymond W. Henn and Andrew H. Merritt of Andrew H. Merritt, Inc.

Mongilardi, E., and R. Tornaghi. 1986. Construction of large underground openings and use of grouts. In *Proceedings-First International Conference-Piling and Deep Foundations*, September, Beijing, China: China Building Industry Press, pp. 1.58-1.76.

Nolting, R.M., F. Duan, and Y. Sun. 1998. Ground support for emplacement drifts at Yucca Mountain, Canadian tunnelling. In *Proceedings from the Annual Conference*. London, Ontario, Canada: The Tunnelling Association of Canada.

O'Rourke, T.D. 1984. *Guidelines for Tunnel Lining Design*. ASCE Technical Committee on Tunnel Lining Design of the Underground Technology Research Council. New York: ASCE.

Peck, R.B., A.J. Hendron, and B. Mohraz. 1972. State of the art of soft-ground tunneling. In *Rapid Excavation and Tunneling Conference Proceedings*. American Institute of Mining, Metallurgical, and Petroleum Engineers and ASCE, Chicago, Baltimore, MD: Port City Press, Inc, pp. 259-286.

Proctor, R.V., and T.L. White, eds. 1977. *Earth Tunneling with Steel Supports*. Youngstown, OH: Commercial Shearing and Stamping Co.

Proctor, R.V., and T.L. White, eds. 1988. *Rock Tunneling with Steel Supports*. Youngstown, OH: Commercial Shearing and Stamping Co.

Ranken, R.E. 1978. Analysis of Ground-Liner Interaction for Tunnels. U.S. Dept. of Transportation Report No. UMTA-IL-06-0043-78-3, 426 p.

Schwarz, L.G., and R.J. Krizek. 1992. Effects of mixing on rheological properties of microfine cement grout. In *Grouting in Geotechnical Engineering*. Proceedings of the conference sponsored by the ASCE Geotechnical Engineering Division, New Orleans, LA, February 10-12. New York: ASCE, pp. 512-525, 1992.

Stephens, P. 2001. Personal communications between Raymond W. Henn and Pat Stephens of Pacific International Grout Company.

Tattersall, G.H., and P.F. Banfill. 1983. *The Rheology of Fresh Concrete*. London: Pittman.

Terzaghi, K. 1946. Rock defects and loads on tunnel supports. In *Rock Tunneling with Steel Supports*, R.V. Proctor and T. White, eds. Youngstown, OH: Commercial Shearing and Stamping Co.

Wang, J. 1993. *Seismic Design of Tunnels, A Simple State-of-the-Art Design Approach*. New York: Parsons Brinckerhoff Inc.

Warner, J., and D. Brown. 1974. Planning and performing compaction grouting. *Journal of the Geotechnical Engineering Division* 100(GT6), Proc. Paper 10606, pp. 653-666.

Weaver, K.D. 1991. *Dam Foundation Grouting*. New York: ASCE, 178 pp.

White, T.L. 1977. Geologic investigations. In *Earth Tunneling with Steel Supports*, R.V. Proctor and T. White, eds. Youngstown, OH: Commercial Shearing and Stamping Co.

Wilson, D., and T. Dreese. 1998. Grouting technologies for dam foundations. In *Proceedings of the 1998 Annual Conference Association of State Dam Safety Officials*, Las Vegas, October 11-14, Paper No. 68.

INDEX

Note: Page numbers in *italics* indicate photos or tables.

39; through the tailshield 102, 104–105

grouting, contact: *see* contact grouting

holding tanks 156
hydration control agents 70

inflow: gases 42–43; groundwater 41–42, 146; liquid 42–43; water 95, 98, 145
injectability 78
injection holes 209–210
injection methods: backfilling 4, 102–105; grout 94, 102–105; parameter recording 169–172; testing 218–226
injection parameter recording, computer monitoring systems 225
injection pressures 38, 158, 181; testing 218–220
inspection forms 192–194; details 199–205

lacustrine deposits 16–17
lagging 45–46
Larimer Poudre Tunnel 36–37
leakage 42
liners: composite 35; design 27, 30; permeability 35; plate 46–47; selection criteria 44; stability 34–37; systems 44–59
liquid inflow 42–43
load transfer 34–37, 87; from ground to structure 40; from structure to ground 38–40
loads, tensile 40
loess 18
lugeon test 42–43

marine deposits 17–18
Marsh funnel test 81–82, 213–214
material testing 210
membranes, gas-proof 31–32
mineral admixtures 67
mix designs: backfilling 116–127; cellular concrete 122–126; concrete

116–121; contact grouting 147–148; flowable fill 127; grout 116–121
mixing 149–155; agitation 149–150; automated batch plants 172–173; batch 154, 156; cellular concrete 154; colloidal 150–155; jet 154; shear 150–155; shear, features 151
mobility 78

NATM: *see* New Austrian Tunneling Method
neat grout: *see* grout, neat
New Austrian Tunneling Method 49, 90
nipples 165
Norwegian Geotechnical Institute index 26
numbering systems, grout hole 194–197

operational requirements 33–43
outflows 42–43
overbreak 27, *27–29*, 111
overcut 20
overexcavation 22–23, 46

packers 164–165
penetrability 78–80
penstocks: backfilling 114–116; defined 99; maximum length factors 99; rock tunnel linings 27; tunnel liners 55; tunnels 38
permeability 144
pipe: backfilling 108–114; concrete cylinder 6; corrugated metal 138; drop 100, 143; grout 100, 102; high-pressure 114–116; precast concrete 55–57, 137; raised 7; reinforced concrete 6; rock tunnel linings 27; shaft lining 91; tunnel liners 55–58; welded steel 55
plant location 165–168
ports: backfill injection 115; crown 108–109, 115; grout 4, 105, 107, 108, 136–138; nipples 165; numbering systems 194–197; springline 108–109, 115